BLACK
STUDENTS

SOME OTHER VOLUMES IN THE
SAGE FOCUS EDITIONS

BLACK STUDENTS

Psychosocial Issues and Academic Achievement

Edited by
Gordon LaVern Berry
and Joy Keiko Asamen

SAGE PUBLICATIONS
The Publishers of Professional Social Science
Newbury Park   London   New Delhi

This book is dedicated to our parents
Marcus and Gertrude Berry
Keigi and Kiyo Asamen

For information address:

SAGE Publications, Inc.
2111 West Hillcrest Drive
Newbury Park, California 91320

SAGE Publications Ltd.
28 Banner Street
London EC1Y 8QE
England

SAGE Publications India Pvt. Ltd.
M-32 Market
Greater Kailash I
New Delhi 110 048 India

Printed in the United States of America

Library of Congress Cataloging-in-Publication Data

Black students : psychosocial issues and academic achievement / edited
   by Gordon LaVern Berry and Joy Keiko Asamen.
       p.   cm. — (Sage focus editions ; 109)
    Bibliography: p.
    ISBN 0-8039-3664-8. — ISBN 0-8039-3665-6 (pbk.)
    1. Afro-American students—Psychology.   2. Academic achievement.
3. Afro-American students—Social conditions.   4. Afro-American
college students—Attitudes.   I. Berry, Gordon L.   II. Asamen, Joy
Keiko, 1953–
LC2731.B57   1990
378.1'8'08996073—dc20   89–35853
FIRST PRINTING, 1989   CIP

Contents

Preface

Few social scientists and health providers in the United States would disagree with the proposition that there is a significant relationship between quality of our past and present sociocultural experiences and the academic or educational achievement of an individual in our schools and colleges. The proposition rests on the premise that general unmet psychosocial needs, especially when accompanied by government policies that foster social and economic inequities, can lead to negative educational and academic achievement in a student group. Similarly most social observers would agree that, among the ethnic minorities, Afro-Americans have made some real gains in terms of their educational achievement since 1970, despite the fact that they have experienced a number of unmet mental, economic, social, and physical health needs. At the same time, Afro-Americans are still represented to an alarming degree among those school-age children and college-level young adults who, because of a number of societal structural factors, have failed to achieve throughout the educational pipeline from kindergarten through college.

Traditional social science and educational approaches used in studying the academic achievement of Black students have frequently attempted to explain what was taking place by employing a rather narrow focus on the deficits found in the family and school settings. Many of these studies have failed to place their academic achievement observations within a framework of the strengths of Black learners, and the uniqueness of the systemic psychosocial and psychoeducational cultural experiences in which they have developed.

This book brings together scholars in the fields of social science, mental health, and education. Their charge was to provide the theory, research, and program models that were not restricted by narrow views concerning the achievement potential of African-American children and college-age students.

Our attempt was to recognize that there are many issues that must be faced in terms of the academic attainment of Afro-Americans. At the same time, there can and must be a commitment to *excellence* from those persons charged with developing the educational potential of Black children, as well as a corresponding commitment from Black Americans themselves. No programs of excellence can be realized, however, unless there is also a commitment to providing for Afro-Americans and all children *equality* of opportunity to reach for their own level of personal achievement.

The reader will note that the topics in the book were arranged to capture a type of growth and educational development perspective. That is to say, the content begins with perspectives on prenatal factors and academic achievement, through selected social and psychological constructs, to educational issues related to college and higher education. Finally, the chapters focus on model programs aimed at making changes in the educational process for Afro-American students from elementary school to the university. The final chapter is a unique and personal perspective from an Afro-American and an achiever in American society.

We want to express our appreciation to Juanita Berry, members of our families, and our friends for their support in the development of this book. Finally, we would like to thank our friends in the Communications Processing Center of the Graduate School of Education for their patience in the preparation of the manuscript.

—Gordon L. Berry
—Joy Keiko Asamen

Introduction

Afro-American Students and Academic Achievement

JOY KEIKO ASAMEN

Social scientists have for a number of years explored those educational issues related to the academic achievement problems of some Afro-American students. Within this context of academic achievement, it must be acknowledged that, for the most part, this book focuses on lower-income Black youth since middle-class and affluent Afro-American students are afforded many of the opportunities denied to those individuals frequently referred to as the underclass. On the other hand, the intent of this book is not to underestimate the profound effect of race on how a person is received in our society irrespective of one's opportunities. In order to comprehend fully the effect of race on the academic achievement of Afro-American students, a brief historical perspective of the educational experiences of African-Americans in the United States will assist the reader.

The education of Afro-American children prior to 1865 was for the most part nonexistent except in rare cases where education was provided by some masters for more efficient labor, sympathetic reformers, and missionaries (Vaughn, 1974; Woodson, 1968). In fact, providing Black Americans with an education during this time of history was often a violation of state laws. To deny Afro-American children an education acted to maintain enslavement, and in consequence, dehumanized the Negroid race. The withholding of education to Afro-American school-age children reflected the mind-set of the time, that is, Blacks were mentally inferior to Whites (Lieberson, 1980). With the end of slavery, Blacks pursued schooling with more self-confidence, but the public system still managed to restrict access to equitable schooling. For example, Congress passed a law in

1864 that was to allow Black students in the District of Columbia access to a fair share of the school funds (U.S. Commissioner of Education cited in Weinberg, 1977). Initially, the school officials chose basically to disregard the measure, but when ordered to divide the funds equally between the White and Black schools, the funds were so divided yet schools were built only for White children and not for Black children.

From 1865 to 1950, the era of *Plessy v. Ferguson* (1896, cited in Tatel, Lanigan, & Sneed, 1986), schooling was not denied to Afro-American children, but the distribution of educational financial support to Black children who attended separate schools from Whites was far from equitable (Bond, 1966; Weinberg, 1977). The difference in revenue between the races is indisputable and continued the cycle of inadequate education to those children of Afro-American heritage. If economic and political deprivation, segregation, and inequality were not enough, Black schools were also subjected to physical intimidation and terrorism.

The period of history from the 1950s forward was a time of numerous transformations. Racial discrimination persisted, but the protest of Afro-Americans against the inequitable treatment by society was more apparent than ever. Afro-American educators, parents, and students began to actively battle the years of inequity and lack of excellence that historically characterized the education of Black Americans in this country (Montgomery, 1970). Segregation in the schools was legally challenged, that is, "separate but equal" was ordered unconstitutional in the famous *Brown v. Board of Education of Topeka* (1954, cited in Tatel et al., 1986). This is not to say that the societal sentiment had changed in the direction of fair education for *all* students. Instead, what we saw was an oppressed minority group developing the self-confidence to take issue with the unfair treatment of the past and present.

With the increasing use of achievement tests, social scientists did not lack support for the notion that Afro-American children showed a significant lag behind their White counterparts (Samuda, 1975; Weinberg, 1977). Would one not expect that this would be the case for any individual subjected to the quality of education offered to the Afro-American student as well as the inherent limitations of the instrumentation that measured achievement?

Of course, the reaction to such bleak findings was that educators now tried to attend to the differential achievement levels of Black children by ability grouping and tracking students (Samuda, 1975). As expected, Whites were significantly represented in the basic, honors, or college preparatory tracks whereas Blacks were over-represented in the special education group.

With the Civil Rights Act of 1964, Congress made a concentrated commitment to the educational needs of Afro-American students (Orfield, 1978). The Department of Health, Education, and Welfare and the Justice Department were made responsible for overseeing the desegregation efforts of our country's schools and colleges. These efforts provided further impetus for Afro-American families to continue their battle for educational equity.

With this brief historical account, it is clear that the current academic standing of many Afro-American students cannot help but be impacted by past social and political events. Much of the prior research on the academic achievement of minority groups has studied the issue by "blaming the victim" or the citing of an intellectual and cultural deficit. The mission of this book is to shift away from such a linear perspective to a more holistic approach that takes into account not only the history of Black Americans but the present economic, political, social, and psychological factors that contribute to shaping a student's ability to achieve. The intention of this book is not to take responsibility away from Afro-American students and their families for improving their educational success but to highlight the systemic forces that may introduce unique challenges to Black Americans.

Part I presents a number of social and psychological influences that contribute to a person's ability to achieve. It begins with a chapter by Kathy Sanders-Phillips who focuses on prenatal and postnatal influences on cognitive development among Afro-American children. She thoroughly examines the interplay between the biological, environmental, and historical/cultural factors that might shape a child's ability to achieve. A critical observation made in this piece is that the influence of health status on cognitive development may be more relevant than the relationship between parental behavior and cognitive development.

Sandra Graham, who looked at the relationship between motivation and academic achievement, proposes that social scientists need to address some core issues prior to arriving at a more scientific understanding of why some Afro-American students may have difficulty in being academically successful. Gloria Johnson Powell examines the construct of self-concept as a dimension of academic achievement. She cites how political, social, and economic factors contribute to the development of the self among inner-city minority group children.

Finally, the first part of the book closes with a chapter by Janice Hale-Benson who looks at the role of the learning environment toward the attainment of academic achievement. She cites that an "incisive analysis of the problem" is necessary to disentangle the complex nature of why a system would consistently keep Afro-Americans in the lower educational and occupational ranks.

Part II looks at family and community factors that affect the academic achievement of Afro-American students. It begins with a chapter coauthored by Roslyn Arlin Mickelson and Stephen Samuel Smith. Cited at the core of poor school outcome for inner-city youth are the "structural forces operating in the national and international political economy."

William D. Parham and Thomas A. Parham tease out the community influences they feel are salient in the development of one's ability to achieve in education. These authors propose that the research in the area of academic achievement relative to minority group status could be enhanced by looking more holistically at the issues, that is, considering variables both internal and external to the children and their families as well as the positive and negative contributions of the Black community. Louis E. Jenkins concurs with taking this more holistic approach in looking at the role of family in fostering the development of an academically successful Afro-American student. His chapter identifies those factors that contribute to both the successful and unsuccessful academic achievement of Afro-Americans.

Part II addresses the increasing problem of Afro-American students prematurely leaving school, which appears to be in sharp contrast to the thinking of many Afro-American families that formal education is the means through which one can "achieve social status and financial security." Romeria Tidwell discusses the factors relevant to the school dropout rate from a minority researcher's perspective.

Part III looks at the personal adjustment of and programmatic considerations for college students. Marcia L. Hall and Walter R. Allen begin this section of the book by presenting a survey study that they conducted in order to describe Afro-American college students at predominately White universities. One observation made in this study is that current Afro-American college students appear to view racism on the parts of individuals within the system, but do not see racism as an institutionally based attitude as their counterparts from the prior decade viewed it.

Shelley Prillerman, Hector F. Myers, and Brian D. Smedley look at the relationship between psychosocial stress, academic achievement, and psychological well-being among Afro-American college students in a data-driven research piece. The effect of stress among all college-age students is an issue of concern for those professionals working in higher education, but for some minority students the college experience might introduce some unique challenges that could impact on a person's psychological welfare and adjustment to the college scene.

Edward "Chip" Anderson addresses the personal attributes, resources, skills, knowledge, and abilities necessary for a college student to academically succeed. He proposes the Gap Theory of Academic Achievement to explain the gaps between what the college students need to achieve and the expectations of the college professors and other institutional factors. From the perspective that a college education is virtually the only avenue for economic and social mobility for a low-income Afro-American student, Chapter 11 provides professionals of higher education with guidelines on how to retain all students, but especially those who may be academically at risk.

Part IV addresses psychosocial interventions and educational leadership strategies related to academic achievement. Unlike prior efforts to explicate the relationship between minority status and academic achievement, this book attempts to propose some specific programmatic directions for enhancing the academic experience of Afro-American students.

Hugh J. Scott introduces this part of the book by clearly specifying the leadership mandates for school administrators who find themselves in mainly Black schools. The ongoing theme of this chapter is the necessity of respecting and appreciating Afro-American children and their parents.

In the next chapter, James P. Comer proposes the School Development Program which is a psychosocial approach to school intervention. He believes that schools must get beyond the traditional educational concerns of curriculum content and teaching approaches to becoming more sensitive to the roles of social and be-havioral sciences and child development on the school as a social system.

Chapter 14 presents some summarizing remarks by Gordon L. Berry who highlights the "changes and challenges" confronting gov-ernmental units, the private sector, the family unit, and the school. He stresses that "excellence and equity" are both necessary for cre-ating meaningful change in the educational status of Afro-American and other low-income and minority students.

In the first paragraph to this introduction, it was stated that this book focuses on lower-income Afro-American youth, but regardless of socioeconomic status, it was argued that race still weighs heavily in our society. Chester M. Pierce clearly expands on this issue in an autobiographical piece as he discusses how race is still significant despite an individual's professional accomplishments and stature. His contribution is suitably presented as an epilogue to this book.

As one moves through the chapters of this book, it becomes ap-parent that the only viable approach to enhancing the academic achievement of African-American youth is to recognize the multi-variate nature of the issue. No one variable can be identified as the cause of why some Black children, youth, and college students are successful academically or face difficulty in succeeding. On the other hand, it is safe to say that one of the major issues that face Afro-American students is the slow movement in our society that recognizes *all* people as equal and entitled to the same life experi-ences, if they should so choose, regardless of one's skin color.

REFERENCES

Bond, H. M. (1966). *The education of the Negro in the American social order.* New York: Octagon Books.

Lieberson, S. (1980). *A piece of the pie.* Berkeley: University of California Press.

Montgomery, M. L. (1970). Our changing school and community. In N. Wright, Jr. (Ed.), *What Black educators are saying* (pp. 272–277). San Francisco: Leswing Press.

Orfield, G. (1978). *Must we bus?* Washington, DC: The Brookings Institution.

Samuda, R. J. (1975). *Psychological testing of American minorities: Issues and conse-quences.* New York: Harper & Row.

Tatel, D. S., Lanigan, K. J., & Sneed, M. F. (1986). The fourth decade of *Brown:* Met-ropolitan desegregation and quality education. *Metropolitan Education, 1,* 15–35.

Vaughn, W. P. (1974). *Schools for all.* Lexington: University Press of Kentucky.

Weinberg, M. (1977). *A chance to learn.* Cambridge: Cambridge University Press.

Woodson, C. G. (1968). *The education of the Negro prior to 1861.* New York: Arno Press and the New York Times.

PART I

Social and Psychological Factors

1

Prenatal and Postnatal Influences on Cognitive Development

KATHY SANDERS-PHILLIPS

Much of the research in infant development since 1970 has been concerned with documenting the existence of learning processes in the human neonate and identifying factors that either facilitate or inhibit learning in infancy and later childhood (Bee et al., 1982; Bradley, Caldwell, & Elardo, 1979; Clarke-Stewart, 1973; Gorski, Lewkowicz, & Huntington, 1987; Lipsitt, 1977, 1986; Lipsitt & Werber, 1981). It now seems quite clear that infants in the first days and months of life are capable of perceiving and responding to the environment and, subsequently, learning from their interactions with the environment (Gorski et al., 1987; Lipsitt, 1986). It also appears that the circumstances—cultural, biological, environmental—that promote early learning also tend to promote the development of later cognitive skills (Kagan, 1979). The variables that affect the nature and quality of the infant's interactions with the environment, and the resulting learning processes, are myriad and complex.

There is much data to suggest that many Black children, particularly those who are raised in circumstances of economic poverty, are at greater risk for later educational failure and/or underachievement (Hale-Benson, 1982). These findings have prompted numerous attempts to identify and examine the factors that may influence academic achievement in Black children. Many studies suggest that the foundations for early learning and educational achievement are laid in the infant's first year of life. It is presumed that early life conditions, such as the level of stimulation to which an infant is exposed and the nature and quality of caretaker–infant interactions in the first year of life, will significantly influence subsequent cognitive de-

18

velopment in the infant (White & Watts, 1973). It is the intent of this chapter to examine these and other significant factors that may influence development and learning in Black infants and to explore whether specific culturally, biologically, or economically based factors may be associated with differences in cognitive development in Black children.

It is important to note at this point that there is little evidence that cognitive development in Black infants is adversely affected in the first two years of life (Bayley, 1965; Sameroff, Seifer, & Zan, 1982). To the contrary, until the age of two, Black infants score as well, and in some instances higher, than other ethnic groups (Bayley, 1965; Broman, Nichols, & Kennedy, 1975; Golden & Birns, 1976; Sameroff et al., 1982). The differences in the scores of Black children versus other ethnic groups, on traditional tests of cognitive development, do not emerge until after two years of age (Sameroff et al., 1982). These findings suggest many avenues of exploration regarding the possible relationship between conditions of infancy in the Black child and later academic achievement. First, the factors that affect academic achievement in Black children appear to be environmentally based. If this were not true, one would expect that Black infants would show deficits in cognitive development in the first two years of life. Second, the findings suggest that the factors associated with academic failure in Black children either exert their influence after the age of two or the influence of these factors is cumulative and, consequently, the effects are not apparent until the child is older, or both. These possibilities will be explored in this chapter.

It is important to remember throughout the following discussion that Blacks in this country do not constitute a homogeneous group (Harrison, Serafica, & McAdoo, 1984). They vary in terms of their economic resources and cultural experiences. One cannot assume, therefore, that the findings from the studies presented in this chapter reflect the broad variation in behavior and experience among Blacks in the United States.

Neonatal Status of Black Infants

Learning processes may be influenced and limited by the biological viability of the infant, but the nature of the caretaking environment can moderate the potentially negative effects of prenatal and perinatal insult. It seems reasonable to conclude, then, that an assessment of learning processes in the Black infant must begin with an evaluation of neonatal status in Black children. It is particularly important to establish whether Black infants are more vulnerable to prenatal or perinatal insult and to assess whether, on the basis of their neonatal status, they may be at higher risk for later learning problems.

Numerous studies have documented the fact that Black infants, as a group, are at higher risk for prenatal and perinatal insult (Birch & Gussow, 1970; Children's Defense Fund, 1985; U.S. Department of Health and Human Services, 1985, 1986). This finding is most dramatic for Black infants who are born into economically disadvantaged families (Birch & Gussow, 1970; Sameroff & Chandler, 1975; Sameroff, 1986). At virtually every level of examination, including complications of pregnancy, labor, delivery, and postnatal events, the number of Black children is disproportionately high. For example, the incidence of maternal complications in pregnancy increases significantly in Black women (Birch & Gussow, 1970; U.S. Department of Health and Human Services, 1985). Black women are much more likely to have toxemia of pregnancy, ectopic pregnancy, hemorrhage of pregnancy and childbearing, hypertension, heart disease, infections during pregnancy, and diabetes during pregnancy (U.S. Department of Health and Human Services, 1985). These problems can adversely affect the development of the fetus and the health status of the newborn infant (U.S. Department of Health and Human Services, 1985, 1986). Prematurity and low birth weight are also significantly higher in Black infants (Birch & Gussow, 1970; Children's Defense Fund, 1985; U.S. Department of Health and Human Services, 1985, 1986). In 1982, Black infants were more than twice as likely to be low birth weight than White infants (Children's Defense Fund, 1985). In general, birth weight increases as the socioeconomic status of the family increases (Birch & Gussow, 1970; U.S. Department of Health and Human Services, 1985). Black women are also more likely to have inadequate diets both preceding and during pregnancy. Therefore, Black infants may be at higher risk for fetal malnutrition (Birch & Gussow, 1970; U.S. Department Health and Human Services, 1985; Zeskind & Ramey, 1981). Black infants also appear to be more vulnerable to exposure to certain infections and some genetic diseases such as sickle-cell anemia (U.S. Department of Health and Human Services, 1985).

Perhaps one of the best measures of the overall health status of a group of people is the incidence of infant mortality (Birch & Gussow, 1970). As might be expected, the infant mortality rate for Black infants in 1980 was almost twice the rate for White infants (U.S. Department Health and Human Services, 1985). Fetal mortality is also greater for non-Whites (U.S. Department of Health. and Human Services, 1985). While a high infant mortality rate among Black infants is of great concern in and of itself, the implications of a high infant mortality rate for the surviving infants are equally serious. Birch and Gussow (1970) have noted that the rate of infant death in any population is an indicator of the level of health hazard to which that population is exposed.

The high infant mortality rate for Black infants not only signals an immediate health crisis for infants who do not survive but it also suggests that those infants who do survive may have been exposed to the same hazards that were responsible for the high rate of infant death. The equally high rate of death in Black infants during the postneonatal period tends to support this point (U.S. Department of Health and Human Services, 1985), and the high rates of infections and illness in Black infants in the first year of life suggest that Birch and Gussow's (1970) contentions are accurate.

The factors that are associated with the poor neonatal status of many Black infants are numerous and complex. They appear to be related to the age and parity of many Black mothers and the fact that many Black mothers are less likely to receive adequate prenatal care (U.S. Department of Health and Human Services, 1985, 1986). There is little doubt, however, that the primary cause of poor neonatal status in Black infants is poverty (Birch & Gussow, 1970). Lack of financial resources is strongly related to maternal health, parity, prenatal care, and other pertinent factors (Birch & Gussow, 1970; U.S. Department of Health and Human Services, 1985). Thus, it is not surprising that both the incidence of prenatal and postnatal complications and the impact on the infant's development are greater in economically depressed populations (Birch & Gussow, 1970; U.S. Department of Health and Human Services, 1985). It is also not surprising that the incidence and impact of these factors on subsequent infant development tends to dissipate as economic resources increase (Birch & Gussow, 1970). However, the improvement in infant outcome as economic resources increase in Black populations is not as great as would be expected. The cumulative impact of poverty on a mother's health and reproductive course is not necessarily erased by current health care and practices (Birch & Gussow, 1970).

Based on the preceding data, one can easily conclude that a significant number of Black infants are at risk for prenatal and perinatal insults that can render them more vulnerable to difficulties in sensory processing, nervous system dysfunctions, and subsequent learning problems. As Lipsitt suggests (1979), babies who experience perinatal complications probably move less, are less visually alert, suck weakly, and engage their environment less. Consequently, they are likely to have fewer opportunities for learning. One might reasonably ask at this point, how and why Black children continue to show average and above-average scores for cognitive development in the first two years of life, as measured by traditional infant assessment scales, despite the prenatal and perinatal hazards to which many of them are exposed. The precocity of Black infants in the first two years of life has been documented in many studies with little explanation for why such differences might exist (Bayley, 1965; Walters, 1967). Some have suggested that the differences reflect the increased maternal availability, nurturance, and/or infant carrying practices in Black mothers (Gerber & Dean, 1966; Ainsworth, 1967).

Freedman (1974) has suggested that such differences may reflect historical differences in the mode of infant transport. In cultures that have traditionally been nomadic, and infants have been frequently carried by caretakers, infants tend to show advanced motor maturity. It is not clear whether cultural practices "shape" infant development or infant development influences cultural practices, but Freedman concludes that there is a strong relationship between cultural practices and biological readiness in infants. Regardless of the origin of advanced motor maturity in Black infants, it is possible, and perhaps probable, that such precocity may have resulted in the ability of Black infants to achieve in spite of neonatal status. In effect, the advanced development of Black infants may serve to compensate, on some level, for earlier prenatal or perinatal insult. This area of research is worthy of much more investigation. The fact that Black infants do not show an overall deficit in cognitive development, and often demonstrate advanced motor development in spite of their documented vulnerability to prenatal and perinatal hazard, is an important and critical finding. Perhaps our efforts to understand learning processes in Black children might be better served if our investigative energies were directed toward the identification of factors that facilitate development in Black infants despite their prenatal and perinatal histories.

Little effort has been made to assess the possible impact of biologically based differences in behavior and development of Black infants on later cognitive development. It is clear that their motor precocity contributes to higher scores on traditional infant assessment measures. The impact that such behavior may have on the nature of the infant's interactions with the environment, which appear to be critical for later cognitive development, has not been adequately explored, but there is evidence to suggest that the level of the infant's motor development can significantly affect maternal behavior and the nature of the infant's experiences with the environment (Escalona, 1973; Green, Gustafson, & West, 1980).

There are other behaviors that may be biologically based that are common to Black infants. Advanced motor behavior, for example, is generally associated with higher activity levels and Morgan (1976) has indicated that Black infants tend to have higher activity rates. Brazelton, Koslowski, and Tronic (1981) have reported that African infants were significantly different from White American babies in a number of behaviors. The African infants scored lower on visual pursuit, irritability, rapidity of buildup, and alertness. They scored higher in cuddliness, reactivity to stimulation, alertness, social interest, and consolability. While one cannot generalize, in the absence of data, from African infants to Black American infants, these findings certainly suggest that biologically based differences may exist. Freedman and his colleagues (1974) have presented a great deal of data that supports the existence of biologically based differences in infants.

In addition, Schachter, Kerr, and Wimberly (1974) have shown that Black infants tend to have significantly higher heart rate levels than other babies. It is not known if there are significant behavioral correlates to these higher heart rates. It is known that variability in heart rate appears to be related to some infant behaviors. Kagan (1979), for example, found that persistent lower heart rate ranges were associated with greater inhibition in infants. Similar studies have not been conducted with Black infants. Nonetheless, it is possible that behavioral differences in Black infants could significantly affect the nature and/or expression of their cognitive development and skills. There is a tremendous need to expand our understanding of the possible differences in behavior and development in Black infants and assess their implications for cognitive development in Black children.

In the next section, we explore the postnatal and environmental factors that may be related to cognitive development in Black children. The discussion is divided into two parts: intrafamilial influences and extrafamilial influences. Intrafamilial influences refer to characteristics of the family system such as patterns of caretaker infant interaction, parental attitudes, and behaviors, and levels of stimulation in the home that are thought to be related to cognitive development in infants. Extrafamilial influences include the economic and social factors that may impact on parental behavior and the family system, but also operate concurrently and independently of the family system, to influence cognitive development in children in ways that might not be recognized as easily.

The results of the following studies must be viewed with some caution. There have been a number of methodological problems in the studies of Black families (Harrison et al., 1984; Myers, 1982). Of particular importance is the fact that many studies have confounded race and economic status. Thus, it is impossible to separate their respective effects. This problem and other methodological problems will be discussed in more detail in a later section of this chapter. Given the problems that have existed in this area of research, however, one must assume that the findings require further study and replication.

Intrafamilial and Extrafamilial Influences on Cognitive Development in Black Infants

Intrafamilial Influences

Most of the studies that have been designed to investigate cognitive development in Black children have focused on the familial environment and, particularly, caretaker–infant interaction as the primary units of analysis (Bee et al., 1982; Sameroff & Chandler, 1975; Sameroff et al., 1982). This approach was and continues to be guided by a number of assumptions that are pervasive in developmental research (Kagan, 1979). As Kagan notes, the first assumption is that a particular set of identifiable external conditions are inevitably associated with a fixed set of consequences for all children. Second, the behaviors that are presumably affected by early experience are stable over time. And third, the nature of the mother–infant bond is the primary determinant of the future psychological and developmental well-being of the child. Kagan further states that these three assumptions have led to the dominant thesis that "frequent, salient and affectively pleasant interactions between infant and mother during the first two years of life produce dispositions that protect the older child against future anxiety and promote cognitive development for an indefinite period" (Kagan, 1979, p. 886). Despite the fact that there is much evidence that these assumptions are not entirely valid, much developmental research in psychology, pediatrics, and psychiatry is based on these premises. The utilization of this approach has led to the identification of the following variables that appear to be related to optimal cognitive development in children (Bee et al., 1982):

High maternal education.

Variety and amount of animate and inanimate stimulation provided in the home including provision of sufficient and appropriate play materials in the home.

Contingent delivery of stimulation, particularly verbal stimulation of and responsivity to the child.

Style of interaction between parent and child particularly affectionate, nonrestrictive and nonpunitive caregiving.

Parents' perception of the child as better than average.

It has been assumed that deficits in any or all of the above are related to poorer cognitive development in children. Collectively, the bulk of the studies on familial environment and its relationship to cognitive development in Black children have indicated that Black parents differ from parents of other ethnic groups in each of the above dimensions. These differences were particularly pronounced when low-income, Black parents were compared to middle-income parents from other ethnic groups. For example, Clarke-Stewart (1973), in her study of interactions between mothers and their infants in Black and White families, reported that Black mothers provided fewer toys for their infants, were more restrictive, and spent more time caring for the child's physical needs. In contrast to White mothers, they talked to their babies less, looked at them less, played with them less, and were less affectionate. Interestingly, Clarke-Stewart (1973) observed that despite these differences, "Judging by children's immediate responses to maternal behaviors, Black mothers' physical and social behaviors also were more effective than were those of White mothers" (p. 57).

Black infants were also judged to be more physically attached to their mothers. Black mothers were found to spend as much time with their infants as White mothers, but they spent more time controlling their infants. Black infants were found to score consistently lower on all measures of competence by 17 months of age. Clarke-Stewart (1973) concluded that children's overall competence is "highly and significantly related to maternal care" (p. 92). Bradley and Caldwell (1976) similarly found that the nature of the early home environment was related to later I.Q. scores for Black children. Although the data were collapsed across racial groups, they found that the quality of stimulation provided, maternal involvement with the child and emotional and verbal responsivity of the mother correlated with infant I.Q. scores. Durrett, O'Bryant, and Dennebaker (1975) have reported that Black parents are more authoritative in their child-rearing practices.

As noted previously, there has been an interesting and important interaction between neonatal status, socioeconomic status, and cognitive development reported by a number of investigators. The data from these studies suggest that socioeconomic status has a pervasive effect on cognitive development and the effect is particularly acute if the infant has been exposed to prenatal or perinatal insult. Zeskind and Ramey (1978, 1981) have shown, for example, that low-birth-weight Black infants who were raised in low-income environments showed significant declines in cognitive development over time. Others have reported similar findings (Sameroff & Chandler, 1975). Two unusually large studies of the effects of perinatal complications on cognitive development in children support these findings. The Kauai study, by Werner, Bierman, and Frence (1971), documented that perinatal complications were consistently related to later cognitive development in children only when combined with poor environmental circumstances. Broman and associated (Broman, Bien, & Shaughnessy, 1985), in a study of 50,000 women and their infants in the United States, also concluded that lower socioeconomic status, higher birth order, and larger family size are significantly related to higher rates of academic failure, particularly in children who have experienced perinatal complications. Sameroff and Seifer (1983) report similar results. Not all of the children in these studies were Black; however, since race and economic status are so often confounded in these studies, one might assume that a significant number of the lower-income families were Black.

In the Sameroff and Seifer study, for example, families from five economic levels were sampled; however, only Black families from the two lowest economic levels were included. Only White families from the three highest economic categories were sampled. Sameroff and Seifer, in interpreting the findings of the above studies, have concluded that developmental outcome, particularly if the infant is biologically vulnerable, is determined or moderated by social status variables. They hypothesize that the critical variable in determining cognitive outcome in infants is the ability of the family to mediate between the child and the environment. "Better conceptions of reality permit a family to reduce the impact of stress on the child and also provide the child with optimal growth experiences" (Sameroff & Seifer, 1983, p. 1260). Poorer conceptions of reality inhibit a family's ability to moderate the effects of a stressful life experience and/or provide special experiences for children with special needs.

Data from the studies presented in this section suggest that Black parents differ in their interactions with their infants, and Black parents provide less stimulating environments for their infants. The investigators also suggest that these environmental differences adversely affect cognitive development in Black children. There is data that refutes these conclusions on a number of levels. First, Bakeman and Brown (1980) have reported in their study of Black mothers and their preterm vs. full-term infants that differences in early interaction did not predict either social or cognitive ability at age three years. Birth status (preterm/full-term) was more predictive of cognitive development. Second, many of the above studies assume that parental behaviors influence infant development, but they do not explore the possibility that the nature of the infant's behavior may strongly influence the parent's behavior. There is considerable evidence that this is the case.

Green et al. (1980) have shown both that an infant's social environment is determined, in part, by the infant's developmental status and that there are consistent differences in infant–mother dyads across time. Field, Widmayer, Stringer, and Ignatoff (1980) also report that low-income Black mothers have higher expectations regarding motor development for their infants and the infants do show optimal motor development. Many of the above studies also fail to examine any positive effects that the caregiving behaviors of Black parents may have had on infant cognitive development and/or fail to discuss the differential effects of caretaking behavior on infant development. For example, Clarke-Stewart (1973) suggests, but does not fully discuss in her summary and conclusions, the fact that her results indicate that the processes involved in mother–child interaction may be different in Black and White homes. That is to say, sources of variation in the environment that are important for White mothers and children may not be for Black families. She suggests, for example, that the number of toys available to Black infants appeared to be a more critical variable for infant development than did variety. The opposite appeared to be true for White families. The correlations between the mother's I.Q. and the child's I.Q. were also higher for Whites than for Blacks. These findings suggest that different factors may be related to cognitive development in infants in Black homes, particularly in low-income Black homes.

Beckwith, Cohen, Kopp, Parmelee, and Marcy (1976) have found that environmental factors may influence different aspects of cognitive development. Sensorimotor development in infants was associated with different maternal and environmental variables than was an infant's developmental quotient. Interestingly, Beckwith et al. (1976) reports that developmental scores were also associated with increased maternal criticism and commands at three months of age. This is not an isolated finding (Beckwith, 1971). It is ironic that the maternal behaviors that Clarke-Stewart identified as negatively affecting cognitive development in Black infants have been found by others to possibly accelerate infant development. These behaviors are thought to reflect achievement concerns on the part of many Black parents (Hale-Benson, 1982; Honzik, 1967).

The findings regarding the level of stimulation in the homes of Black infants in the previously discussed studies have also been contradicted by subsequent findings. Boykin (1978) and Field et al. (1980) have reported that the level of stimulation in the homes of Black children provide an abundance of stimulation, intensity, and variation. Also, as Kagan, Kearsley, and Zelazo (1980) have reported, variety can be generated in different ways and in different contexts of care. Variety of stimulation need not be measured solely by the number of caretaker–infant interactions. Variety connotes change and change can occur in any setting.

Sameroff and Seifer's (1983) observation that infants who have experienced perinatal complications tend to have a poorer cognitive outcome is an important finding. Their attribution of this outcome to social status variables may be correct; however, their conclusion that the behavior, or conceptions of reality on the part of the family, is the salient feature of low-income status may be faulty.

In the next section we explore extrafamilial factors that are associated with social status that may independently and concurrently affect infant cognitive development. As we shall see, the circumstances of poverty, in combination with perinatal insult, may override the influence of specific parental behaviors on cognitive development in children.

Extrafamilial Influences

The above studies illustrate the importance of social status variables in predicting infant outcome. Lower social status in our society connotes less respect and prestige relative to occupation, less power to influence the institutions of the community, less availability of educational and occupational opportunity, and fewer economic resources (Harrison, Serafica, & McAdoo, 1984; Hess, 1970). Low-income ethnic families of color are also often stigmatized in terms of assumed inferior traits or characteristics (Harrison et al. 1984). Thus, lower social status offers children experiences that are both different and unequal with respect to the resources and rewards of the society (Hess, 1970). These differences in access to the resources of the society can influence child development in lower socioeconomic status families, but the most critical variable for cognitive development in children may be the lack of financial resources in low-income families.

In focusing their primary attention on patterns of interaction between Black, low-income parents and their children, investigators such as Clarke-Stewart may have failed to adequately evaluate the very significant effect that lack of financial resources can have on child development, particularly in the cognitive sphere. Lack of financial resources in families most often results in inadequate nutrition for children and adults, poor or nonexistent medical care, and inadequate housing (Birch & Gussow, 1970). These factors, in turn, can have major and deleterious effects on children's development, health, and cognitive skills.

Most of the previous studies have failed to evaluate the impact of these variables on cognitive development in low-income Black children nor did they attempt to control for these variables across groups. It may be impossible, in fact, to equate these variables across groups of ethnically diverse families. Yet, there is overwhelming evidence that poverty exerts a pervasive and cumulative effect on cognitive development in low-income children (Birch & Gussow, 1970).

Few studies have specifically examined the role that inadequate nutrition and poor medical care have played in the cognitive development of Black children in our society. The relationship between malnutrition, poor health status, illness, and delays in physical and cognitive development is well recognized and well documented in other parts of the world. In other countries it has been recognized that educational failure is part of a cycle of poverty. When the levels of malnutrition and infant illness are extreme, cognitive deficits first appear in children during infancy (Ford Foundation, 1983). In Chile, for example, 78% of the young low-income children show significant deficits in cognitive development, whereas only 2% of the middle-income children show similar delays. Infant mortality in such countries is also very high.

In the United States, the rate of infant mortality among low-income groups, particularly Black low-income groups, approaches that of developing countries. Although the levels of malnutrition and illness during early childhood may not equal the rates in other countries, the following statistics certainly suggest that low-income children of all races, and particularly low-income Black children, suffer poorer health, malnutrition, and undernutrition in numbers that far exceed those of children from higher-income groups. In some parts of the United States, debility and illness rates for low-income American children approach the rates for children in Bangladesh (Ford Foundation, 1983). The following statistics regarding health status in Black children reflect the fact that such children are more likely to be living in poverty and are more likely to continue to suffer poorer health throughout the first years of life. In 1983, for example, almost one half of Black children were living in poverty and the median income of Black families was less than six tenths that of

White families (Children's Defense Fund, 1985). Black children living with a sole female caretaker are the poorest group of children in our nation and their family income declined 28.39% from 1977 to 1982. Up to 27% of Black children did not see a doctor at all in 1983; they are much less likely to have health insurance, and the number of Black preschool children who were not immunized against childhood diseases ranged from 61.5% to 70.6%.

The rate of illness and infection in Black and non-White children is also significantly higher. Up to 18.8% of non-White children had active cases of tuberculosis in 1979 (Children's Defense Fund, 1985). There is also substantial evidence that low-income Black children are more likely to have elevated blood lead levels, infections, and pneumonitis in the first two years of life (Adebonojo, 1973). In addition, between one fifth and one third of Black children have hemoglobin levels that fall below the White median hemoglobin level (Children's Defense Fund, 1985). This is one indicator of poor nutritional status and anemia. Jelliffe and Jelliffe (1973) have concluded that the most prominent indicators for malnutrition in the United States include low-income, single-parent household, and lack of consistent health care. The Black child is likely to have fewer well-child and health maintenance checkups, and more frequent hospitalizations for more serious and life-threatening illnesses (Adebonojo, 1973).

The above statistics clearly indicate that low-income Black children are at higher risk for health problems, poorer health, and malnutrition. It is also clear that poor health status is inextricably related to later cognitive development (Ford Foundation, 1983; Wolman, 1973). Poor health, infrequent medical care, and malnutrition/undernutrition result in poor physical and cognitive development and may affect central nervous system development (Birch & Gussow, 1970; Ford Foundation, 1983; Wolman, 1973). These factors can affect later problem-solving ability, language, personal–social development, general intelligence, sensory integration, and visual-perception skills (Wolman, 1973). There is also much evidence that the effects of poor health status and malnutrition are cumulative, producing greater deficits as the child grows and develops (Wolman, 1973). The consequences of poor health and inadequate nutrition on cognitive development in children are most severe when the deprivation begins prenatally (i.e., the mother suffers poor health and inadequate nutrition), extends through infancy, and continues throughout early childhood (Birch & Gussow, 1970; Ford Foundation, 1983; Wolman, 1973).

Perhaps the best support for the impact that health status has on cognitive development comes from the success of intervention programs with low-income families that stress both parent–infant interaction and continued medical care. Intervention programs that incorporate medical care and supervision appear to offer more promise for facilitating optimal cognitive development in children than programs that focus exclusively on parent–infant interaction (Birch & Gussow, 1970; Morris, 1973; Ullman, Kotok, & Tobin, 1977; Seigel, Gillings, Campbell, & Guild, 1986). Seigel et al. (1986) have reported that a regionalized perinatal program that included identification of high-risk pregnancies and high-risk infants, obstetric and newborn consultation and referral services, and nutrition consultation was successful in reducing infant morbidity in the targeted population. Mothers who participated in the program also reported significant gains in language development in their infants, and infants in the study region had higher mean scores on developmental tests. Infants in the study region also had better developmental reflex maturity, and maternal involvement with infants was greater in the study region. Indirect support for the potential value of intervention programs that stress caretaker–infant interaction and health also comes from studies that suggest that the nature and extensiveness of a family's social network and social support system can facilitate cognitive development in a child (Bee et al., 1982; Cochran & Brassard, 1979). Presumably, as one's social network and social support system increases, the number and variety of potential sources of influence on the child's cognitive development increase. The sources of influence may include individuals and/or systems that promote and/or increase the probability that a child will receive better health care and/or nutrition.

Summary

The above evidence indicates that Black children, particularly low-income Black children, are more vulnerable to prenatal, perinatal, and postnatal health hazards. They are also more likely to suffer from poorer health, lack of medical supervision, and inadequate nutrition. These environmental realities can, and do, decrease the probability that any of these children will be able to realize and achieve their full academic potential. The effect of poverty and lack of financial resources is pervasive and cumulative. Poverty begins to affect a child's cognitive development when it impacts the health and nutritional status of a pregnant woman and, thus, increases the probability that a child will be exposed to prenatal and/or perinatal complications. It continues its deleterious effect as the low birth weight or premature infant continues to suffer from inadequate nutrition and lack of medical care. The effect of poverty on cognitive development may not be as apparent in the period of infancy, however. Perhaps the effects of undernutrition, infections, and illness, because they are not as extreme in this country as in others, are not as apparent until later ages in children in this country. The cumulative effect of poverty on cognitive development becomes significant, however, as a child grows and develops and cognitive demands on that child increase.

The focus on poverty and its effects on health and cognitive development in low-income Black children is not intended to negate the importance of intrafamilial influences on cognitive development. Certainly, consistent and effective caretaking facilitates cognitive growth. This discussion is designed to illustrate the importance of evaluating health status in children and its relationship to cognitive development. It is also designed to encourage developmental researchers to broaden their conceptualization of social status factors that influence cognitive development in children to include the economic and social influences on development. Third, this discussion should indicate that comparative studies of parental behavior that do not evaluate the health status of children may be unproductive. Not only do poverty and health variables correlate with cognitive development in children but they have an important and critical impact on parental behaviors (Wolman, 1973). Thus, many low-income Black parents may be responding to their children in ways that may obviously, and not so obviously, ensure biological survival of the infant. They may promote behaviors that are adaptive for the environmental context in which the child lives, and may or may not be adaptive for our current educational system.

In addition, the health status of the infant affects parental perceptions and behavior (Green et al., 1980; Field et al., 1980). Many Black infants may behave differently because of their health status and Black parents may be responding in very typical ways. This discussion is also not designed to neglect other sources of influence (e.g., school systems, peers) on cognitive development in Black children; these sources are very real and important. It was the intent of this chapter, however, to examine the conditions of infancy in Black children and assess possible relationships to cognitive development.

Our efforts to facilitate academic achievement in Black children cannot be limited to changes in curriculum and/or the development of intervention programs to "modify" caretaker–infant interaction in Black families. The exclusive focus on social, psychological, and educational remedies for educational underachievement may, as Birch and Gussow (1970) have suggested, lead us to neglect the health-related factors that directly and indirectly influence the developing child and alter his or her ability to profit from educational experiences. Our attempts to intervene in the education of Black children and the caretaking activities of Black families might be more successful and beneficial if we directed our efforts to the improvement of health care and nutrition for children in these families. In addition, we need to ensure that access to continued health care and adequate nutrition is provided to those low-income families who include infants who have experienced prenatal and/or perinatal complications. Clearly, these are the children who are most vulnerable to later learning problems. It is becoming increasingly clear that there are many psychological, biological, and environmental factors that contribute to cognitive development in children. Among these, however, the access to continued health care and adequate food intake may be the most critical and modifiable determinants of cognitive development in children.

Directions for Future Research

As mentioned earlier in this chapter, there have been a number of methodological and/or conceptual problems in research on Black families. (For an extensive review see Harrison et al., 1984; Myers, 1982.) These include:

The full range of economic levels in Black families has not been adequately sampled in previous studies; thus, one cannot begin to separate the effects of poverty and ethnicity.

Data across ethnic groups has often been collapsed for the purposes of analyses. Consequently, it is virtually impossible to assess whether ethnic difference exist and to examine the direction of the effects (positive vs. negative).

Many studies have implicitly or explicitly been based on the assumption that the behavior of middle-income parents is preferred, normative, and effective. The norms, values, and goals of parenting in ethnic and low-income families have not been adequately assessed.

Many studies have assumed equivalence of culture, color, and class. It may not be possible to legitimately compare the behavior of different ethnic groups within the same economic level since the impact of ethnicity may differ, even within the same economic group.

Many studies have ignored or failed to adequately assess the impact of the child's behavior on the parents' behavior. Thus, it is difficult to determine whether parental behavior differs in response to infant traits.

Most studies have failed to examine the influence of health status on cognitive development. The correlation between health status and cognitive development may be higher than the correlation between parental behavior and cognitive development.

The assessment of prenatal and postnatal influences on cognitive development in Black children offers many avenues for future research. There is a critical need for research that focuses on both the similarities and differences in child development within Black families across various economic groups. This approach would allow assessment of the impact of poverty on general development, cognitive skills, health status, and parental behavior. Second, equal attention should be paid to behaviors and environmental circumstances in Black families that facilitate competence in Black children in spite of the health hazards to which they are exposed. Clearly, Black parents are engaging in behaviors that are effective and productive and Black children do prosper despite adverse environmental conditions. The mechanisms by which this productivity occurs should be identified so that effective methods of fostering optimal development in Black children within the context in which they develop can be enumerated.

We must also begin to evaluate within-family variations in child development in Black families in an effort to identify those environmental, behavioral, and/or constitutional variables that are associated with optimal development. In sum, we must begin to evaluate a child's skills in the total context of his or her development. This would include examination of the impact of constitutional/biological factors, transactions with the environment, and historical/cultural events. It is the cumulative effects of these experiences that are critical to subsequent development. To evaluate and understand less is irresponsible.

REFERENCES

Adebonojo, F. O. (1973). A comparative study of child health care in urban and suburban children. *Clinical Pediatrics, 12,* 644–648.

Ainsworth, M. S. (1967). *Infancy in Uganda.* Baltimore MD: Johns Hopkins University Press.

Bakeman, R., & Brown, J. V. (1980). Early interaction: Consequences for social and mental development at three years. *Child Development, 51,* 199–207.

Bayley, N. (1965). Comparisons of mental and motor test scores for ages 1–15 months by sex, birth order, race, geographical location and education of parents. *Child Development, 36,* 379–411.

Beckwith, L. (1971). Relationships between attributes of mothers and their infants' I.Q. scores. *Child Development, 42,* 1083–1097.

Beckwith, L., Cohen, S. E., Kopp, C. B., Parmelee, A. H., & Marcy, T. G. (1976). Caregiver–infant interaction and early cognitive development in preterm infants. *Child Development, 47,* 579–587.

Bee, H. L., Barnard, K. E., Eyres, S. S., Gray, C. A., Hammond, M. A., Snyder, C., & Clark, B. (1982). Prediction of I.Q. and language skill from perinatal status, child performance, family characteristics, and mother–infant interaction. *Child Development, 3,* 1134–1156.

Birch, H. G., & Gussow, J. D. (1970). *Disadvantaged children: Health, nutrition, and school failure.* New York: Harcourt, Brace, and World.

Boykin, A. W. (1978). Psychological/behavioral verve in academic/task performance: Pretheoretical considerations. *Journal of Negro Education, 47,* 343–354.

Bradley, R. H., & Caldwell, B. M. (1976). The relation of infants' home environments to mental test performance at fifty-four months: A follow-up study. *Child Development, 47,* 1172–1174.

Bradley, R. H., Caldwell, B. M., & Elardo, R. (1979). Home environment and cognitive development in the first two years: A cross-lagged panel analysis. *Developmental Psychology, 15,* 246–250.

Brazelton, T., Koslowski, B., & Tronic, E. (1981). Racial differences in newborn heart rate level. *Psychophysiology, 11,* 220.

Broman, S. H., Bien, E., & Shaughnessy, P. (1985). *Low achieving children: The first seven years.* New Jersey: Lawrence Erlbaum.

Broman, S. H., Nichols, P. L., & Kennedy, W. A. (1975). *Prenatal and early developmental correlates.* Hillsdale, NJ: Lawrence Erlbaum.

Children's Defense Fund. (1985). *Black and White children in America: Key facts.* Washington, DC: Author.

Clarke-Stewart, K. A. (1973). Interactions between mothers and their young children: Characteristics and consequences. *Monographs of the Society for Research in Child Development,* Serial No. 152, *38,* 6–7.

Cochran, M. M., & Brassard, J. A. (1979). Child development and personal social networks. *Child Development, 50,* 601–616.

Durrett, M. E., O'Bryant, S., & Dennebaker, J. W. (1975). Child-rearing reports of White, Black, and Mexican American families. *Developmental Psychology, 11,* 871.

Escalona, S. K. (1973). The differential impact of environmental conditions as a function of different reaction patterns in infancy. In J. Westman (Ed.), *Individual differences in children* (pp. 145–157). New York: John Wiley.

Field, T. M., Widmayer, S. M., Stringer, S., & Ignatoff, E. (1980). Teenage lower-class Black mothers and their preterm infants: An intervention and developmental follow-up. *Child Development, 51,* 426–436.

Ford Foundation, (1983). Child survival/fair start. A working paper.

Freedman, D. G. (1974). *Human infancy: An evolutionary perspective.* Hillsdale, NJ: Lawrence Erlbaum.

Gerber, U., & Dean, R. F. (1966). Precocious development in newborn African infants. In Y. Brackbill & G. Thompson (Eds.), *Readings in infancy and childhood* (pp. 120–126). New York: Free Press.

Golden, M., & Birns, B. (1976). Social class and infant intelligence. In M. Lewis (Ed.), *Origins of intelligence: Infancy and early childhood.* New York: Plenum.

Gorski, P. A., Lewkowicz, D. J., & Huntington, L. (1987). Advances in neonatal and infant behavioral assessment: Toward a comprehensive evaluation of early patterns of development. *Developmental and Behavioral Pediatrics, 8,* 39–50.

Green, J. A., Gustafson, G. E., & West, M. W. (1980). Effects of infant development on mother–infant interactions. *Child Development, 51,* 199–207.

Hale-Benson, J. E. (1982). *Black children: Their roots, culture, and learning styles.* Baltimore, MD: Johns Hopkins University Press.

Harrison, A., Serafica, F., & McAdoo, H. (1984). Ethnic families of color. In R. D. Parke (Ed.), *Review of child development research* (Vol. 7, pp. 329–371). Chicago: University of Chicago Press.

Hess, R. D. (1970). Social class and ethnic influences on socialization. In P. H. Mussen (Ed.), *Carmichael's manual of child psychology* (Vol. 2, pp. 457–557). New York: John Wiley.

Honzik, M. (1967). Environmental correlates of mental growth. *Child Development, 38,* 337–364.

Jelliffe, D. B., & Jelliffe, E. F. (1973). The at-risk concept as related to young child nutrition programs. *Clinical Pediatrics, 12,* 65–67.

Kagan, J. (1979). Family experience and the child's development. *American Psychologist, 25,* 41–48.

Kagan, J., Kearsley, R. B., & Zelazo, P. R. (1980). *Infancy: Its place in human development.* Cambridge, MA: Harvard University Press.

Lipsitt, L. P. (1977). The study of sensory and learning processes of the newborn. *Clinics in Perinatology, 4*(1), 163–186.

Lipsitt, L. P. (1979). Critical conditions in infancy: A psychological perspective. *American Psychologist, 34,* 973–980.

Lipsitt, L. P. (1986). Learning in infancy: Cognitive development in babies. *The Journal of Pediatrics, 109,* 172–182.

Lipsitt, L. P., & Werner, J. S. (1981). The infancy of human learning processes. In E. S. Collin (Ed.), *Developmental Plasticity* (pp. 101–133). New York: Academic Press.

Morgan, H. (1976). Neonatal precocity and the Black experience. *Negro Educational Review, 27,* 129–134.

Morris, A. G. (1973). Parent education for child education being carried out in a pediatric clinic playroom. *Clinical Pediatrics, 12,* 235–239.

Myers, H. F. (1982). Research on the Afro-American family: A critical review. In B. Bass, G. Wyatt, & G. Powell (Eds.), *The Afro-American family: Assessment, treatment, and research issues.* New York: Grune Stratton.

Sameroff, A. J. (1986). Environmental context of child development. *Journal of Pediatrics, 109,* 192–200.

Sameroff, A. J., & Chandler, M. J. (1975). Reproductive risk and the continuum of caretaking causality. In F. D. Horowitz, M. Hetherington, S. Scarr-Salapatek, & G. Seigel (Eds.), *Review of child development research* (Vol. 4, pp. 187–244). Chicago: University of Chicago Press.

Sameroff, A. J., & Seifer, R. (1983). Familial risk and child competence. *Child Development, 54,* 1254–1268.

Sameroff, A. J., Seifer, R., & Zan, M. (1982). Early development of children at risk for emotional disorder. *Monographs of the Society for Research in Child Development, 47.*

Schachter, J., Kerr, J., & Wimberly, F. (1974). Racial differences in newborn heart rate level. *Psychophysiology, 11,* 220.

Seigel, E., Gillings, D., Campbell, S., & Guild, P. (1986). Controlled evaluation of rural regional perinatal care: Developmental and neurologic outcomes at one year. *Pediatrics, 77,* 601–616.

U. S. Department of Health and Human Services. (1985). *Health status of minorities and low income groups* (DHHS Publication No. (HRSA) HRS-P-DV85-1). Washington, DC: U.S. Department of Health and Human Services, Health Resources and Services Administration, Bureau of Health Professions, Division of Disadvantaged Populations.

U.S. Department of Health and Human Services (1986). *Report of the Secretary's task force on Black and minority health, Vol. 6: Infant mortality and low birthweight.* Washington, DC: Author.

Ullman, R., Kotok, D., & Tobin, J. R. (1977). Hospital-based group practice and comprehensive care for children of indigent families. *Pediatrics, 60,* 873–880.

Walters, C. E. (1967). Comparative development of Negro and White infants. *Journal of Genetic Psychology, 110,* 243–251.

Werner, E. E., Bierman, J. M., & France, F. E. (1971). *The children of Kauai.* Honolulu: University of Hawaii.

White, B., & Watts, J. (1973). *Experience and environment.* Englewood Cliffs, NJ: Prentice-Hall.

Wolman, I. J. (1973). Some prominent developments in child nutrition: 1972. *Clinical Pediatrics, 12,* 72–82.

Zeskind, P. S., & Ramey, C. T. (1978). Fetal malnutrition: An experimental study of its consequences on infant development in two caretaking environments. *Child Development, 49,* 1155–1162.

Zeskind, P. S., & Ramey, C. T. (1981). Preventing intellectual and international sequelae of fetal malnutrition: A longitudinal transactional and synergistic approach to development. *Child Development, 52,* 213–218.

2

Motivation in Afro-Americans

SANDRA GRAHAM

There is a simple premise guiding this chapter: Much of the chronic school failure of Black or Afro-American children can be understood as reflecting problems in motivation. Far too many minority children perform poorly in school not because they lack basic intellectual capacities or specific learning skills but because they have low expectations, feel hopeless, lack interest, or give up in the face of potential failure. These are motivational concerns and they are just as important to understanding academic achievement among Blacks as is our more traditional focus on basic cognitive processes. In this chapter, the research on a number of prominent motivational variables studied among Blacks is critically examined. Such a critique is perhaps long overdue; the psychological study of minority motivation has not kept pace with our need to better understand the role of nonintellective factors in school performance.

Two distinct approaches to the study of motivation in Blacks will be examined. As the historically dominant school of thought, the personality approach to minority motivation will be examined first. Personality psychologists study underlying traits or dispositions within people that are thought to reflect motivation. In the field of minority motivation, the traits most often examined, and the ones to be reviewed in this chapter, are need for achievement and locus of control.

A second, more contemporary perspective examined in this chapter is what we might label the cognitive approach to motivation. Here we are concerned not with underlying traits or dispositions but rather with an individual's cognitions (e.g., perceptions, evaluations, causal inferences) as determinants of achievement-related behavior. For example, when Black children do well or poorly on a test, what are their beliefs about the causes of these outcomes? Are there different motivational consequences for the student who attributes failure in math to lack of aptitude versus poor instruction? As intimated in these examples, the particular cognitions examined here are causal attributions, or inferences about why outcomes occur. Causal attributions are central to a theory or motivation that has proved to be exceedingly rich and applicable to a wide range of phenomena relevant to Blacks (see Graham, 1988). One of the particular goals for this chapter is to indicate how attribution theory can offer a useful conceptual framework for examining motivational patterns in Blacks.

Within both the personality and cognitive approaches to motivation, most of the research with Blacks has been conducted within a comparative racial framework. This is, Blacks are compared with Whites or other ethnic groups on the motivational variable of interest. Inasmuch as this continues to be the dominant research paradigm, I will concentrate in this review on the comparative racial literature.

Personality Approach to Motivation: Need for Achievement

Need for achievement (Nach), or the achievement motive, is a relatively stable feature of personality reflecting the desire to do things well and to compete against a standard of excellence. Individuals who are high in the achievement motive appear to be interested in excellence for its own sake rather than for the rewards it brings. Given a choice between easy, moderate, or difficult tasks, such individuals find tasks of moderate difficulty most attractive. These are the students, for example, who work hard to excel but might not necessarily elect the most advanced courses. In a similar vein, such highly motivated individuals tend to be moderate risk takers and to have realistic aspirations.

Historically, the study of achievement motivation as a personality trait began in 1938 when Henry Murray observed that individuals vary in their tendency or desire to accomplish difficult things and to do this as quickly and as independently as possible (Murray, 1938). Murray labeled this tendency the need to achieve and he devised the Thematic Apperception Test (TAT) to measure variations in the strength of this motive. Interest in the achievement motive continued to grow thereafter, with something of a "Golden Age" occurring from about 1950 to 1965. David McClelland and his colleagues were the first psychologists to study need for achievement experimentally and this work culminated in the publication of *The Achievement Motive* in 1953 (McClelland, Atkinson, Clark, & Lowell, 1953). John Atkinson furthered this experimental tradition with a theory of achievement motivation that dominated motivation research throughout the 1960s (see Atkinson, 1964).

It is not surprising that need for achievement would attract the attention of researchers concerned with motivation among minority groups. Paralleling the experimental research on motive measurement and its behavioral correlates was a growing interest in the relationship between achievement need and social mobility. McClelland's (1961) ambitious attempt to relate the achievement motive to economic growth of nations underscored the linkage between the study of personality structures on the one hand and status and social mobility on the other. Given this orientation, it was but a short leap to suggest that ethnically (and thus socially) different groups in this country might also differ in their achievement needs.

A second factor accounting for the popularity of achievement motive research among Blacks stemmed from efforts to uncover the developmental antecedents of achievement needs. McClelland (1951) maintained that patterns of child rearing played a critical role in the child's achievement motivation. In support of this contention, several studies reported that motive strength in children was related to particular family socialization patterns such as high achievement (mastery) training, especially from the mother; training in early independence and self-reliance, especially from the father; and high levels of parental nurturance (Winterbottom, 1953; Rosen, 1959; Rosen & D'Andrade, 1959). The view of the family fostered by these patterns was quite the opposite of the portrayal of Black family life at the time. Black families in the 1950s and 1960s were characterized as disorganized, unstable, largely father-absent, and harshly authoritarian (e.g., Rainwater, 1966; Moynihan, 1965). Social scientists of the day therefore found it easy to relate differences in family structure between Blacks and Whites to differences in their achievement needs.

For the present review, 14 studies on need for achievement were identified where the primary goal of the study was to compare Blacks and Whites. Table 2.1 lists these studies in chronological order, along with each study's sample characteristics (e.g., number, ages, and socioeconomic status of subjects), type of measure used, and overall direction of findings.

Turning first to sample characteristics, it is evident that 4 of the 14 studies included only male participants. This is not surprising inasmuch as females also tended to be neglected in the achievement motivation research of McClelland and Atkinson. Socioeconomic status of participants tended to be low (7 studies) or unspecified, suggesting that participants of both races were not represented across all social class groupings. This seems to be typical of most comparative racial research, but this methodological issue will be discussed later in the chapter.

What do the data show regarding differences between Blacks and Whites in motive strength? Most previous reviews have concluded that Whites have higher achievement needs than Blacks (see Cooper & Tom, 1984). The last column of Table 2.1 shows the direction of findings in the present review. It also is evident here that the majority of studies (9 of 14) report at least one set of findings showing differences favoring Whites over Blacks. But a closer examination of the pattern of findings in Table 2.1 reveals a picture more complex than what is indicated by a simple numerical count. Specifically, there appear to be at least three unanswered questions raised by the comparative racial literature on need for achievement.

Are there developmental differences in the pattern of comparative racial differences? Perhaps most apparent in Table 2.1 is the fact that all of the investigations documenting differences in favor of Whites were conducted with children. In the three experiments involving adult populations, there was either no reported difference in motive strength between the two racial groups or, as in Lefkowitz and Fraser (1980), differences favoring Blacks over Whites. There is some evidence in the noncomparative literature that Nach scores of Blacks increase with age (e.g., Schroth, 1976), but clearly the necessary developmental research has not been carried out. It is uncertain, then, whether racial differences in motive strength endure past childhood and adolescence.

Are reported racial differences influenced by the method of motive measurement? Most of the comparative racial studies employed the TAT or other TAT-like projective techniques. Respondents write

Table 2.1.   Comparative Racial Research on Need for Achievement

Study	Sample	Socio-economic Status (SES)	Method of Assessment	Direction of Findings
Musen (1953)	100 9- to 14-year-old males	Low	TAT Cards	White > Black[a]
Rosen (1959)	954 8- to 14-year-old males of ethnic groups	Varied	TAT Cards	White > Black, all ethnic groups but French Canadians
Lott & Lott (1963)	300 high school seniors	Mid-SES White, Low-SES Black	French Test of Insight	White > Black, all Ss NSD[b] subsample matched for SES and IQ
Mingione (1965)	350 3rd to 7th graders and high school	Low	Projective (TAT-like line drawings)	White > Black in 2 studies
Mingione (1968)	255 5th to 7th graders, White, Black, Puerto Ricans	Low	Projective (TAT-like sentences)	NSD
Veroff & Peele (1969)	1000 5th to 7th graders before and after desegregation	Unspecified	Behavioral (Risk taking, task choice)	White > Black, both measures before and after desegregation
Turner (1972)	518 7th & 8th graders, males	Varied	TAT cards	White > Black, all Ss and within SES groups except lowest
McClelland (1974)	365 adults (18–49 years)	Unspecified	TAT cards	NSD
Hall (1975)	160 junior college students	Low/Low Middle	French Test of Insight	NSD

Table 2.1.   Continued

Study	Sample	Socio-economic Status (SES)	Method of Assessment	Direction of Findings
Travis & Anthony (1975)	150 high school juniors and seniors in segregated vs. integrated schools	Varied	Objective (EPPS Nach subscale)	Black > White in both school types
Ramirez & Price-Williams (1976)	180 4th graders	Unspecified	Projective (TAT-like line drawings)	White > Black, Nach; Black > White family ach. imagery
Debord (1972)	292 11-year-old males	Low	TAT cards with oral responses	White > Black, low achievers only
Ruhland & Feld (1977)	197 1st and 4th graders	Low	Projective (Story completion) Behavioral (Risk taking, task choice)	NSD autonomous: projective & behavioral White > Black social comparison: projective & behavioral
Lefkowitz & Fraser (1980)	63 college students	Unspecified	TAT cards; Objective (Hermans PMT)	NSD TAT Black > White PMT

[a]Indicates greater motive strength in Whites than Blacks.
[b]Indicates no differences between racial groups in motive strength.

imaginative stories picturing individuals engaged in some activity and these stories are then scored for amount of achievement imagery. The TAT has often been criticized for its poor reliability and this critique has a particular history in the literature on Blacks. As early as 1949, some researchers argued that the White stimulus figures presented in traditional TAT cards do not elicit imagery at all among Blacks (e.g., Thompson, 1949). Several researchers have drawn on this early work to argue that the achievement motive, as well as its primary method of assessment, are culturally biased. In truth, the racial data on the TAT are not as biased as the arguments would lead us to believe. Within the achievement literature, several studies have compared the achievement imagery reported by Blacks given Black versus White TAT cards. Although Blacks do sometimes write longer stories given same-race TAT cards, there is no strong evidence that the motive scores of Blacks are significantly influenced by the racial characteristics of the stimuli (see Lefkowitz & Fraser, 1980 for a recent review).

But lest we dismiss the measurement issue prematurely, it is also worth pointing out that two of the three studies in Table 2.1 showing higher motive strength in Blacks than Whites used objective rather than projective measures of Nach. For example, Travis and Anthony (1975) used the Nach subscales of the Edwards Personal Preference Schedule, which employs a forced choice format, whereas Lefkowitz and Fraser (1980) employed the Hermans Primary Motivation Test, a Likert-type instrument. Once again, there is more uncertainty than resolution in the question of whether racial differences in motive scores are dependent on the way we measure the construct.

Is the achievement motive itself too narrowly defined to yield meaningful racial comparisons? It has often been argued that that the conception of achievement motivation guiding empirical research is biased toward a very Western view of individually motivated human behavior (see Maehr, 1974). If this is so, then it may not be reasonable to study this construct as a measure of motivation in a particular minority group if, for example, the emphasis in that culture is on family or group achievement rather than on individual accomplishment. Unfortunately, only one comparative racial study attempted to define achievement motivation in a broader cultural context. Ramirez and Price-Williams (1976) had children write imaginative stories to TAT-like stimuli. They then scored the children's stories for both individual achievement imagery, as defined by McClelland et al. (1953), and for what they termed *family* achievement imagery. In essence, this scoring entailed reference to achievement or accomplishments from which the family would benefit or from which recognition from family members would be achieved. As shown in Table 2.1, Blacks displayed greater motive strength than Whites when the construct was defined in this manner.

In sum, questions such as those raised above make one wonder about the interpretability of racial differences in the achievement motive. The meaning of reported differences becomes less clear once factors such as age of respondents, motive measurement, and definition of achievement motivation itself are taken into account. It is also evident that the comparative racial literature consists of little more than studies that measure motive strength. None of the theoretical work on the behavioral correlates of high Nach has been incorporated into the comparative literature. As already indicated, high need for achievement is associated with intermediate risk taking, realistic aspirations, and preference for tasks of intermediate difficulty (see Atkinson, 1964). Yet only two of the studies listed in Table 2.1 (Veroff & Peele, 1969; Ruhland & Feld, 1977) examine any of these behavioral correlates. At best, this leaves us with an incomplete picture of racial differences on a personality variable that is central to the study of achievement motivation.

Personality Approach to Motivation: Locus of Control

Locus of control is the second major personality characteristic studied in comparative racial research on motivation. Originally formulated by Julian Rotter, locus of control refers to stable and generalized beliefs about personal responsibility for outcomes (Rotter, 1966). At one extreme is the internal—the individual who thinks of herself as completely responsible for her behavior and reinforcements. At the other extreme is the external—the individual who sees powerful others, luck, or circumstances beyond his control as responsible for outcomes (Rotter, 1966). Internals tend to blame themselves for failure and accept praise for deserved triumphs. Externals, in contrast, neither blame themselves for failure nor do they view success as caused by their own efforts and abilities. Furthermore, people who are relatively internal have been shown to be more likely to exert effort to control their environment, to be less susceptible to social influence, better information seekers, more achievement oriented, and better psychologically adjusted than external (see Lefcourt, 1982).

Locus of control has been an enormously popular personality construction. Although its own "Golden Age," say, the late sixties and the decade of the seventies, has passed, there is still a good deal of interest among motivational psychologists in the characteristics of people who assume personality responsibility for achievement outcomes. Perhaps more so than any other variable, locus of control has also been central in the study of motivation in Blacks. In the landmark Equality of Educational Opportunity Study (EEOS), James Coleman and his colleagues reported that perceived control accounted for more of the variance in Black school achievement than any other variable studied, including school, teacher, and family factors (Coleman et al., 1966). With the publication of the Coleman report, locus of control emerged as the variable that attracted the most attention among researchers directly concerned with the noncognitive determinants of Blacks' school achievement.

A second factor is its conceptual similarity to other factors known to be related to social class and racial group status. For example, in the 1960s a major focus in both psychological and sociological analyses of poverty was the concept of powerlessness (e.g., Seaman & Evans, 1962). Definitions of powerlessness also imply response-outcome independence; indeed, the concept is sometimes used interchangeably with external locus of control. Not surprisingly, then, the prevailing view in the control literature is that Blacks are more external than Whites.

What does the research actually show? Thirty-one studies were identified that examined locus of control in a comparative racial framework (see Table 2.2). These investigations appear in Table 2.2, again ordered chronologically. Given the large number of studies, they are further grouped by age of respondents (school-age children versus older adolescent and adult populations).

Research with Adolescents and Adults

Among adolescents and adults, the most widely used measure of locus of control is the Rotter Internal-External (I-E) Scale (Rotter, 1966). A 29-item scale, the Rotter I-E has a forced choice format that pits an internal belief against an external one. For example, the respondent is asked to choose between: "In my case getting what I want has little or nothing to do with luck" or "Many times we might just as well decide what to do by flipping a coin." (The second is the external item.) Nine of the studies listed in Table 2.2 used the Rotter I-E as the measure of locus of control. Five showed differences favoring

(text continued p. 53)

Table 2.2. Comparative Racial Research on Locus of Control

Study	Sample	Socio-economic Status (SES)	Method of Assessment	Direction of Findings
Adults and Older Adolescents				
Lefcourt & Ladwig (1965)	120 prison inmates	Low	Rotter I-E; Expectancy	White > Black on I-E[a] Black more atypical expectancy shifts
Scott & Phelan (1969)	120 hardcore unemployed males	Low	Rotter I-E	White > Black
Ducette & Wolk (1972)	667 juniors and seniors in 3 high schools	Low-SES Black, Mid-SES White	Rotter I-E	NSD[b]
Edwards (1974)	8th to 11th graders, boys	Varied	Rotter I-E	NSD
Garcia & Levenson (1975)	194 college students	Mid-SES White, Low-SES Black	Levenson Scale	NSD on International scale White > Black on Chance, Powerful Others
Jacobson (1975)	127 11th to 12th graders	Unspecified	Rotter I-E; Crandall IAR	Rotter I-E: NSD IAR: White > Black on I-items, NSD on I-items Scale
Hall (1975)	160 junior college students	Low/Low Middle	Rotter I-E inc. personal control and control	NSD
Farley et al. (1976)	30 college students	Unspecified	Rotter I-E	White > Black

(continued)

Table 2.2. Continued

Study	Sample	Socio-economic Status (SES)	Method of Assessment	Direction of Findings
Levy (1976)	429 13- to 16-year-old males	Low, Middle	Rotter I-E	White > Black
Gaa & Shores (1979)	300 college juniors	Unspecified	Domain-specific LOC scale	For academic: Black > White in success, NSD in failure
				For physical: NSD
				For social: White > Black in success and failure
Helms & Giorgis (1980)	164 college students	Unspecified	Rotter I-E	White > Black overall
				White > Black Personal Control Subscale
				White > Black Control Ideology Subscale
Gaa et al. (1981)	204 Black, White, Chicano high school students	Unspecified	Domain-specific LOC scale	For academic: NSD in success, Black > White in failure
				For social: White > Black in success and failure
				For physical: NSD in success, White > Black in failure

Younger Adolescents and Children

Study	Sample	Socio-economic Status (SES)	Method of Assessment	Direction of Findings
Battle & Rotter (1963)	80 6th & 8th graders	Varied	Children's Picture I-E, Bialer Scale	White > Low-SES Black on both

Table 2.2.   Continued

Study	Sample	Socio-economic Status (SES)	Method of Assessment	Direction of Findings
Lessing (1969)	558 8th & 11th graders	Low, Middle	Personal Control Scale	White > Black
Solomon et al. (1969)	262 4th to 6th graders	Low, Middle	Crandall IAR	NSD
Milgram et al. (1970)	92 6-year-olds	Low-SES Black, Low, Mid-SES White	Children's Picture I-E	NSD
Gable & Minton (1971)	24 high school students	Low	Children's I-E	NSD
Milgram (1971)	80 1st, 4th, 7th, & 10th graders	Low, Low Middle	Bialer Scale	NSD
Pedhazur & Wheeler (1971)	70 5th to 6th graders	Unspecified	Bialer Scale	White > Black
Shaw & Uhl (1971)	211 2nd graders	Low, Upper Middle	Bialer Scale	White > Black in upper middle only
Zytkowkee, Strickland, & Watson (1971)	132 14- to 17-year-olds	Low	Bialer Scale	White > Black
Garrett & Willoughby (1972)	162 5th graders	Unspecified	Crandall IAR	Black > White on I+ White > Black on I–
Strickland (1972)	300 11- to 13-year-olds	Low-SES Black, Varied SES White	Nowicki-Strickland Scale	White > Black

(continued)

Table 2.2.   Continued

Study	Sample	Socio-economic Status (SES)	Method of Assessment	Direction of Findings
DuCette et al. (1972)	40 8- to 11-year-old males with behavior problems or normal	Low	Crandall IAR	For problem Ss: Black > White on I+, White > Black on I− For normal Ss: NSD
DuCette et al. (1972)	40 9- to 11-year-old males	Low	Crandall IAR	White > Black
Gruen et al. (1974)	1,100 White, Black, Spanish-American 2nd to 6th graders	Low, Low Middle	Gruen et al. I-E Scale	White > Black
Burbach & Bridgeman (1976)	274 5th graders	Unspecified	Crandall IAR	*NSD
Will & Verdin (1978)	281 7th graders	Varied	Nowicki-Strickland Scale	White > Black
Wolf et al. 1982)	368 10- to 17-year-olds	Unspecified	Nowicki-Strickland Scale	White > Black
Martin & Cowles (1983)	78 6- to 7-year-olds	Varied	Stephens-Delys RC Interview (open-ended)	NSD
Brown et al. (1984)	161 3rd- & 6th-grade class leaders	Varied	Crandall IAR	White > Black overall White > Black on I+ White > Black on I− for females only

aIndicates greater internality in Whites than Blacks.
bIndicates no differences between racial groups on internality.

Whites over Blacks; that is, Whites were reported to be more internal than Blacks; and four showed no differences in locus of control as a function of race.

One of the major criticisms of locus of control as originally defined by Rotter is the unidimensionality of the construct. While Rotter assumed that his instrument measured a single underlying construct, critics have argued that the perception of control is actually a multidimensional construct. Some have argued, for example, that the I-E scale actually measures several independent dimensions, including (a) a political or powerful others dimension; (b) a chance, fate, or luck dimension; (c) an internal or personal control dimension; and (d) a just or unjust world dimension (see Ashkanasy, 1985).

Such distinctions have proved particularly important in the racial literature. Gurin, Gurin, Lao, and Beattie (1969) factor analyzed responses of more than 1,500 Blacks to the Rotter I-E. They uncovered two independent dimensions that accounted for almost all of the variance in the Rotter I-E items. These dimensions were labeled (a) *personal control,* which refers to how much control one feels he or she personally possesses; and (b) *control ideology,* which refers to how much control one feels individuals have in general. Gurin et al. (1969) and later Lao (1970) reported that Blacks who were internal on personal control achieved better in school, expressed more self-confidence, and had higher aspirations than those who were external on these items. On the other hand, perceived internality on control ideology was unrelated to any of these achievement variables.

The implication of the Gurin et al. finding is that locus of control may need to be more broadly defined before meaningful racial comparisons can be made (see Kinder & Reeder, 1975). For comparative racial research, one wonders whether Blacks are reported to be more internal than Whites when subscales such as those identified by Gurin et al. are included. Unfortunately, the necessary empirical work has not been done to examine this question. Only two investigations reported in Table 2.2 specifically looked at subscales of the Rotter I-E score, and the reported findings were quite inconsistent. Whereas Hall (1975) found no racial differences in the overall I-E score or subscale scores, Helms and Giorgis (1980) reported differences favoring Blacks over Whites on all three measures (i.e., Blacks were more internal than Whites). Three other studies with adolescents and adults followed a multidimensional approach to locus of control using measures other than the I-E (Gaa & Shores, 1979; Gaa, Williams, & Johnson, 1981; Garcia & Levenson, 1975). But these investigations also do not offer a clear picture of the presence or absence of racial differences.

Research with Children

Nineteen studies that tested grade-school children and younger adolescents were identified. Three measures of locus of control have been extensively used in this research. As evident from Table 2.2, a number of the earlier studies used the Bialer LOC Scale (Bialer, 1961) and the Nowicki-Strickland Scale (Nowicki & Strickland, 1973). Both are forced-choice paper and pencil measures where children respond "yes" or "no" to a series of questions about control beliefs. The first comparative racial study with children used the Bialer Scale (Battle & Rotter, 1963), as did four other investigations conducted in the early 1970s (see Table 2.2). Four of these five investigations reported that Whites were more internal than Blacks. Three studies using the Nowicki-Strickland also reported that White children were more internal than their Black counterparts.

A more widely used measure of locus of control is Crandall's Intellectual Achievement Responsibility Scale (IAR) (Crandall, Katkovsky, & Crandall, 1965). The IAR is different from other locus of control measures in several respects. First, all of the items relate to school achievement rather than more general beliefs about control. Second, unlike the other measures, the IAR provides separate subscores for positive and negative outcomes. Thus, respondents can receive an overall score measuring degree of internality as well as scores on subscales measuring perceived internality for success (I+) and failure (I−).

Seven studies in Table 2.2 used the IAR to assess locus of control in a comparative racial framework. (We include the study by Jacobson (1975) even though participants were somewhat older). Two investigators (Solomon, Houlihan, & Parelius, 1969; Burbach & Bridgeman, 1976) showed no differences between racial groups on either I+ or I− subscales. On the other hand, only one study (DuCette, Wolk, & Friedman, 1972) unequivocally showed differences favoring Whites over Blacks, although these authors did not report subscale scores. In the other four studies, the results were more mixed. DuCette, Wolk, and Soucar (1972) found that Blacks assumed more personal responsibility for success than did Whites, whereas Whites were the more internal group for failure. However, these racial differences emerged only for "problem" children—that is, those boys who had been referred to a mental health facility for series behavior disruptions in their classroom. A comparable group of normal 8- to 10-year-old males showed no such racial differences in locus of control. Jacobson (1975) and Brown, Fulkerson, Furr, Ware, and Voight (1984) similarly reported that Whites were more internal for success, but Garrett and Willoughby (1972) reported the opposite. Given personal responsibility for failure, it is not clear that there are differences between the racial groups. Overall, then, studies employing the IAR are less clear than the studies using the Bialer or Nowicki-Strickland Scales. Like the studies with adults, once the construct is defined more complexly, the differences between Blacks and Whites become more equivocal.

The final group of studies with children employed instruments less widely used in comparative racial research. The large-scale studies by Lessing (1969) and Gruen, Korte, and Baum (1974) used forced-choice measures. In both of these studies, Whites were reported to be more internal than Blacks. On the other hand, open-ended answering is the response mode for the Children's I-E used in three studies (Battle & Rotter, 1963; Milgram, Shore, Riedel, & Malasky, 1970; Gable & Minton, 1971), and the Stephens-Delys Scale used in one study (Martin & Cowles, 1983). Of the four investigations using such operant measures, the only one reporting racial differences was the early study by Battle and Rotter (1963).

Critique of the Personality Approach to Motivation

Close to 50 studies comprise the comparative racial literature on need for achievement and locus of control that is presented in Tables 2.1 and 2.2. If I were to characterize this research in one sentence, I would say that it is fundamentally descriptive: It reports similarities and differences between Blacks and Whites on the personality variables of interest. Often we find differences favoring Whites over Blacks; we may then feel compelled to look for reasons why these differences do not adequately portray motivation in Blacks. Such reasons may pertain to measurement, age group of respondents, demographic variables, or any number of legitimate methodological factors. On the other hand, when we find similarities between the two racial groups, then often the case is closed. Nothing more is said about general motivational principles or even guidelines for future research. But it is not especially mortifying to read that Blacks have less need for achievement than Whites, nor is it particularly gratifying to read that they are more internal on locus of control, if neither of these personality characteristics is very informative about achievement-related behavior. The following example supports this line of reasoning.

It is reasonably well documented that internality on locus of control and academic achievement are positively correlated (see Cooper & Findley, 1983). Much of the more recent comparative research suggests that Blacks are no less internal than Whites, yet they consistently do more poorly in school. What, then, is the relationship between perceived control and academic achievement among Blacks? Are we to believe that the two are unrelated? If so, then what are the correlates of high achievement among Blacks if perceived control is not a likely candidate? We need conceptions of motivation that have the theoretical richness to link motivational constructs with achievement-related behavior. We turn now to a cognitive approach to motivation with this goal of greater richness in mind.

The Cognitive Approach to Motivation: Causal Attributions

Cognitive motivational psychologists place heavy emphasis on the role of thought, rather than personality, as a determinant of behavior. They assume that people strive to explain, understand, and predict events, all of which requires constant processing of information relevant to the self and the environment. Among the most important of these thoughts are causal attributions or cognitions about *why* outcomes such as success or failure occur. From an attributional perspective, we might want to know the minority student's answer to such questions as "Why did I flunk math?" or "Why does my teacher dislike me so?" It is no accident that these examples describe failure situations, for we are more likely to engage in causal search given negative or unexpected events (see Weiner, 1985,

1986). Attributional search is therefore functional because it may impose order on a sometimes uncertain environment.

Attribution theorists have identified a number of causes that individuals enlist to explain achievement outcomes, including ability, effort, task factors, luck, and help or hindrance from others. Among the dominant causes, ability and effort appear to be the most important. That is, in explaining achievement outcomes, individuals attach the most importance to what their perceived competencies are and how hard they try.

What difference does it make if individuals attribute failure to, for example, low ability versus lack of effort? Consider first the student who attributes exam failure to low ability. Low ability typically is perceived to be a stable and enduring causal inference and is not subject to one's personal control. Hence, the student who displays this attributional pattern is likely to expect failure to occur again. A low expectancy for success, in turn, is believed to lead to performance decrements and to giving up in the face of failure. Indeed, there are a number of theoretical conceptions outside of the attributional framework that document the debilitating consequences of self-statements such as "I cannot" (Bandura, 1977). Failure attributions to low effort, on the other hand, need not lead one to expect failure to occur again since effort is volitionally controllable and may vary from situation to situation. Low effort attributions, then, should lead to the maintenance of achievement strivings in the face of failure. For example, research on attribution retraining has shown the adaptiveness of training helpless children to attribute failure to lack of effort rather than to low ability because effort self-ascriptions lead to greater persistence and to improvement in the quality of performance (see Dweck, 1975). In sum, attribution theory provides a model of motivation stating that following an achievement outcome individuals search for the causes of that outcome, such as whether it was due to ability or effort, and that particular causal attributions have distinct psychological and behavioral consequences.

Table 2.3 contains the comparative racial studies on casual attributions. The total number of studies is surprisingly small, given the centrality of attribution theory in current motivation research. Even within this relatively small literature, two methodologies generally have been employed in comparative racial research. The studies listed in Table 2.3 are ordered to reflect these two paradigms.

Table 2.3. Comparative Racial Research on Causal Attributions

Study	Sample	Socio-economic Status (SES)	Method of Assessment	Direction of Findings
		Comparative-Hypothetical		
Shaw & Schneider (1969)	57 7- to 19-year-olds	Varied	Responsibility Attributions	White > Black for younger Ss in use of causal cues
Weiner & Peter (1973)	300 4- to 18-year-olds	Unspecified	Evaluative Judgments	White > Black use of intent and effort cues
Banks et al. (1977)	40 16- to 18-year-olds	Unspecified	Evaluative Judgments	NSD[a] high-interest tasks
Lipton & Garza (1977)	343 Black, White, Mexican-American junior high school students	Unspecified	Responsibility Attributions	White > Black use of outcome and causal dues
McMillan (1980)	174 4th to 5th graders	Unspecified	Evaluative Judgments Others	White > Black use of effort and ability cues
Whitehead et al. (1982)	364 junior high school students	Unspecified	Attribution Ratings	NSD
Wong et al. (1988)	80 junior high school students	Unspecified	Open-ended Attributions	NSD
		Comparative-Own Performance		
Friend & Neale (1972)	20 5th graders	Mid and Low SES	Attribution Ratings; Rank Order Attributions	NSD Ratings; White > Black Rank Order ability, effort for failure
Willig et al. (1983)	397 4th to 8th graders, Black, White, and Hispanic	Varied	Attribution Ratings	White > Black ability and task dif. for failure

NSD for success |

Table 2.3. Continued

Study	Sample	Socioeconomic Status (SES)	Method of Assessment	Direction of Findings
Powers & Rossman (1984)	149 remedial junior college	Unspecified	MMCS	NSD for success Black > White for failure on effort
Graham (1984)	176 6th graders	Middle and Low	Attribution Ratings for Failure	Mid-SES Black > Other groups on effort
Graham & Long (1986) Experiment 2	171 7th graders	Middle and Low	Attribution Ratings	Mid-SES White < Other groups on luck for success
				Mid-SES White > Other groups on task dif. for failure
				Mid-SES Black > Other groups on teacher for failure
Hall et al. (1986)	80 junior high school students	Unspecified	Attribution Ratings for Science	NSD

aIndicates no difference between racial groups.

One type of study employed a role playing methodology to examine causal inferences about the outcomes of hypothetical others. For example, Shaw and Schneider (1969) investigated children's attributions of responsibility in hypothetical situations that varied causal and outcome information. In a similar design, Weiner and Peter (1973) examined evaluative judgments (reward or punishment) in contexts that varied intent, attribution (effort and ability), and outcome information. The overall goal of such studies in a comparative racial framework is to ascertain whether Blacks and Whites differ in their understanding and use of basic attributional principles such as the use of causal information as guides to evaluating others. As indicated in Table 2.3, most of the earlier studies do find racial differences. For example, Weiner and Peter (1973), McMillan (1980), and Lipton and Garza (1977) reported that Black children use effort information less systematically than do their White counterparts in the administration of rewards and punishments. The implicit message in studies of this type harkens back to a belief from the earlier motivation literature that minority children attach less value to effort as a cause of achievement outcomes (see Katz, 1969).

The second type of comparative racial study examines attributions of Black and White students following success or failure at a specific achievement task. The first study of this type (Friend & Neale, 1972) found that Whites rated ability and effort as more important causes of failure at a laboratory task whereas Blacks rated the external factors (task difficulty and luck) as relatively more important. These findings were of course compatible with the then-dominant view supported by locus of control research that Blacks were more externally oriented than Whites.

More recent studies using both types of methodologies have challenged these prevailing views of Blacks as more externally oriented in their attributions or less sensitive to the value of effort. In the studies of hypothetical outcomes, Whitehead, Smith, and Eichorn (1982) and Wong, Derlaga, and Colson (1988) report no racial differences in attributional judgments about others. In the research involving actual self-perception, the more contemporary studies report no differences between Blacks and Whites (Graham & Long, 1986; Hall, Howe, Merkel, & Lederman, 1986) or differences favoring Blacks over Whites (Graham, 1984; Powers & Rossman, 1984). For example, Graham (1984) documented a particularly adaptive attributional pattern among middle-class Blacks following failure on a puzzle-solving task. Relative to the other demographic groups studied, middle-SES Black children were more likely to attribute failure to lack of effort and less likely to endorse task difficulty, low ability, or luck as causes for nonattainment of their goal.

One potential drawback of the studies on self-perception is their emphasis only on the content of casual inferences to the virtual exclusion of other important principles of an attributional theory of motivation. As such, the comparative racial literature suffers from some of the same criticisms lodged against the personality approach reviewed earlier. Documenting similarities and differences between ethnic groups in the endorsement of particular attributions is only one part of casual thinking: It may be less interesting for comparative racial research than particular processes underlying attributional thinking and how ethnic groups might differ in the way they use these processes.

Affective Cues from Others and Self-Perception

As already indicated, one of the most important attributions that we make about ourselves relates to ability self-perceptions. Recall that low ability as a cause for failure often undermines self-esteem, lowers expectations for the future, and leads to the belief that there is no response in one's repertoire to alter the course of failure. There is hardly a more maladaptive attributional pattern. For the motivational psychologist concerned with attributions in failure-prone Black students, one might then ask, What factors are known to influence ability attributions for performance?

In achievement contexts, it seems reasonable to assume that what a teacher communicates to students might be an important source of attributional information. While it is unlikely that a teacher will often directly tell a student "You are dumb," such messages may be subtly and unintentionally communicated by, for example, affective displays of teachers. In attribution theory we have a set of well-documented attribution-affect linkages that allow us to address this question. Specifically, we know that affective displays of sympathy versus anger are the consequences of particular attributions. Sympathy is elicited by failure attributed to lack of ability (imagine the teacher's reaction to the retarded child who continually experiences academic difficulty). In contrast, anger is the dominant reaction to failure due to lack of effort (think of the teacher's response to the gifted child who never completes assignments).

We also have evidence that affective displays of sympathy or anger are used by students to infer that they personally are low in ability versus lacking in effort (Graham, 1984). In other words, we gain information about ourselves based on the affective communications of others. Thus, if the causes of failure are somewhat ambiguous, as is often the case in classroom contexts, and the teacher communicates to the student, "I pity you," the student is more likely to think he is low in ability than if the teacher expresses anger in response to the student's poor performance.

We know that these affect-to-attribution self-perceptions are quite prevalent in this culture. Indeed, they have been documented in both Black and White adolescents who differ in social class (Graham, 1984). The intriguing question now for the study of minority motivation is whether Blacks are more likely to be the targets of sympathetic feedback from teachers and thus the recipients of low-ability cues. There is some indirect evidence that teachers of minority children are perceived as sympathetic and that being characterized in this manner is linked to low achievement among students (Kleinfeld, 1972). A motivational principle relating sympathy from others to low-ability self-perception might help explain why a seemingly positively intended emotion can have unintended negative consequences.

Note that this focus is different than that more typically followed in the study of motivation in Blacks. Rather than focus on Black–White differences per se, we study general motivational principles. The principles apply to both Blacks and Whites. The two ethnic groups just fall at different points along some basic construct such as, in this case, degree of prior failure and vulnerability to pity from others.

Conclusions

A great deal of material has been covered in this chapter, for I have attempted to review a substantial portion of the theoretical and empirical literature on motivation in Blacks. Irwin Katz, who undertook a similar review in 1969, concluded that our accumulated knowledge in the field was no more scientific than "the conventional wisdom of the teacher's lounge" (Katz, 1969, p. 23). I wish to conclude the present review on a less sober note. With greater hope for progress in the field, I suggest the following three principles as guidelines for the study of motivation in Blacks.

First, the study of motivation in Blacks must be concerned with the cognitive as well as personality factors that guide achievement-related behavior. A major point emphasized in this chapter is how theoretically impoverished a purely personality approach is to minority motivation. We know which cognitive constructs are most central in the study of minority motivation. They include perceptions of control, expectations for the future, and interpersonal evaluation, among others. We need a theoretical framework for the study of motivation in Blacks that can incorporate all of these cognitive variables with one set of interrelated constructs.

Second, the study of motivation in Blacks must recognize the complex relationship between ethnicity and social class in this society. Even a cursory glance at the description of the studies presented in Tables 2.1, 2.2, and 2.3 reveals how unsystematically social class was addressed in the research. More often than not, the socioeconomic status of participants is unspecified. This becomes problematic for comparative racial research because race and social class are confounded: We do not know whether reported differences or similarities are due to the racial or the class factor.

A more subtle implication of this confounding is revealed in one of my own comparative racial studies on causal attributions (Graham, 1984). It was reported in that study that middle-SES Blacks displayed a particularly adaptive attributional pattern that was different from that of Whites and lower-status Blacks (see Table 2.3). Such systematic race and class effects have not previously been documented. What is clear, then, to the motivational psychologist interested in comparative racial study is how infrequently the research has focused on economically advantaged Black populations. Middle-class Blacks have often been ignored altogether in the literature because many investigators only make comparisons between low-SES Blacks and middle-SES Whites or because middle-SES Blacks do not fit our stereotypes of either deviant minorities or special populations. One researcher, for example, justified his neglect of middle-class Blacks by describing them as "uninteresting persons who present neither social pathology nor remarkable success." (Fortunately I can no longer recall the exact source of this pernicious statement.) This view, as well as the confounding of race with class in much previous research, has operated to obscure the Black middle class as a potentially rich source of information about motivational processes in minority populations.

Finally, the third principle states that the study of motivation in Blacks must be particularly sensitive to the dynamics of failure. There is an unfortunate educational reality in this society: Minority children are overrepresented in the ranks of those who experience chronic school failure. Let us not forget that Black children are three times more likely than Whites to be in mentally retarded classes, but only half as likely to be in programs for the gifted or talented. Let us be reminded that one of every five Black students drops out before the end of high school, whereas those who remain are anywhere from two to three years behind grade level in the basic subjects. There are no signs that this dismal picture of failure is improving. I stated at the beginning of this chapter that motivational psychologists are concerned with the nonintellective factors accounting for school performance. A theoretical framework for the study of motivation in Blacks must therefore be particularly capable of addressing how individuals think, feel, and act in response to nonattainment of goals.

REFERENCES

Ashkanasy, N. (1985). Rotter's internal–external scale: Confirmatory factor analysis and correlation with social desirability for alternative scale formats. *Journal of Personality and Social Psychology, 48,* 1328–1341.

Atkinson, J. (1964). *An introduction to motivation.* Princeton, NJ: Van Nostrand.

Bandura, A. (1977). Self-efficacy: Toward a unifying theory of behavioral change. *Psychological Review, 84,* 191–215.

Banks, C., McQuater, G., & Hubbard, J. (1977). Task-liking and intrinsic–extrinsic orientations in Black adolescents. *Journal of Black Psychology, 5,* 61–71.

Battle, E., & Rotter, J. (1963). Children's feelings of personal control as related to social class and ethnic group. *Journal of Personality, 31,* 482–490.

Bialer, I. (1961). Conceptualization of success and failure in mentally retarded and normal children. *Journal of Personality, 29,* 303–320.

Brown, D., Fulkerson, K., Furr, S., Ware, W., & Voight, N. (1984). Locus of control, sex role orientation, and self-concept in Black and White third- and sixth-grade male and female leaders in a rural community. *Developmental Psychology, 20,* 717–721.

Burbach, H., & Bridgeman, B. (1976). Relationship between self-esteem and locus of control in Black and White fifth grade students. *Child Study Journal, 6,* 33–37.

Coleman, J., Campbell, E., Hobson, C., McPartland, J., Wood, A., Weinfeld, F., & York, R. (1966). *Equality of educational opportunity.* Washington, DC: U.S. Government Printing Office.

Cooper, H., & Findley, M. (1983). Locus of control and academic achievement: A literature review. *Journal of Personality and Social Psychology, 44,* 419–427.

Cooper, H., & Tom, D. (1984). Socioeconomic status and ethnic group differences in achievement motivation. In R. Ames & C. Ames (Eds.), *Research on motivation in education* (Vol. I, pp. 209–242). New York: Academic Press.

Crandall, V., Katkovsky, W., & Crandall, V. (1965). Children's beliefs in their own control of reinforcements in intellectual–academic achievement situations. *Child Development, 36,* 92–109.

DeBord, L. (1972). The achievement syndrome in lower class boys. *Sociometry, 40,* 190–196.

DuCette, J., & Wolk, S. (1972). Locus of control and levels of aspiration in Black and White children. *Review of Educational Research, 42,* 493–504.

DuCette, J., Wolk, S., & Friedman, S. (1972). Locus of control and creativity in Black and White children. *Journal of Social Psychology, 88,* 297–298.

DuCette, J., Wolk, S., & Soucar, E. (1972). Atypical patterns in locus of control and nonadaptive behavior. *Journal of Personality, 40,* 287–297.

Dweck, C. (1975). The role of expectations and attributions in the alleviation of learned helplessness. *Journal of Personality and Social Psychology, 31,* 674–685.

Edwards, D. (1974). Blacks versus Whites: When is race a relevant variable? *Journal of Personality and Social Psychology, 29,* 39–49.

Farley, F., Cohen, A., & Foster, A. (1976). Predicting locus of control in Black and White college students. *Journal of Black Studies, 6,* 299–304.

Friend, R., & Neale, J. (1972). Children's perceptions of success and failure: An attributional analysis of the effects of race and class. *Developmental Psychology, 7,* 124–128.

Gaa, J., & Shores, J. (1979). Domain specific locus of control among Black, Anglo, and Chicano undergraduates. *Journal of Social Psychology, 107,* 3–8.

Gaa, J., Williams, R., & Johnson, S. (1981). Domain specific locus of control orientations of Anglo, Black, and Chicano adolescents. *Journal of Psychology, 107,* 185–190.

Gable, R., & Minton, H. (1971). Social class, race, and junior high school students' belief in personal control. *Psychological Reports, 29,* 1188–1190.

Garcia, C., & Levenson, H. (1975). Differences between Blacks, and Whites' expectations of control by chance and powerful others. *Psychological Report, 37,* 563–566.

Garrett, A., & Willoughby, R. (1972). Personal orientation and reactions to success and failure in urban Black children. *Developmental Psychology, 7,* 92.

Graham, S. (1984). Communicating sympathy and anger to Black and White children: The cognitive (attributional) antecedents of affective cues. *Journal of Personality and Social Psychology, 47,* 40–54.

Graham, S. (1988). Can attribution theory tell us something about motivation in Blacks? *Educational Psychologist, 23,* 3–21.

Graham, S., & Long, A. (1986). Race, class, and the attributional process. *Journal of Educational Psychology, 78,* 4–13.

Gruen, G., Korte, J., & Baum, J. (1974). Group measure of locus of control. *Developmental Psychology, 10,* 683–686.

Gurin, P., Gurin, G., Lao, R., & Beattie, M. (1969). Internal–external control in the motivational dynamics of Negro youth. *Journal of Social Issues, 25,* 29–53.

Hall, E. (1975). Motivation and achievement in Black and White junior college students. *Journal of Psychology, 97,* 107–113.

Hall, V., Howe, A., Merkel, S., & Lederman, N. (1986). Behavior, motivation, and achievement in desegregated junior high school science classes. *Journal of Educational Psychology, 78,* 108–115.

Helms, J., & Giorgis, T. (1980, November). A comparison of locus of control and anxiety level of African, Black American, and White American college students. *Journal of College Student Personnel,* 503–509.

Jacobson, C. (1975). The saliency of personal control and racial separatism for black and white southern students. *Psychological Records, 25,* 243–253.

Katz, I. (1969). A critique of personality approaches to Negro performance with research suggestions. *Journal of Social Issues, 25,* 13–27.

Kinder, D., & Reeder, L. (1975). Ethnic differences in beliefs about control. *Sociometry, 38,* 261–272.

Kleinfeld, J. (1972). Effective teachers of Indian and Eskimo children. *School Review, 83,* 301–344.

Lao, R. (1970). Internal–external control and competent and innovative behavior among Negro college students. *Journal of Personality and Social Psychology, 14,* 263–270.

Lefcourt, H. (1982). *Locus of control.* Hillsdale, NJ: Lawrence Erlbaum.

Lefcourt, H., & Ladwig, G. (1965). The American Negro: A problem in expectancies. *Journal of Personality and Social Psychology, 4,* 377–380.

Lefkowitz, J., & Fraser, A. (1980). Assessment of achievement and power motivation of Blacks and Whites, using a Black and White TAT, with Black and White administrators. *Journal of Applied Psychology, 65,* 685–696.

Lessing, E. (1969). Racial differences in indices of ego functioning relevant to academic achievement. *Journal of Genetic Psychology, 115,* 153–167.

Levy, M. (1976). Deferred gratification and social class. *Journal of Social Psychology, 100,* 123–135.

Lipton, J., & Garza, R. (1977). Responsibility attribution among Mexican-American, Black, and Anglo adolescents and adults. *Journal of Cross-Cultural Psychology, 8,* 259–273.

Lott, A., & Lott, B. (1963). *Negro and White youth.* New York: Holt, Rinehart, & Winston.

Maehr, M. (1974). Culture and achievement motivation. *American Psychologist, 29,* 887–895.

Martin, S., & Cowles, M. (1983). Locus of control among children in various educational environments. *Perceptual and Motor Skills, 56,* 831–834.

McClelland, D. (1951). *Personality.* New York: William Sloane.

McClelland, D. (1961). *The achieving society.* Princeton, NJ: Van Nostrand.

McClelland, D., Atkinson, J., Clark, R., & Lowell, E. (1953). *The achievement motive.* New York: Appleton-Century.

McClelland, L. (1974). Effects of interviewer–respondent race interactions on household interview measures of motivation and intelligence. *Journal of Personality and Social Psychology, 29,* 392–397.

McMillan, J. (1980). Children's causal attributions in achievement situations. *Journal of Social Psychology, 112,* 31–39.

Milgram, N. (1971). Locus of control in Negro and White children at four age levels. *Psychological Reports, 29,* 459–465.

Milgram, N., Shore, M., Riedel, W., & Malasky, C. (1970). Level of aspiration and locus of control in disadvantaged children. *Psychological Reports, 27,* 343–350.

Mingione, A. (1965). Need for achievement in Negro and White children. *Journal of Consulting Psychology, 29,* 108–111.

Mingione, A. (1968). Need for achievement in Negro, White, and Puerto Rican children. *Journal of Consulting and Clinical Psychology, 32,* 94–95.

Moynihan, D. (1965). Employment, income, and the ordeal of the Negro family. In T. Parsons (Ed.), *Full citizenship for the Negro American.* Boston: Houghton Mifflin.

Murray, H. (1938). *Explorations in personality.* New York: Oxford University Press.

Mussen, P. (1953). Differences between the TAT responses of Negro and White boys. *Journal of Consulting Psychology, 17,* 373–376.

Nowicki, S., & Strickland, B. (1973). A locus of control scale for children. *Journal of Consulting and Clinical Psychology, 40,* 148–154.

Pedhazur, L., & Wheeler, L. (1971). Locus of control and need achievement. *Perceptual and Motor Skills, 33,* 1281–1282.

Powers, S., & Rossman, M. (1984). Attributions for success and failure among Black, Hispanic, and Native American community college students. *Journal of Psychology, 117,* 27–31.

Rainwater, L. (1966). Crucible of identity: The Negro lower class family. *Daedalus, 95,* 172–216.

Ramirez, M., & Price-Williams, D. (1976). Achievement motivation in children of three ethnic groups in the United States. *Journal of Cross Cultural Psychology, 7,* 49–60.

Rosen, B. (1959). Race, ethnicity, and the achievement syndrome. *American Sociological Review, 24,* 417–460.

Rosen, B., & D'Andrade, R. (1959). The psychosocial origins of achievement motivation. *Sociology, 22,* 185–218.

Rotter, J. (1966). Generalized expectancies for internal versus external control or reinforcements. *Psychological Monographs, 80*(1) (Whole No. 609).

Ruhland, D., & Feld S. (1977). The development of achievement motivation in Black and White children. *Child Development, 48,* 1362–1368.

Schroth, M. (1976). Sex and grade level differences in need achievement among Black college students. *Perceptual and Motor Skills, 43,* 135–140.

Scott, J., & Phelan, J. (1969). Expectancies of unemployable males regarding source of control of reinforcement. *Psychological Reports, 25,* 911–913.

Seaman, M., & Evans, J. (1962). Alienation and learning in a hospital setting. *American Sociological Review, 69,* 772–782.

Shaw, M., & Schneider, F. (1969). Negro–White differences in attribution of responsibility as a function of age. *Psychonomic Science, 16,* 289–291.

Shaw, R., & Uhl, N. (1971). Control of reinforcement and academic achievement. *Journal of Educational Research, 64,* 226–228.

Solomon, D., Houlihan, K., & Parelius, R. (1969). Intellectual achievement responsibility in Negro and White children. *Psychological Reports, 24,* 479–483.

Strickland, B. (1972). Delay of gratification as a function of race of the experimentor. *Journal of Personality and Social Psychology, 22,* 108–112.

Thompson, C. (1949). The Thompson modification of the Thematic Apperception Test. *Journal of Protective Techniques, 13,* 469–478.

Travis, C., & Anthony, S. (1975). Ethnic composition of schools and achievement motivation. *Journal of Psychology, 89,* 271–279.

Turner, J. (1972). Structural conditions of achievement among Whites and Blacks in the rural South. *Social Problems, 19,* 496–508.

Veroff, J., & Peele, S. (1969). Initial effects of desegregation on the achievement motivation of Negro elementary school children. *Journal of Social Issues, 25,* 72–91.

Weiner, B. (1985). An attributional theory of achievement motivation and emotion. *Psychological Review, 92,* 548–573.

Weiner, B. (1986). *An attributional theory of motivation and emotion.* New York: Springer-Verlag.

Weiner, B., & Peter, N. (1973). A cognitive-developmental analysis of achievement and moral judgments. *Developmental Psychology, 9,* 290–309.

Whitehead, G., Smith, S., & Eichorn, J. (1982). The effects of subject's race and other's race on judgments of causality for success and failure. *Journal of Personality, 50,* 194–202.

Will, E., & Verdin, J. (1978). Social desirability response bias in children's locus of control reports. *Psychological Reports, 43,* 924–926.

Willig, A., Harnisch, D., Hill, K., & Maehr, M. (1983). Socio-cultural and educational correlates of success–failure attributions and evaluation anxiety in the school setting for Black, Hispanic, and Anglo children. *American Educational Research Journal, 20,* 385–410.

Winterbottom, M. (1953). *The relation between childhood training in independence to achievement motivation.* Unpublished doctoral dissertation, University of Michigan.

Wolf, T., Monny, S., MacHunter, S., & Berenson, G. (1982). Factor analytic study of children's Nowicki-Strickland locus of control scale. *Educational and Psychological Measurement, 42,* 333–337.

Wong, P., Derlaga, V., & Colson, W. (1988). The effects of race on expectancies and performance attributions. *Canadian Journal of Behavioral Science, 20,* 29–39.

3

Defining Self-Concept as a Dimension of Academic Achievement for Inner-City Youth

GLORIA JOHNSON POWELL

Introduction

For many, the global self-concept is an overall view of self and is a crucial factor in determining human behavior (Combs & Snygg, 1959; Hayakawa, 1963; Rogers, 1951). Arising from the experience of self as object (James, 1961) and as a global construct, the self-concept consists of the awareness of the totality of one's self-knowledge that is derived from a history of interactions with others and the evaluation of one's coping ability.

In the frameworks of several theorists (Combs & Snygg, 1959; Gordon, 1968; Rogers, 1951; Sears & Sherman, 1964), the global self-concept plays a significant role in initiating and guiding behavior and is equated with motivation. Thus, variations in human behavior that span a wide range of performance situations have been attributed to individual differences in global self-concept.

Of particular interest are the studies that support the theory that academic achievement constitutes one area of behavior that is assumed to be associated with global self-esteem (Purkey, 1970; Wylie, 1974; Hawridge, Chalupsky, & Roberts, 1968). Indeed, several investigators have found that the academic achievement problems of inner-city minority group children may be the consequence of inadequate global self-concept (Ausubel & Ausubel, 1963; Erikson, 1966; Kvaraceus, 1965; Witty, 1967). However, there is no conclusive support for the assumption that there is a significant relation between global self-concept and academic achievement in any population (Powell, 1979).

The confusion over the relationship between self-concept and academic achievement may well be due to the context in which self-concept emerges, particularly major environmental stressors, which will be discussed in another section of this chapter. The dispute regarding whether or not Afro-American children have positive or negative self-concepts is to assume that all Afro-American children are alike; the diversity of the group is ignored and only socioeconomic status is considered, but even within the same class there is diversity in values, life-styles, aspirations.

Sowell (1981) has noted that the geographic distribution of Afro-Americans distorts national statistical comparisons. In fact, the geographic distribution of the population affects both Black–White comparison and comparisons with other ethnic groups. In a six-city study of self-concept among Afro-American (AF–AM) students in racially isolated minority (RIM) schools outside of the Southeast and segregated southern AF–AM schools, the total self-concept scores of the students in southern AF–AM schools were significantly higher than those in RIM schools in other regions of the country (Powell, 1985). However, on the subscales there were considerable regional differences as well as some differences amongst the six cities.

At this juncture the reader may well be left with a definition of motivation, but may be more confused about global self-concept and how it develops. What follows is a brief discussion of the process of self-concept as well as definition of terms so that the reader will be able to understand better the correlates of academic achievement and the many dimensions of self-concept.

The Dimensions of Self-Concept

After the early differentiation of self from the animate and inanimate worlds, the process of self-concept continues to evolve and becomes more social in nature. The process becomes more accelerated with the development of language. Then the self-concept begins to involve identification with others, interjection from others, and expansion into interpersonal relationships. Indeed, there is no value judgment more significant to a person and more decisive in one's psychological development and motivation than the estimates that one poses on him- or herself (Branden, 1969). The nature of an individual's self-evaluation has profound effects on the individual's thinking processes, emotions, desires, values, and goals. To understand a person psychologically, one must understand the nature and degree of his or her self-esteem and the standards by which one judges him or herself. Self-esteem is a subset of global self-concept, which is composed of the ideas and attitudes that are part of the self-evaluation process. Self-esteem has two interrelated aspects: (a) a sense of personal efficacy and (b) a sense of personal worth. More expansively, it is the integrated sum of self-confidence and self-respect as well as the conviction that one is competent to live and worthy of living.

The process by which individuals acquire evaluation has become an important construct to understand complex human behavior. Consequently, the self has been of interest to sociologists, psychologists, psychiatrists, and philosophers. It has become a particular interest of educators who seek to find answers regarding the educational underachievement and lack of motivation to learn, especially among inner-city minority youth.

Webster and Sobieszek (1974) examine the concept of Cooley's (1902) social self with testable models that focus on such topics as (a) self-evaluation and performance expectations as well as the sources of each; (b) status characteristics of evaluations; (c) multiple sources of evaluation and the formation of expectations; (d) cognitive maximization and behavioral motivation. Referring to the works of Charles Horton Cooley (1902), George Herbert Mead (1934), Harry Stack Sullivan (1947), Ewing Goffman (1959), and Carl Rogers (1961), Webster and Sobieszek (1974) reiterate the axiom of the reflected self, which is that a person's self-concept is considered to be dependent on observing the reactions and opinions of others toward the individual. In short, there is no meaningful way to speak of the existence of a person or his personality without the shaping effects of his contact with others. This concept is very important in understanding the development of self-concept among inner-city minority youth.

The Ethnic Identity

Racial awareness is part of the human process of establishing self-identity. Most studies on ethnic identity and racial preferences have no control for social class and those that have show mixed results. For those who have membership in an ethnic minority group, such membership appears to be a factor in the early development of ethnic awareness. It does appear that minority group children of lower socioeconomic status (SES) tend to be more accepting of their own ethnicity than those of middle- and upper-social-class groups. The explanation offered for such a finding may well be due to the fact that lower-class groups develop their own cultural patterns and values and may reject dominant definitions of success. Afro-American children appear to be more concerned with color differences and racial cues than their White peers. It has also been noted that geographical residence of the sample is an important factor in interpreting the ethnic identification process (MacAdoo, 1970; Powell, 1973). Spurlock (1973) suggests caution in interpreting the impact of the 1960s. Although Afro-American children may declare "Black is beautiful," such a declaration may be only a reaction formation, an attempt to protect the self against a hostile world and provide the self with feelings of unity and self-acceptance.

Barriers to Self-Actualization for Inner-City Minority Children

Self-concept is a very important aspect of mental health because it contributes to the individual's ability to participate as a fully functioning person and to realize her own potentialities. Maslow's (1954) concept of self-actualization stresses the importance of the maximal development of human potential and the individual's basic need for and drive toward becoming and being all that she is capable of being. According to Maslow, the need for self-actualization can only be met by fulfilling the psychological needs; safety needs (or security); needs for love, affection, and belonging; esteem needs; and the need for self-actualization. One has only to look at the statistics on the health and mental health of inner-city minority families to understand that Maslow's humanistic psychology does not apply here. The data to follow will lend credence to this view.

In 1984, the National Association for the Advancement of Colored People and the National Urban League convened a Black Family Summit Conference to discuss the growing number of Afro-American children under age 18 who live with one parent. The overwhelming majority (90%) of those one-parent families are headed by females. The vast majority of Afro-American female-headed households live in poverty. Indeed, female-headed households are 4.6 times more likely to be poor than two-parent households or households headed by a man. The increasing feminization of poverty means that 70.6% of 4.6 million Afro-American children live in poverty in female-headed households (McLoyd, 1986). These families are concentrated in urban industrialized cities—the urban ghetto or the inner city.

Of particular importance is the sequelae of unemployment and poverty on the mental status of the mothers as single heads of household. Data from a study of one-month prevalence of psychiatric disorders in the United States from the Epidemiologic Catchment Areas (ECA) collected by the National Institute of Mental Health showed that the separated and divorced group had two and one-half times the rate of affective disorders than the rate found among the married (Regier et al., in press). Affective disorders were found at significantly higher rates in females and concentrated particularly in the 25 to 44 age group. In addition, the strongest correlates of all of the anxiety disorders are (a) a low SES, (b) being female, and (c) being separated or divorced (Weissman, Leaf, Beazer, Karno, & Bruce, in press).

The ECA data also show that women are more likely to be depressed than men, and among women, non-Whites generally show higher rates of depression. In addition to having the highest rates for depression, women in the 25 to 44 age group also have the highest rates of mental illness. The second highest rates are found in females 15 to 24 years of age. High rates of depression seem to be associated with stresses from life conditions, especially single parenthood, low income, poor education, and responsibility for young children. The lower the age of the youngest child, the higher the likelihood of depression.

Depressed mothers, during their interaction with their children, spend more time prohibiting or prescribing action and less time in nurturing with help or emotional support. In their observations of depressed mothers, Belle and Corfman (1979) observed them to use dominating and hostile-aggressive styles with their children and they were less likely to comply with their children's request. Depressed mothers have also been noted to have a sense of learned helplessness and a lack of self-efficacy. The children of depressed parents have a model of learned helplessness that may get translated into anger and early rebellion, ineffectual problem-solving skills, and a lack of personal efficacy. Needless to say, the quality of parenting needs to be examined as a variable of self-concept as well as academic achievement.

Finally, it must be remembered that the socialization process that shapes the self-concept of Afro-American youth is enclosed in a caste system with psychosocial and economic consequences for their significant others and themselves. In such a world, self-actualization may be realized by few.

In 1982, unemployment for Afro-Americans was 18.9%. Afro-Americans are consistently underrepresented in the managerial and professional occupations, constituting 6% of the work force. One out of every three Afro-Americans or 34% lives below the poverty line. The Report of the Secretary's Task Force on Black and Minority Health (Heckler, 1985) states that minority group people have not benefited fully or equitably from the unprecedented explosion in scientific knowledge in medicine to diagnose, treat, and cure diseases.

Violence in the Afro-American community has become a topic of prominent concern. The psychological forces at work to produce "Black on Black homicide" are at once simplistic and complex. Gang violence especially has taken its toll on Afro-American youth and is related to how such youth view education as something meaningful for their futures.

Infant mortality among Afro-Americans is twice as high as that for Whites: In 1960, Afro-Americans had 44.3 deaths per 1000 live births and nonminorities had 22.9 deaths; in 1981, Afro-Americans had 20 deaths per 1000 live births, and nonminorities had 10.5 deaths. Afro-Americans have a life expectancy reached by nonminorities in the early 1950s. In 1900, life expectancy was 47.3 years for Whites and 33 years for Afro-Americans. In 1983, life expectancy for nonminorities was 75.2 years and for Afro-Americans it was 69.6 years.

Given the sociocultural environment in which many Afro-American children subside, some of the variables responsible for the disparity in academic performance could be expected. The educational system has not risen to the challenge to provide the kind of experiences that minority groups need to realize their self-actualization. It is ridiculous to assume that educational institutions can provide the same curriculum for such a wide diversity of students, but yet it persists in doing so. However, necessary fundamental changes in American education are impossible without a thorough examination of why things are as they are.

The Linkages to Academic Achievement for Afro-American Students

Self-concept, as a global construct, consists of the awareness of the totality of one's self-knowledge emanating from a history of interactions with others and evaluations of how one has coped with life. The global self-concept whose role it is to initiate and guide behavior has been equated with motivation, and inadequacies in global self-concept have been repeatedly implicated as a casual factor in the academic achievement problems of inner-city minority children (Ausubel & Ausubel, 1963; Erikson, 1966; Kvaraceus, 1965; Witty, 1967). There is the tendency to presume that academic achievement constitutes a socially desirable, equally relevant and integral aspect to all students' lives such that individuals with good global self-concepts will perform successfully in academic areas.

Jordan (1981) notes that the notion of total congruence between global and academic self-concepts stands contrary to the accumulating support for multidimensional models of self-concept and for multifaceted nature of self-cognitions that reflect the complexity of the social environment as suggested by Lewis and Brooks-Gunn (1979) and Weintraub, Brooks, and Lewis (1977). In short, there has been a confounding of global and academic self-concepts. Herein lies a plausible explanation for the equivocal literature that has accumulated on inner-city minority students. Research to date on self-concept and academic achievement has often neglected to include separate assessments of motivation because of the belief that self-concept is sufficient to account for motivation. Spears and Deese (1973) advocate assessing self-perceptions as well as the extent to which competence in school performance is needed or sought by the individual. It may well be the case that school success can be possible only if an individual feels capable of this success, or when such success is significant in supporting the feeling of competence. Thus, the need for academic competence can be viewed as a situation-specific facet of motivation. Jordan's (1981) study found no relation between global self-concept and academic achievement. Instead, academic self-concept and need for academic competence accounted for the variance in academic achievement.

Lay and Wakstein (1985) found that Afro-Americans at the same level of test performance exhibit greater self-esteem than Whites on a series of self-rated abilities. In addition, the level of self-esteem among Afro-Americans depends less on academic achievement in high school than does the level of self-esteem among Whites. It is suggested that among minority group students, self-esteem and self-concept may be better predictors of educational attainment than SAT scores and academic rank.

In a longitudinal study of stability and change in self-perception and achievement among Afro-American adolescents, Hare (1985) noted that from preadolescence to adolescence, Afro-American youth reported instability and decline in self-concept of academic ability. The explanation given for this phenomenon was the increased awareness that Afro-American adolescents acquired regarding their relative academic deficiency compared to White youth. On the general self-esteem measure, the Afro-American group showed a larger number of changes that were in the positive direction than did the White group. Although Afro-American adolescents appeared to be changing and feeling good about themselves in certain areas, they knew that their school performance was not good. It can be theorized that Afro-American adolescents are feeling relatively better, but doing relatively worse. The importance of studying the sources as well as the levels of self-esteem becomes obvious.

Academic and school items may not be significant predictors of general self-esteem. Previous studies on self-concept and academic achievement (Bledsoe, 1967; Campbell, 1967; Epps, 1969) confirm the findings of Hare (1977), who found that school esteem was not a predictor of general self-esteem among Afro-American youth as it was for middle-class White children. Physical appearance is generally considered a predictor of general self-esteem, indicating that racial physiognomy may still be a crucial variable in self-esteem development for Afro-American children.

There are other studies that have tried to delineate the aspects of self-concept and motivation for academic achievement. Most noteworthy is the study by Coleman et al. (1966) that reported that motivational variables accounted for more variance in the academic achievement of minority group youth than any other variable investigated. Gurin and Epps (1974) found that Afro-American youths with a high sense of personal efficacy performed better academically than their counterparts who lacked this component of self.

Bowman and Howard (1985) propose that the socialization of proactive orientations regarding racial barriers can increase the sense of personal efficacy and promote academic performance and upward mobility. To test their hypothesis, a three-generation family sample was obtained from a national cross-section sample of 2,167 Afro-American youths, 14 to 24 years of age, who were members of the youngest cohort of the larger three-generation family sample. Building on earlier work that emphasized the importance of differential to blocked opportunity (Ogbu, 1974, 1978), the results indicated that familial socialization of proactive orientations toward blocked opportunities improves the mobility prospects of Afro-American youth by enhancing their sense of personal efficacy and effectiveness in academic roles. Indeed, several studies have suggested that Afro-American families have operated as buffers between racial barriers in the larger society and individual family members (Comer & Poussaint, 1975; Jackson, McCullough, & Gurin, 1981). Youth whose parents transmitted a consciousness of racial barriers were able to attain better grades than those who were taught nothing about their racial status.

Defensive and strategic interracial protocol fosters behavioral adaptation in a variety of social roles, particularly by helping to modulate and channel race-related emotions (Poussaint, 1967). In order to achieve, it is necessary for Afro-Americans to monitor their affective reactions to race-related frustrations daily and sublimate more enduring rage and hostility toward racial injustice in pro-social ways.

Thus, the theme to achieve successfully in school as a way to gain the knowledge to overcome racism and make the world a better place for other Afro-Americans is a theme that many Afro-American youth have been able to identify with in the past and still resonate in the present. In Powell's (1973) study of school desegregation in three southern cities, she was impressed with the segregated Afro-American schools in which teachers openly talked about racial oppression and how to overcome and cope with such vicissitudes through education and social action.

Coping and Self-Concept

Afro-American children are more likely to encounter values in the larger culture that are not synchronic with the socialization patterns of their families and communities. Consequently, the entrance into school may threaten their identity because their way of acting, being in the world, and perceiving the world seem incompatible with what is expected of them at school. The combination of teacher expectations, peer pressure, and the ensuing identity crisis leads to poor performance (Ingraham, 1988).

In examining the coping and adaptation process of Afro-Americans in the inner city, Myers and King (1983) note that there are new models of competent coping available that define appropriate standards, methods, and processes of functioning that have been tested in their reality. According to Myers and King (1983), "illness, dysfunction, and incompetence are the natural by-products of the concrete reality of the urban Black child. Adapting to it and learning to cope with its pressures can result only in survival, not mastery" (pp. 295–296). Finally, the fact that many Afro-American children enter school with such vulnerability puts them at high risk for dysfunctional patterns of cognitive and emotional responses to the school environment. Before they reach junior high school, alienation has begun to set in.

Newmann (1981), in enumerating the ways in which student alienation can be reduced, emphasizes the fact that schoolwork that is "incongruent with a student's cultural commitments can assault self-esteem" (p. 555). He advocates the creation of communality within the school to engage the student in a working/learning process that stimulates social integration, collective identity, and a collective commitment to cultural heritage, norms, and values.

Schools must establish a new agenda and teachers must obtain new skills to meet the challenge of education for the inner-city Afro-American child. Society must expand its commitment to educational equity, and to the health and welfare of children above the level of mere survival. It must provide every child with the opportunity to experience Maslow's self-actualization.

Conclusions

Self-concept has been assumed to be directly associated with motivation, especially motivation for academic achievement. The most dramatic contradiction to this assumption was a study on self-concept in six cities in which academic achievement was not related to high or low self-concept and vice versa (Powell, 1973, 1979, 1985).

Indeed, Afro-American children in segregated schools had higher self-concept scores than White students in segregated or desegregated schools regardless of SES, educational attainment of parents, academic achievement, and family composition. However, it was interesting to note that the Afro-American students in segregated schools had higher percentages of students going to colleges than segregated Afro-American students in the three cities outside of the Southeast. Clearly, there was some relationship between expectations of significant others, self-efficacy, and educational attainment. Given such data, can we assume that the academic achievement problems of inner-city minority children may be the consequences of inadequate global self-concept?

Self-concept and self-esteem have been bounced around in the literature often without any specific definitions of each or any focus on the relationship between the two. Rosenberg's (1979) book concerning the self is noteworthy in that is presents the many dimensions of the self-concept. Most important, the self-concept involves identification with others, interjection from others that projects into self-evaluation as well as interpersonal relationships. Self-esteem encompasses a sense of personal efficacy and a sense of personal worth.

The real linkage to academic achievement for Afro-American children is academic self-concept. Academic self-concept is enhanced by pro-social strategies for coping with racism and overcoming the blocked opportunities that youngsters may encounter because of racism. The pro-social strategies for coping with racism provide a self-enhancing channel for the anger and frustration and use that psychic energy to create a feeling of self-efficacy and self-worth. However, the pro-social strategies for overcoming racism presuppose that the significant others that the student incorporates into his or her sense of self can articulate those concepts and model them.

As Comer (1980) notes, the school staff is no longer a natural extension of parental authority. Television and radio bring attitudes and values from around the world. Many young people capable of high academic achievement wonder whether the psychological and social stress of competition is desirable. Comer (1980) found that societal forces and the complexity of the school itself have the potential of rendering any people powerless. Consequently, the inner-city minority child perceives an environment of powerless adults at school and at home, and thus lacks the models of self-efficacy needed to overcome the vicissitudes of growing up poor and Black.

REFERENCES

Ausubel, D. R., & Ausubel, R. (1963). Ego development among segregated Negro children. In H. A. Passow (Ed.), *Education in depressed areas* (pp. 237–271). New York: Bureau of Publications, Teachers College, Columbia University.

Belle, D., & Corfman, E. (1979). Depression and low income female-headed families. In *Families today* (Vol. 1, Science Monographs No. 1, NIMH, DHEW Publication No. ADM 79–815). Washington, DC: U.S. Government Printing Office.

Bledsoe, J. (1967). Self-concept of children and their intelligence, achievement, interests, and anxiety. *Childhood Education, 43,* 436–438.

Bowman, P. J., & Howard, C. (1985). Race-related socialization, motivation, and academic achievement: A study of Black youths in three-generation families. *Journal of American Academy of Child Psychiatry, 24,* 134–141.

Branden, N. (1969). *The psychology of self-esteem.* Los Angeles: Nash.

Campbell, P. B. (1967). School and self-concept. *Educational Leadership, 24,* 510–515.

Coleman, J. S., Campbell, E., Hobson, E., McFarland, J., Mood, A., Weinfeld, F., & York, R. (1966). *Equality of educational opportunity.* Washington, DC: U.S. Government Printing Office.

Combs, A., & Snygg, D. (1959). *Individual behavior* (rev. ed.). New York: Harper.

Comer, J. P. (1980). *School power.* New York: Free Press.

Comer, J. P., & Poussaint, A. F. (1975). *Black child care: How to bring up a healthy Black child in America.* New York: Simon & Schuster.

Cooley, C. H. (1902). *Human nature and the social order.* New York: Scribner.

Epps, E. G. (1969). Correlates of achievement among northern and southern urban Negro students. *Journal of Social Issues, 25,* 55–70.

Erikson, E. H. (1966). *The concept of self in race relations.* Washington, DC: American Academy of Arts and Sciences (ERIC Document Reproduction Service, No. ED 012730)

Goffman, E. (1959). *The presentation of self in everyday life.* Garden City, NY: Doubleday.

Gordon, I. J. (1968). *A test manual for the how I see myself scale.* Gainsville: Florida Educational Research and Development Council.

Gurin, P., & Epps, E. (1974). *Black consciousness, identity, and achievement.* New York: John Wiley.

Hare, B. R. (1977). Racial and socioeconomic variations in preadolescent area—Specific and general self-esteem. *International Journal of Intercultural Relations, 1,* 31–51.

Hare, B. R. (1985). Stability and change in self-perception and achievement among Black adolescents: A longitudinal study. *Journal of Black Psychology, 11,* 29–42.

Hawridge, D. C., Chalupsky, A. B., & Roberts, A. O. (1968). *A study of selected exemplary programs for the education of disadvantaged children* (USOE Report, Project No. 089013). Washington, DC: DHEW, Office of Education.

Hayakawa, S. I. (1963). *Symbol, status, and personality.* New York: Harcourt, Brace, and World.

Heckler, M. (1985). *The report of the Secretary's Task Force on Black and Minority Health, vol. I: Executive summary.* Washington, DC: U.S. Department of Health and Human Services.

Ingraham, C. L. (1988). Self-esteem, crisis, and school performance. In J. Sandoval (Ed.), *Crisis counseling intervention and prevention in the schools* (pp. 21–34). Hillsdale, NJ: Lawrence Erlbaum.

Jackson, J., McCullough, W., & Gurin, G. (1981). Group identity within Black families. In H. MacAdoo (Ed.), *Black families* (pp. 252–263). Beverly Hills, CA: Sage.

James, W. (1961). *Psychology: The briefer course.* New York: Harper & Row.

Jordan, T. J. (1981). Self-concepts, motivation, and academic achievement of Black adolescents. *Journal of Educational Psychology, 73*(4), 509–517.

Kvaraceus, W. (1965). *Negro self-concept: Implications for school and citizenship.* New York: McGraw-Hill.

Lay, R., & Wakstein, J. (1985). Race, academic achievement, and self-concept of ability. *Research in Higher Education, 22*(1), 43–64.

Lewis, M., & Brooks-Gunn, J. (1979). *Social cognition and the acquisition of self.* New York: Plenum.

MacAdoo, J. (1970). *An experimental study of racial attitude change in Black preschool children.* Ann Arbor: University of Michigan. (ERIC Document Reproduction Service, No. ED 062497)

Maslow, A. H. (1954). *Motivation and personality.* New York: Harper & Row.

McLoyd, V. (1986). Coping with unemployment and the feminization of poverty. *The University of Michigan Center for Afro-American and African Studies Newsletter, III*(1), 1–6.

Mead, G. H. (1934). *Mind, self, and society.* Chicago: University of Chicago Press.

Myers, H. F., & King, L. M. (1983). Mental health issues in the development of the Black American child. In G. J. Powell, J. Yamamoto, A. Romero, & A. Morales (Eds.), *The psycho-social development of minority group children* (pp. 275–306). New York: Brunner/Mazel.

Newmann, F. M. (1981). Reducing student alienation in high schools: Implications of theory. *Harvard Educational Review, 51*(4), 546–564.

Ogbu, J. V. (1974). *The next generation.* New York: Academic Press.

Ogbu, J. V. (1978). *Minority education and caste.* New York: Academic Press.

Poussaint, A. (1967, August 20). A Negro psychiatrist explains the Negro psyche. *New York Magazine,* pp. 58–80.

Powell, G. J. (1973). *Black Monday's children: The effects of school desegregation on southern school children.* New York: Appleton-Century-Croft.

Powell, G. J. (1979, May). *Self-concept, school desegregation, and academic achievement among Afro-American children.* Paper presented at the annual meeting of the American Educational Research Association, Chicago.

Powell, G. J. (1985). Self-concepts among Afro-American students in racially isolated minority schools: Some regional differences. *Journal of American Academy of Child Psychiatry, 24*(2), 142–149.

Purkey, W. W. (1970). *Self-concept and school achievement.* Englewood Cliffs, NJ: Prentice-Hall.

Regier, D. A., Boyd, J. E., Burke, J. D., Ree, D. S., Myers, J. K., Kramer, M., & Locke, B. Z. (in press). *One month prevalence of psychiatric disorders in the U.S. based on five epidemiologic catchment area sites.*

Rogers, C. (1951). *Studies in client centered psychotherapy.* Washington, DC: Psychological Service Center Press.

Rogers, C. (1961). *On becoming a person.* Boston: Houghton.

Rosenberg, M. (1979). *Conceiving the self.* New York: Basic Books.

Sears, P. S., & Sherman, V. S. (1964). *In pursuit of self-esteem.* Belmont, CA: Wadsworth.

Sowell, T. (1981). *Ethnic America: A history.* New York: Basic Books.

Spears, W. D., & Deese, M. E. (1973). Self-concept as cause. *Educational Theory, 23,* 144–152.

Spurlock, J. (1973). Some consequences of racism for children. In C. V. Willie, B. M. Kramer, & B. S. Brown (Eds.), *Racism and mental health* (pp. 147–165). Pittsburgh: University of Pittsburgh Press.

Sullivan, H. S. (1947). *Conceptions of modern psychiatry.* Washington, DC: W. H. White Psychiatric Foundation.

Webster, M., & Sobieszek, B. (1974). *Source of self-evaluation: A formal theory of significant others and social influence.* New York: John Wiley.

Weintraub, M., Brooks, J., & Lewis, M. (1977). The social network: A reconsideration of the concept of attachment. *Human Development, 20,* 31–47.

Weissman, M. M., Leaf, P. J., Beazer, D. G., Karno, M., & Bruce, M. L. (in press). Affective disorders in five United States communities. *Psychological Medicine.*

Witty, P. A. (Ed.) (1967). *The educatonally retarded and disadvantaged: The sixty-sixth yearbook of the National Society for the Study of Education.* Chicago: University of Chicago Press.

Wylie, R. C. (1974). *The self-concept: A review of methodological considerations and measuring instruments.* Lincoln: University of Nebraska Press.

4

The School Learning Environment and Academic Success

JANICE HALE-BENSON

Bruce Hare (1987) places the blame for the endangered status of Black youth on the structural inequality of the American educational and occupational systems. He suggests that theories about the biological and cultural inferiority of Black people serve to justify the race, class, and gender inequalities found in American society. He states further that:

> The myth of equal opportunity serves as a smoke screen through which the losers will be led to blame themselves, and be seen by others as getting what they deserve. One might simply ask, for example, how can both inheritance of wealth for some and equal opportunity for all exist in the same social system? (p. 101)

Bowles and Gintis (1976) point out that unequal distribution of wealth, power, and privilege is, and historically has been, the reality of American capitalism, and that such a system *must* produce educational and occupational losers.

Hare (1987) argues that in addition to the inherent intergenerational inequality caused by inheritance, the educational system, through its unequal skill giving, grading, routing, and credentialing procedures plays a critical role in fostering structured inequality in the American social system. The occupational structure simply responds to the schools when it slots people into hierarchical positions on the bases of the credentials and skills given by the schools.

The dire statistics on the compendium of problems of Black youths are well known. This chapter considers how Black children endowed with innate equal childhood potential arrive at such a disadvantaged youth status. It is suggested here that Black children do not enter school disadvantaged, but they emerge from school disadvantaged.

There is no question that the masses of Black children are disproportionately located in families that suffer the turmoil of unemployment, single-parent heads of households, and low-paying occupational positions. These factors cause them to be at high risk for family instability and deprivation.

The question considered in this chapter is in what way the schools reproduce failure for Black children generation after generation. The activity of the schools is considered as a central issue because schools are the major socializing institution of the society. Students who drop out or are pushed out of schools are disconnected from the future. The other problems confronting Black youth such as teen pregnancy, crime, drugs, and unemployment emanate from school failure.

It has been pointed out elsewhere (Hale-Benson, 1986) that one explanation for the difficulties Black children experience in school may be their participation in a culture that is very different from the culture that designed the school. It is essential to lay the foundation for delineating this culture and for identifying those points of mismatch between it and Euro-American culture that may have educational consequences for Black children.

I locate myself clearly among the theorists who trace the genesis of Black culture to the African heritage, while acknowledging that there are other theories. This method has generated a great deal of discussion, because the evidence supporting each theory is inconclusive. In *Black Children: Their Roots, Culture, and Learning Styles* (Hale-Benson, 1986), I argue for examining this cultural core for Black children in general while acknowledging that lower-income children are most severely affected by the dual socialization that is required to straddle Afro-American and Euro-American cultures. In this chapter, I would like to go a step further and consider scholarship that examines the specific interethnic code conflict that transpires between Black children and White teachers that results in failure over time for Black children.

Ray McDermott (1987) offers an interesting analysis in which he defines Black Americans as being a pariah group in American society. He observes that each generation of children renew their parents' life-styles, oblivious to the oppression that the host group brings down upon their heads. The structural inequality thesis points out that the host population works actively to defeat the efforts of each and every pariah child to beat the cycle of degradation. Racial markers, low prestige dialects, school failure, occupational specialities, and life-styles tag each new generation for low-ascribed status.

However, McDermott sets forth the thesis of *achieved failure.* He points out that inherited disadvantage as simple tagging is a simplistic explanation. Overt ascription is frowned upon legally and in popular ideologies. Yet, the pariah boundaries remain firm throughout the society and in school systems. Even without formal institutionalized ascription, pariah status survives into each generation.

Each new pariah generation affirms the soundness of this classificatory system because it learns and exemplifies the behavior essential to the system's maintenance. Rather than regarding themselves blinded by prejudice, the hosts maintain that they are using standards of evaluation that are used uniformly for all people regardless of race or ethnic identity. What McDermott (1987) examines is, "how is it that what is there for them to see is in fact there?" (p. 176). He analyzes that pariah groups do not enter school disadvantaged; they leave school disadvantaged. Ascription of status does not account for all of this disadvantage, nor do the inherent characteristics of the pariah population account for the disadvantage. Clearly the pariah group regards the host behavior as oppressive. Likewise, the host group regards the pariah behavior as inadequate. McDermott suggests that the way in which the two groups learn about each other is the central problem. Misunderstandings take place very often in the early grades and the results are disastrous.

McDermott maintains that children must achieve their pariah status. This status is neither totally ascribed nor naturally acquired by the children. Interethnic code differences cause miscommunication between the teacher and the children. This miscommunication deteriorates the relations until the children begin to form alternatives to the teacher's organization of the classroom. The children construct this new social organization in an attempt to become visible. The result is more condemnation of their behavior and the teacher becomes the administrator in charge of failure. In McDermott's view, school failure becomes an achievement because it is a rational adaptation made by children to human relations in host schools. Children produce pariah–host statuses in their interactions with each other and their teachers.

Young children are very vulnerable to messages of relationship. It is pointed out elsewhere (Hale-Benson, 1986) that Black children are very adept at nonverbal communication and sensitive to affective cues. McDermott points out that young children upon entering school are more sensitive to relational messages than they are to information transfer.

Erikson (1968) discussed formative experiences during puberty by noting that "it is of great relevance to the young individual's identity formation that he be responded to and be given function and status as a person whose gradual transformation makes sense to those who begin to make sense to him" (p. 156). The teacher plays an important role in organizing the statuses and identities of children in the classroom. One example of the social organization of status and identity in the classroom is the division of the class into ability groups (McDermott, 1987). This division is made to simplify the administration of the classroom and determines the level of work, as well as the interpersonal interaction and the kind of feedback received from the teacher.

McDermott notes that rarely do children reject their assignment even if assigned to the lowest status groups. They most often accept their assignment as if it makes sense. A child who did not accept his assignment might work harder to catch up with the rest of the class. The reason that revolt is rarely attempted, he suggests, is that generally in schools that contain host children, the teacher assigns them to groups using criteria that the children use in dealing with each other or that their parents use and the rest of the community uses in dealing with the children. Essentially, the teacher, the children, and the community are in agreement. Even if a child is placed in a low-status group, it does not have a disastrous effect if it makes sense. "The politics of everyday life in the classroom will be identical to the politics of everyday life outside the classroom and the children's world will be in order" (McDermott, 1987, p. 183).

The social organization of minority children by a host group teacher does not proceed as smoothly. There is a reduced possibility that a host group teacher will organize the classroom into the same ability groups that the minority community might perceive. Through ability grouping, children receive messages of relationship from the teacher. If the wrong children are assigned to the lower-ability group, they will reject the messages of relationship from the teacher. They will demand a political reorganization of the classroom and a relationship that is more in keeping with their self-concepts.

If the teacher is insensitive to their demands, no matter how subtle, then the remainder of the year the teacher and the children will be engaged in small battles over the status and identities of the children. The resolution of these battles will determine whether anything gets done in the classroom. Thus, we can see that the politics of daily classroom life determine the amount of information transfer and the development of abilities and disabilities.

McDermott points out that the root of pariah/host group divisions begin with small political arenas constituted by dyads and slightly larger groups. Abilities and disabilities arise based on a person's tendency to attend to, think about, and manipulate selected aspects of his or her environment.

A chronic educational problem is the high rate of learning disabilities found among Black children. Rates of functional Black illiteracy are estimated to be around 50% (Thompson, 1966) as compared to 10% for White Americans and only 1% for Japan (Makita, 1968). There have been a number of explanations for this disproportionality that generally suggest some genetic inferiority or cultural deprivation. McDermott suggests that illiteracy is caused by selective inattention developed in the politics of everyday life in the classroom.

The social work between White teachers and Black children in the areas of status and identity is such a failure that the children turn off and physiologically shut down. The children disattend reading materials and choose to join their peers in the pupil subculture within the class, which results in reading disabilities and school failure. Deprivation theorists generally place the fault on the child or the child's culture. However, achieved failure theorists suggest that achievement has been measured using a biased set of standards. McDermott asserts that achievements take place in social context. Instead of looking at the skills stored in children's bodies, we must look at the social contexts in which the skills are turned into achievements.

Scores on perceptual, intelligence, attitude, language, and even neurological tests are remnants of the practical work of persons in a specific situation. Test scores have discernible roots in the social world in which they take place. Tests do not reveal much about the mental capabilities of any subject, but they do tell us much about the social processes in which a subject is engaged.

Cazden (1970) has described Black children who do badly on language tests in formal situations and very well in informal situations; the opposite is true for White children. McDermott points out that tests can tell us a great deal about the thinking underlying the social acts to be performed during the test. Reading is an act that may align the Black child with incompatible forces in the social universe. In the classroom social organization produced by the politics of everyday life, reading takes its place as part of the teacher's "ecology of games" (Long, 1958). To read is to buy into the teacher games and all of the statuses and identities that accompany them. Not to read is to buy into the peer group games and the accompanying statuses and identities. In some sense, reading failure becomes a social accomplishment that is supported and rewarded by the peer group.

This phenomenon is not measured by tests. The battle lines that determine whether a child learns to read or not are drawn by the statuses and identities made available by the teacher and the peer group. McDermott analyzes that "if the teacher and the children can play the same games, then reading and all other school materials will be easily absorbed" (p. 186).

Several researchers (Allitto, 1969; Hostetler & Huntington, 1971) have noted the success of educational settings directed by teachers who are members of ethnic and dialect minorities for their own children. This contrasts with the failure of educational settings directed by outsiders. When the classroom is divided into two separate worlds, with teachers and children playing different games, it results in a social reorganization of the classroom in which the teacher's authority and information transfer are challenged.

A pivotal issue that is related to reading instruction is a struggle for attention. The politics of everyday life, according to McDermott, get inside a child's body and determine what will be perceived; the child learns how not to attend to printed information, and as a result, shows high rates of reading disabilities. The relationship between a high rate of illiteracy and continued pariah status is clear.

Jackson (1968) found in a study of gaze direction that more than 90% of host children had their eyes fixed on the teacher or reading material at a given time. In Harlem elementary schools, the teachers spent more than half their day calling children to attention (Deutsch, 1963). Attention patterns seem to be the crux of the struggle in pariah education (Roberts, 1970).

In pariah classrooms, there are teacher games and peer group games. The side one chooses will determine who one pays attention to. To attend to the teacher is to give the teacher a leadership role; to attend to the peer group is to challenge the teacher's authority. McDermott (1987) analyzes, "Those who attend learn to read; those who do not attend do not learn how to read" (p. 190).

Language Codes

In addition to a shift in perceptual properties, there are subtle but significant changes in use of language among Black children as they move through elementary school. Pariah children code switch when addressing pariah people and host people. However, the job of code switching is difficult when the teacher regards the child as ignorant for using one code and the child's peer group rejects him for using the other.

William Labov (1964, p. 91) has delineated stages in the acquisition of nonstandard English:

1. Up to age 5: Basic grammatical rules and lexicon are taken from parents.
2. Ages 5 to 12, the reading years: Peer group vernacular is established.
3. Adolescence: The social significance of the dialect characteristics of his friends become gradually apparent.
4. High school age: The child begins to learn how to modify his speech in the direction of the prestige standard in formal situations or even to some extent in casual speech.

McDermott points out that the second and third stages are important because during the school years the two become mutually exclusive.

Labov and Robins, (1969) compared the use of language of street gang members, Black children they regard as lames, and White lower-income children in the community. The lames are Black children who, although they are in contact with the gangs, still participate to some extent in the teacher's ecology. Labov demonstrates a rank ordering of the three groups' use of language that parallels their participation in school with the gang showing the most extreme deviance from standard English, the Whites deviating least, and the lames falling in between. He points out that the linguistic difference does not cause the school alienation; rather, it is an index of the extent to which the groups have bought out of the games of the school. Adoption of the peer group's linguistic code and alienation from school develop together.

Labov and Robins (1969) have documented the fact that participation in formal peer group organizations and deployment of their linguistic codes correlate very closely with reading scores. None of the 43 gang members was able to achieve a reading score on grade level and most were two years behind the national average. McDermott (1987) points out that "printed materials appear to send few meaningful cues to those interested in improving their status among their peers" (p. 194).

McDermott reports that a series of sociometric tests administered to sixth-grade Black children in the lowest achievement track consistently placed the nonreaders at the center of all peer group activities. Similar tests that were administered in an all-Black fifth grade that was nontracked showed that the nonreaders were at the center of most peer group activities. He summarizes that "Reading skills do not recommend an actor for leadership. Indeed, the acquisition of such skills can exclude an actor from the peer group ecology of games" (McDermott, 1987, p. 194).

Summary of Achieved Failure Perspective

Pariah children in host classrooms learn in a very subtle way to behave in new, culturally appropriate ways that will cause them to acquire pariah status. The process of learning to behave in a culturally appropriate way in a Black classroom that is administered by a White teacher involves learning to attend to cues produced in the peer group and learning to disattend teacher- and school-produced cues such as demands for attention or the introduction of new tasks such as reading.

McDermott suggests that these attention patterns are deeply programmed in the central nervous system. When the child attempts to attend to cues that are outside of his normal perceptual patterns, he fails. In this way, when many Black children fail in reading, it appears to be the result of a neurological impairment. The children are not actually impaired at all; they have merely learned over time to attend to different stimuli in a school situation. However, this phenomenon results in their being categorized as disabled and treated as inferior.

Communicative Code Differences

Spindler (1959) has demonstrated that middle-class teachers attend to middle-class children and label them the most talented and ambitious children in the class. School success follows parallel patterns. Lower-class children over time give up trying and amass failing "institutional biographies" (Goffman, 1963) as they move through school because they are unable to give evidence of their intelligence in terms of the limited code that teachers use for evaluating children.

Black children are particularly at risk for being overlooked because of a nonrecognition of Afro-American culture and the strengths that emerge from that culture. It is pointed out elsewhere (Hale-Benson, 1986) that Western social science overly emphasizes linguistic and logicomathematical skills in assessing intelligence. Even these skills must be demonstrated in patterns that approximate those used by Anglo-Americans to be recognized by the educational system.

Skills that emerge from Black culture are only recognized when they are extraordinary and marketable to the capitalist ecosystem such as the athletic skills of Michael Jordan or the musical skills of Michael Jackson. When these skills are exhibited in early childhood as a part of a pattern, that if nurtured could support the self-esteem and achievement of Black children, they are virtually ignored.

Rist (1970) analyzes the effect of dividing a kindergarten classroom into three ability groups: the fast, slow, and nonlearners at tables 1, 2, and 3, respectively. The teacher's subjective evaluations were shown by Rist to be rooted in the teacher's evaluation of the children's physical appearance and interactional and verbal behavior. At table 1 were children with neater and cleaner clothes, with lighter skin, and dressed more appropriately for weather conditions. Class leaders and direction givers were also clustered at table 1. The children in the low tables spoke less in class, used heavy dialect, and seldom spoke to the teacher.

By the time the children were in the third grade, the ones who started out at the lower tables were still at the lower tables. Once a child is tracked, it is difficult for him or her to break loose. The lower the table, the less instructional time the child receives. Each child is well on the way to amassing the institutional biography that will follow him or her from year to year through the school. This sorting process continues until each year more and more are sorted out until a select few reach college. McDermott (1987) states that the "select few make it to college on the basis that they are most like their teachers" (p. 198).

Given Labov's speech data, the children at table 3 are not neurologically impaired slow learners. McDermott predicts that by sixth grade, the children at table 3 will talk the most, be the most popular, and be the best dressers in the class. There is nothing wrong with their native ability. They will just be directing their achievement efforts away from the school. The reason these children were not selected for achievement in their early years has to do with the communicative code conflict between them and their teachers. If they are not able to work out this code conflict in the early years, the children at the lower tables take flight into their own subculture, which becomes oppositional to the classroom culture constructed by the teacher.

A key to the construction of this alternative classroom culture is the fact that children are assigned to the lower groups together. Therefore, there are larger numbers to construct the revolt and it becomes more powerful. There is a normal developmental shift away from the teacher and toward the peer group in fourth, fifth, and sixth grade. Therefore, the achievement gap between Black and White children becomes most apparent in late elementary school.

The children in the host classroom have three choices (McDermott, 1987). They can take the school as a source of identity as do the children at table 1; or they can take the peer group as a source of identity as do the children at tables 2 and 3—many of these children are transformed into gangs by late elementary school; or they can accept the teacher's definitions of them and their abilities and passively fail through school into pariah status—the choice represented by children at the lower tables. These children not only fail in school but also fail in their identity work. Children are better off who dispute the messages of relationship sent by the teacher and cause disruption in the classroom, because they have a better chance of constructing a solid ego in their community that could lead to achievement by an alternative route. The children who passively accept subordinate status do not disrupt the calm classroom status quo, but emerge from the educational experience with a weak ego.

McDermott points out that the host group teachers do not create this code difference. Both the children and the teachers participate in ethnic group traditions that they bring to school. In the early years, teachers make the difference because they are not as adaptable as the children. However, in later years, as the peer group gains strength, the children force the distinction between their code and the teacher's code. In making their code make a difference, they are learning how to produce pariah status for themselves vis-à-vis the host group.

Ethnic Group Identity and Mobility

McDermott ponders the question of why Blacks do not fare as well as other ethnic groups in working out the politics of the classroom. A possible explanation is found in the work of Robert Havighurst (1976) who suggests a compatibility between the White Anglo-Saxon Protestant American middle-class mainstream and the ethnic cultures of European Whites, Jews, Chinese, and Japanese. It seems that Blacks and Hispanics must shed more of the beliefs, values, attitudes, and behavioral styles associated with their ethnicity in order to acquire the somewhat divergent culture of the middle-class mainstream. There is a dual socialization of straddling of the two cultures required for upward mobility.

The theory has been developed (Hale-Benson, 1986) that at the root of achievement and disciplinary difficulties of Black children is a lack of understanding of Afro-American culture and child rearing, as well as a lack of recognition of the mismatch between this culture and the Euro-American-oriented culture of the school. The research of Donald Henderson and Alfonzo Washington (1975) is an example of investigations of Afro-American cultural patterns that may have implications for educational practices. They first affirm that Black children are culturally different from White children. This difference can be directly attributed to the fact that Black children mature in communities that are culturally different from the communities of the broader society.

Afro-American males participate in a distinctive culture that is distinguished from that of Euro-American males and Afro-American females (Hale-Benson, 1986). Nonrecognition of this culture accounts for the disproportionality of Black males in assignment to lower-ability tracks and disciplinary measures in school. Christine Bennett and J. John Harris (1982) studied the disproportionality of suspensions and expulsions of male Black students in order to identify the causes. The findings of this study reveal some surprising characteristics of disrupting students. They found that serious disrupters come to school with a strikingly high sense of personal efficacy. They also report positive feelings about school. When they get into trouble, they tend to feel that their punishment has been reasonable and fair.

The researchers suggest that even though the disruptive students have a sense of overall personal efficacy, they lack a sense of personal efficacy concerning the school. Bennett and Harris suggest further that this contrast in feelings of personal and school efficacy may help explain the disproportionate numbers of males who are suspended and expelled from schools. Bennett and Harris point out that males in our society tend to have a higher sense of efficacy than females. Thus, it is possible that males have higher self-expectations for school success and feel greater frustration with failure in school. They suggest that conflicting levels of personal and school efficacy may result in more "disturbance" or "acting out."

The findings of this study suggest that school programs designed to help "disruptive" students should build feelings of school "efficacy." Programs should use decision-making strategies and other activities to "give kids a stake in the school." They recommend that such programs may be especially important for males and should begin early in the elementary school. There is also evidence that Black males suffer because there is a preference for the behavioral styles of females in educational settings. Not only is Afro-American culture not understood and appreciated but there is also a preference for female culture.

Cornbleth and Korth (1980) suggest that, in addition to the Euro-American cultural orientation of the school, the teachers in their study reported that White females had a higher potential as learners than White males, Black females, and Black males, in that order.

They linked the characteristics of White females (reserved, efficient, orderly, quiet) with learning potential. They also designated the characteristics of Black males (outspoken, aggressive, outgoing) as being linked with low potential as learners.

Hare (1987) notes that as early as preadolescence, Black children show a trend toward higher peer self-esteem than White children and higher ratings of the importance of being popular and good at sports. His research corroborates that of Bennett and Harris (1982) in noting that Black children do not differ from White children in general self-esteem or in home self-esteem, but tend toward lower school self-esteem, which is accompanied by significantly lower standardized reading and mathematics performance. There seems to be a shift from school to peers that solidifies by late elementary school as pointed out above by McDermott.

Given the vulnerability and family turmoil of particularly lower-income Black youth, this shift toward the positive strokes and affective support of the peer group is a flight from the failure and ego damage of the school. Hare defines Black youth culture as a long-term failure arena. On a short-term basis, Black youths exhibit competent, adaptive behavior and achieve in the arenas that are open to them. They demonstrate streetwiseness, excel in playground sports, sexuality, domestic, and child-rearing chores, supplementing family income and taking on other aspects of adult roles at an early age.

Even though this youth culture provides alternative outlets for achievement, it offers little hope of long-term legitimate success. Rather, it carries with it the danger of drafting the youths into the self-destructive worlds of drugs, crime, and sexual promiscuity. Hare observes that the collectively negative schooling experiences of Black youth produce this antischool sentiment. The accompanying availability of positive peer group experiences and the inability of youths to perceive the long-term consequences of adolescent decisions cause the youths to make what appears to be a logical decision to shift from the school to the peers.

Connecting Black Children to the Future

The implications from this statement of the problem are clear. The overriding goal of the Black community must be connecting Black children to the future. This can only be done after an incisive analysis of the problems that they face and an identification of the quicksand and landmines that they confront as they move from early childhood through adolescence.

Clearly, more empirical research is needed to answer questions concerning Black child development. The following areas are suggestions for future studies that are based on a research agenda proposed by Spencer, Brookins, and Allen (1985): (a) Afro-American cultural orientations related to the socialization of these children; (b) research to examine the class structure of Black communities; (c) interactions between class and race in Black life; (d) role of peers in Black child socialization; (e) implications of changing Black family structure; (f) Black children and the success and failure in the school setting; (g) Black children and the occupational opportunity; (h) self-evaluation and self-esteem issues related to Black children; (i) Black families interface with other societal institutions; (j) biopsycho-social factors in Black child development; (k) ecological determinants of Black child development; (l) societal change as a conditioning factor in Black child development; (m) sex differences and Black child development; (n) cross-cultural implications involving Afro-American children and their relationship to the African diaspora; (o) reframing and redefining appropriate theories, measures, and methods for studying Black child development.

The system that consistently maintains the position of Black Americans at the bottom of the educational and occupational ladder is extremely complex. It is critical that we go beyond the statistics and provide incisive analysis of the problem. Only then can we focus our efforts and dwindling resources on the agonizingly slow process of trying to effect meaningful change for a generation of Black youths. At present, we are truly at risk for losing an entire generation.

REFERENCES

Allitto, S. (1969). The language issue in Communist Chinese education. In C. Hu (Ed.), *Aspects of Chinese education* (pp. 43–59). New York: Teachers College Press.

Bennett, C., & Harris, J. J., III. (1982). Suspensions and expulsions of male and Black students: A study of the causes of disproportionality. *Urban Education, 16*(4), 339–423.

Bowles, S., & Gintis, H. (1976). *Schooling in capitalist America.* New York: Basic Books.

Cazden, C. (1970). The situation: A neglected source of social class differences in language use. *Journal of Social Issues, 26*(2), 35–60.

Cornbleth, C., & Korth, W. (1980). Teacher perceptions and teacher–student interaction in integrated classrooms. *Journal of Experimental Education, 48,* 259–263.

Deutsch, M. (1963). The disadvantaged child and the learning process. In A. Passow (Ed.), *Education in depressed areas.* New York: Teachers College Press.

Erikson, E. (1968). *Identity: Youth and crisis.* New York: Norton.

Goffman, E. (1963). *Stigma.* Englewood Cliffs, NJ: Prentice-Hall.

Hale-Benson, J. (1986). *Black children: Their roots, culture, and learning styles.* Baltimore: Johns Hopkins University Press.

Hare, B. (1987). Structural inequality and the endangered status of Black youth. *Journal of Negro Education, 56*(1), 100–110.

Havighurst, R. J. (1976). The relative importance of social class and ethnicity in human development. *Human Development, 19,* 56–64.

Henderson, D. H., & Washington, A. G. (1975). Cultural differences and the education of Black children: An alternative model for program development. *Journal of Negro Education, 44,* 353–360.

Hostetler, J., & Huntington, G. (1971). *Children in Amish society: Socialization and community education.* New York: Holt, Rinehart, & Winston.

Jackson, P. (1968). *Life in the classroom.* New York: Holt, Rinehart, & Winston.

Labov, W. (1964). Stages in the acquisition of standard English. In R. Shuy (Ed.), *Social dialects and language learning* (pp. 77–104). Champaign, IL: National Council of Teachers of English.

Labov, W., & Robins, C. (1969). A note on the relation of reading failure to peer-group status in urban ghettos. *Florida FL Reporter, 7*(1), 54–57, 167.

Long, N. (1958). The local community as an ecology of games. In N. Polsby, R. Dentler, & P. Smith (Eds.), *Politics of social life, an introduction to political behavior* (pp. 407–415). Boston: Houghton Mifflin.

Makita, K. (1968). The rarity of reading disability in Japanese children. *American Journal of Orthopsychiatry, 38,* 599–614.

McDermott, R. (1987). Achieving school failure: An anthropological approach to literacy and social stratification. In G. Spindler (Ed.), *Education and cultural process: Anthropological approaches* (2nd ed). Prospect Heights, IL: Waveland.

Roberts, J. (1970). *Scene of the battle: Group behavior in urban classrooms.* New York: Doubleday.

Rist, R. (1970). Student social class and teacher expectations, *Harvard Educational Review, 40,* 411–451.

Spencer, M., Brookins, G. K., & Allen, W. R. (1985). *Beginnings: The social and affective development of Black children.* Hillsdale, NJ: Lawrence Erlbaum.

Spindler, G. (1959). The transmission of American culture. In G. Spindler (Ed.), *Education and culture, 1963.* New York: Holt, Rinehart, & Winston.

Thompson, L. (1966). *Reading disability.* Springfield, IL: Charles C Thomas.

PART II

Family and Community Factors

5

Inner-City Social Dislocations and School Outcomes: A Structural Interpretation

ROSLYN ARLIN MICKELSON and STEPHEN SAMUEL SMITH

One of the most explosive and controversial political and theoretical debates in sociology and public policy concerns the social problems facing the urban Black underclass.[1] Virtually no scholar or responsible political figure disputes that the social dislocations plaguing members of the underclass include high rates of poverty, unemployment, disease, drug abuse, incarceration, criminal victimization, leaving school, and poor academic performance. But agreement stops shortly afterward. Although the controversy has many aspects, in the 1980s it has pivoted around two questions: (a) Have government policies exacerbated these problems? (b) To what extent are these problems exacerbated, if not caused, by the behavior and attitudes of those most affected by them?

It is obviously beyond the scope of this chapter to treat the many ramifications of these questions. Instead, we focus on just one: the relationship between educational outcomes and the social dislocations facing the underclass. Our fourfold aims are reflected in the organization of this chapter. In the first section we summarize the empirical literature on the relationship between school outcomes for Black youth and the social problems mentioned above. Next, we delineate the terms of the debate over the causes of the social dislo-

AUTHORS' NOTE: The authors wish to thank Iris Carleton-LaNey, Michael Pearson, and Melvin L. Oliver for their helpful suggestions.

cations. In the third section we bring the literature on school out-comes to bear on the controversy surrounding the plight of the underclass. And finally, we offer suggestions for public policy.

School Outcomes and Social Dislocations

Family Composition and Educational Outcomes

During the last three decades, the Black female-headed family has been viewed both as a social dislocation itself (Gilder, 1981; Moynihan, 1965; Murray, 1984) and as a prime cause of other ones like drug abuse, juvenile delinquency, and teen pregnancy. More re-cently, it has been cited as a direct factor in Black students' poor achievement and high rates of school leaving. The relationship be-tween family background and school outcomes has been well known since Hollingshead's (1949) *Elmtown's Youth* and, of course, the Coleman report (Coleman et al., 1966). However, the relationship between achievement and family composition, per se, is more com-plicated and much less researched.

Recently, Milne and her associates (Milne, Meyers, Rosenthal, & Ginsburg, 1986) argued that, net of other factors, children from female-headed households do not achieve as well in school as those with two parents in the home. The benefits of having two parents are greater for elementary than for secondary students, and are greatest for Black elementary students. However, they note that for all chil-dren, the effect of the number of parents in the home is primarily transmitted through intervening variables. Family income stands out as the most important of these, particularly for Black students (Milne et al., 1986). However, the strength and substantive signifi-cance of these findings have been questioned by Heyns and Catsambis (1986). Yet the results, even as they stand, indicate that in and of itself, family composition should not be held responsible for poor school performance, since low family income among female-headed households is a crucial intervening variable.

Sexual Activity and Early Pregnancy

Just as there is a well-known empirical connection between lower family income and female-headed households, there is a well-known link between poverty, minority status, poor basic academic skills, and early parenthood. Poor teens are 2.5 times more likely to become parents than are nonpoor teens. Minority teens are 27% of the population, but 40% of teen parents (Children's Defense Fund [CDF], 1988). Adolescents with poor academic skills are more likely to be teenage parents than those with average skills, regardless of race. And poor youths with lower than average academic skills are 5.5 times more likely to be teen parents than similar adolescents who are not poor and who have average skills.

Teenage parents, both males and females, often leave school. Among sophomores, 50% of mothers and 33% of fathers drop out of school. Some will eventually get a general equivalency diploma (GED), but data suggest that the earlier adolescents become parents, the less likely they are to finish high school. Among married teen parents, 6 of 10 mothers and 7 of 10 fathers drop out of school (CDF, 1988).

The birth of a child clearly has a disastrous effect on high school completion for most adolescent parents. But what about school performance and early sexual activity, the behavioral antecedent to parenthood? Evidence shows that poor skills and achievement levels are associated with early sexual activity and failure to contracept (CDF, 1988; Fine, 1988; National Academy of Science, 1987). It remains difficult to establish the direction of causality between poor achievement and sexual activity. Nevertheless, the empirical links are clear between, on the one hand, early sexual behavior and out-of-wedlock births, and on the other, low achievement and high rates of dropping out of school.

Drug Abuse and School Outcomes

Drug use and abuse are widespread throughout U.S. society, but prevalence of use is greater among adolescents in larger metropolitan areas (Johnson, O'Malley, & Bachman, 1987). Drug use and abuse, like teen pregnancy and juvenile delinquency, have a long-established record of covariation with both poor achievement and dropping out of school. Researchers have long sought to distinguish whether drug use simply covaries with poor school outcomes because they both are caused by common antecedents (like family instability and poverty), or whether drug use itself, net of all other factors, has a direct effect on lowered performance and dropping out of school.

Using data from the National Longitudinal Survey of Youth, Mensch and Kandel (1988) report that the earlier adolescents become involved with drugs and sexual activities, the higher the likelihood that they will drop out, and the more socially unacceptable the substance (heroin compared to marijuana), the stronger the association. The researchers argue that since various factors that could determine both drug use and dropping out of school were controlled in their multivariate analysis, the results lead to the conclusion that dropping out of school is a partial function of drug use itself (Mensch & Kandel, 1988).

Their data also suggest that drug use and abuse have an indirect effect on dropping out by lowering adolescents' school performance, and a direct effect on achievement by detracting from active participation in classroom activities, paying attention to teachers, doing homework, and perhaps by impairing cognitive functioning. Drug use also reinforces membership in deviant adolescent subcultures (like gangs) that, in turn, support lack of attachment to school (Mensch & Kandel, 1988).

Juvenile Delinquency, Crime, and School Outcomes

There is clearly a difference between misbehavior in school and juvenile delinquency (defined as behavior that results in some degree of formal, sustained interaction with the criminal justice system). Many juvenile offenders also get into trouble in school well before they catch the attention of the police. At the same time, most adolescents with school behavioral problems do not end up in jail. This section will begin by discussing the relationship between misbehavior in school and school outcomes, and then move on to a discussion of bona fide juvenile delinquency and school outcomes.

Criminologists tend to approach the covariation of poor school performance and misbehavior by positing the direction of causality from academic failure to misbehavior, while sociologists point out that there is also a casual path from misbehavior to school performance. There is a large body of research that suggests that good behavior in school is a prerequisite for learning. In fact, correlational research consistently shows that a good disciplinary climate is a key school-level variable associated with achievement (Baker, 1985;

Coleman, Hoffer, & Kilgore, 1982; DiPrete, 1981; Purkey & Smith, 1983). In a recent study of students in tenth and later in twelfth grade, Myers and his associates (1987) examined the direction of causality between the two factors. They found that while misbehavior causes poor academic performance, poor academic performance also causes misbehavior. Not surprisingly, adolescents from single-parent families have greater classroom discipline problems and lower academic performance than similar students from two-parent families (Myers, Milne, Baker, & Ginsberg, 1987).

According to the Children's Defense Fund, between 100,000 and 400,000 youths pass through the criminal justice system each year. Most (75%) are charged with status offenses or crimes against property, drug, and alcohol abuse rather than violent acts (CDF, 1988). Most of the adolescents in detention are significantly behind their peers academically. Among detained juveniles with an average age of 15.5 years, 75% read below the seventh-grade level, 32% read below the third-grade level, and 80% are below grade level in math. (CDF, 1988). Once in detention, most teens experience a virtual cessation of their education. While incarcerated, they are in overcrowded conditions where the educational training facilities available to them are generally poor. The psychological and physical dislocation they experience makes attending school and learning anything while in jail very difficult. Once released, lingering involvement with the criminal justice system complicates returning to regular school.

As the previous discussion suggests, there is a systematic relationship between school misbehavior, juvenile delinquency, and lower school performance and dropping out of school. These forces affect Black youth disproportionately. Blacks from single-parent homes who also live in troubled neighborhoods are more likely than their counterparts who do not share their demographic profiles to associate with delinquents, to have attitudes favorable to delinquency and, therefore, to violate the law. And the total effect of single-parent homes on delinquency is much larger for Blacks than for non-Blacks (Matsueda & Heimer, 1987).

This description of the relationship of Black family organization and delinquency should not be taken as an indictment of single Black mothers for their child-rearing practices. As will be shown in subsequent sections of this chapter female-headed household are an intervening variable in the relationship between structural factors (like the deindustrialization of central cities) and juvenile delinquency. Viscusi (1986), Joe (1987), and Duster (1987) show that these same structural factors responsible for family instability are those that underlie delinquent behavior as well. As Cloward and Ohlin note, racial differences in delinquent behavior are more than likely due to a history of restricted opportunity and a sense of resignation (Cloward & Ohlin, 1960).

High School Dropouts

Reports on high school drop-out rates are quite variable. They differ tremendously because of the ways in which they are calculated. The drop-out rate calculated from U.S. Census data and the high school attrition rate computed from state-level school enrollment data show widely different rates and probably represent lower and upper limits to the true rate according to Rumberger (1987). The U.S. Census Bureau computes the drop-out rate as the proportion of a given age cohort that is not enrolled in school and has not completed high school. In contrast, the attrition method shows the proportion of a given entering high school class that graduates. In 1984, average national attrition rates for persons ages 18 to 19 were 29.1% compared with age cohort drop-out rates of 15.2% (Rumberger, 1987).

Rumberger's (1983, 1987) work describes the magnitude and correlates of dropping out of high schools. While he claims no one really knows what causes adolescents to drop out, there are definite social correlates. More than half of all Black male dropouts and 30% of female dropouts cite school-related reasons, like disliking school or being expelled. Economic reasons were cited by 23% of Black males and 15% of females. Pregnancy and marriage account for almost half of the reasons given by Black women for leaving school. Rumberger (1987) cautions, however, that these should be considered symptoms rather than causes of dropping out.

Too often research focuses on individual, rather than structural factors, for dropping out. Coleman and Hoffer's (1987) analysis of the differential drop-out rate in public and Catholic schools illustrates the importance of community in reinforcing academic norms and sustaining a child's schooling (Mensch & Kandel, 1988). Rumberger (1987) notes that the economic consequences of dropping out are not the same for all adolescents. The relative economic disadvantage of dropping out is larger for Whites than for Blacks and Hispanics. While there may be less of an economic incentive for minorities to stay in school, minorities are actually more likely than Whites to stay in school once SES and other predictors of dropping out are taken into account (Mensch & Kandel, 1988).

The thrust of all of these empirical findings is that poor school outcomes are in general linked to the constellation of other social dislocations that characterize underclass life. If not quite a seamless web, the interrelations among all of them are profound and multidimensional. Establishing the fundamental causes of poor school outcomes and the other social dislocations requires us to consider the heated political and academic debate swirling around the plight of the underclass.

The Theoretical Debate: Culture of Poverty Resuscitated

For most of the 1980s, the terms of debate about the plight of the underclass have been set by a critique of the previous liberal social welfare policy consensus and the theories underlying it. Associated with writers such as Auletta (1982), Gilder (1981), Lemann (1986), Loury (1985), and Murray (1984), this critique is most popularly called a neoconservative critique, a label with which, despite some ambiguity, we find no reason to quibble. The essence of this critique is to place the burden of change squarely on the shoulders of the Black community by arguing that the norms and values of the underclass are responsible for its problems.

In a much quoted article, Nicholas Lemann (1986) states this proposition most blatantly, "In the ghettos . . . it appears that the distinctive culture is now the greatest barrier to progress by the Black underclass, rather than either unemployment or welfare" (1986, p. 35). Similarly, Loury (1985) argues the academic gap between Black and White youngsters is a direct result of the behaviors and values of Black inner-city children and their parents, which he claims are distinct from the values of successful, middle-class Blacks. Along with Gilder (1981), Lemann (1986), and Murray (1984), Loury (1985) argues that the Black community must first heal itself:

It is now beyond dispute that many of the problems of contemporary

> Black American life lie outside the reach of effective government action, and require for their resolution action that can only be undertaken by the Black community itself. These problems involve at their core the values, attitudes, and behaviors of individual Blacks. (p. 10)

In essence, the neoconservative alleged links between cultural values, family instability, and "social pathologies" are basically a resuscitation of Lewis's culture of poverty thesis (Lewis, 1966, 1968). Lewis (1968) describes the culture of poverty as "both an adaptation and reaction of the poor to their marginal position in a class stratified, highly individualized, capitalist society" (1968, p. 188). Children absorb the values of their parents and larger subculture and are, therefore, not able to take advantage of changing and expanding opportunities.

The neoconservative thesis, just like the earlier culture of poverty theory, places the blame for social dislocations on its victims while it conceals, or at best underplays, the social structural causes of poverty and the social havoc it wreaks (Ryan, 1971; Sampson, 1987; Valentine, 1968; Wilson, 1988). The weakness of the neoconservative approach can be seen by scrutinizing two of its most crucial lines of argument. The first involves the high rates of violent crime. One aspect of the neoconservative approach denies any empirical linkage between unemployment and crime rates (Wilson & Herrnstein, 1985). Another draws upon the subculture-of-violence literature (Wolfgang & Ferracuti, 1967; Curtis, 1975) to argue that underclass crime rates reflect the distinctively violent aspect of the culture of poverty.

In response to such claims, Duster (1987) points out that unemployment no more causes crime than wealth causes health, but in either case it would be foolish to conclude that there is no systematic linkage or association. He notes Viscusi's (1986) study of unemployed Black males that explicitly concludes that a fundamental influence on their criminal behavior is the role of economic factors such as labor force participation (cited in Duster, 1987). And Sampson's (1987) work provides a devastating critique of the notion that a Black subculture of violence underlies Black crime rates when he demonstrates that crime rates among Whites with similar economic profiles are comparable to those of Blacks. Using racially desegregated crime rates in 150 U.S. cities, Sampson (1987) also shows that "persistently high rates of Black crime appear to stem from the structural linkages among unemployment, economic deprivation and family disruption in urban Black communities" (p. 349).

A second proposition crucial to the neoconservative argument is the alleged effect of welfare policy on Black family structure. It is argued that liberal welfare state policies allegedly entice women to forego marriage and to have more children (Gilder, 1981; Murray, 1984). Wilson (1988) responds to this claim with evidence that neither welfare receipt nor benefit levels have an effect on out-of-wedlock births, and the effects of transfer payments on marriage stability are inconclusive. He cites Ellwood and Bane (1984) who go further: "Welfare does not appear to be the underlying cause of the dramatic change in family structure" (cited in Wilson, 1988, p. 81).

The theoretically sophisticated and carefully documented scholarship of Wilson, Ellwood and Bane, Duster, Viscusi, and Sampson constitutes a devastating critique of these two elements of the neoconservative argument. In essence, culture of poverty theories minimize the links between culture and structure, and the few linkages that are hypothesized cannot be substantiated empirically. If the neoconservative argument rests on such thin reeds, what is an alternative model for understanding rising levels of female-headed households, increased drug abuse, out-of-wedlock births among teens, high crime rates, and poor school outcomes?

A Structural Thesis: Joblessness, Family Instability, and Social Dislocation Among Poor Blacks

Best exemplified by Wilson's *The Truly Disadvantaged* (1988), the liberal response to the neoconservative argument emphasizes the dynamic interplay between underclass characteristics and the changing structure of social and economic opportunities in the central cities. Wilson shows how urban minorities are especially vulnerable to structural economic changes such as the shift from goods-producing to service-producing economy, the polarization of the labor market into low-wage and high-wage sectors, and the relocation of manufacturing out of central cities.

This interplay of forces is particularly evident in regard to education and jobs. The aforementioned economic transformations have been accompanied by changes in the educational requirements of the remaining central city jobs (Wilson, 1988). Specifically, inner-city job growth has been in occupations that require very high levels of education. So, despite the increases since 1970 in the absolute educational attainment of Blacks, there is a growing gap between the educational requirements of new central city jobs and the educational credentials of young Blacks who live there. The loss of blue-collar jobs traditionally held by inner-city Black males and the growth of the tertiary sector (high-level management of finance and commerce) has had dire consequences for the labor force participation of Blacks. Consequently, the percentage of Black males in the labor force fell sharply between 1960 and 1984 (Wilson, 1988). Ironically, the rise in unemployment among young Black males is due to another recent structural change—the entrance of mature women into the paid labor force, primarily in low-level service jobs (Duster, 1987; Wilson, 1988).

Lichter (1988) confirms that the geographic mismatch between where Blacks live and where jobs are located contributes to the growing Black underclass. In his study of race differences in urban underemployment he finds that the underemployment gap between Blacks and Whites increases over time, and that the significance of race and the effects of poor education and youthful age also increase over time.

From a structural perspective, the role of joblessness among young Black inner-city men is the key to understanding the rise in female-headed families (Sampson, 1987; Wilson, 1988). Wilson shows that while the structure of the American economy has changed a great deal in the past five decades, labor force participation of White males has been relatively stable, with the exception of a decrease in those over 55 (due primarily to early retirement) and a slight increase in young White males during the last decade. However, the same is not true of Black men. Black male labor force participation has declined from 84% (compared to 82% for Whites) in 1940 to 67% in 1980 (compared to 76% for Whites). The rate of employment for young Black males is 55% (Wilson, 1988).

Wilson shows how these economic changes in inner cities had profoundly negative effects on Black family stability. He notes that the normative pattern for Black inner-city families during the second quarter of this century was a two-parent, male-headed household. In 1940, 72% of Black families with children under 18 were male-headed. Female-headed families began to increase during the sixties, so that by the mid-1980s, 48% of Black families with children under 18 were female-headed.

Wilson also identifies several demographic correlates of the changes in metropolitan Black family structure. First, there have been tremendous changes in Black fertility and martial status. Over the past 45 years, the percentage of premarital pregnancies legitimated by marriage has decreased while the proportion of Black women who never marry has increased. Married Black women have fewer babies and divorced women are less likely to remarry. Second, Black teens are having children at earlier ages and higher rates than ever before (this is also true of White teens). In 1980, 68% of births to Black women between the ages of 15 and 24 were out of wedlock, and 30% of Black women had at least one child before age 20. Next, Black women have higher divorce and separation rates than do White women, and young Black mothers today are increasingly forming their own households rather than remaining at home with their parents. All of these changes are exacerbated by changes in the age structure so that there is an increasing proportion of Black women relative to marriageable Black men (this is largely due to the extraordinary mortality and incarceration rates for young Black males). Nevertheless, Wilson (1988) concludes that "the weight of the evidence on the relationship between employment status of men, family life, and married life suggests that the increasing rate of joblessness among Black men merits serious consideration as a major underlying factor in the rise of single mother and female-headed households" (p. 82).

The social correlates of living in a Black female-headed household are well known. In 1982, the poverty rate for married couples was 7.6% (total population), while for Black female-headed households it was 56.2%. Consequently, in inner-city areas, 78% of poor Black families are headed by single women (Wilson, 1988). It now becomes clearer why female-headed households are often an intervening variable in the relationship between the structural forces that transformed the economic base in the central cities and incidents of drug abuse, juvenile delinquency, teenage parenthood, and poor school outcomes. It is important to note that the evidence suggests female-headed households are primarily an intervening, not casual, factor in these social dislocations.

The Opportunity Structure, Students' Understanding of Reality, and School Outcomes

While the structural approach of the previous section provides a broad framework for understanding the situation facing the underclass, it says very little about the role of human agency in this process. In this section, we attempt to show how human agency mediates between structural factors and school outcomes. We focus on several theorists whose emphasis on students' perceptions and attitudes about education and opportunity enables them to delineate the mechanisms by which this occurs. Although these scholars focus on aspects of student culture, their work is distinguished from that of culture of poverty theorists by careful attention to the dialectical relationship between structure and cultural forms.

The theoretical sweep of Paul Willis's (1977) *Learning to Labor: How Working Class Youth Get Working Class Jobs* makes it an appropriate starting point even though his data are drawn from an ethnographic study of White working class males in a high school in England's industrial north. He describes the lived culture of the "lads," which holds that well-behaved, good students are "earholes" (because they are passive and compliant like the organ after which they are named), in which behavior that leads to good grades is deemed feminine, and in which manual labor, high levels of alcohol consumption, and sexist and racist behavior are romanticized as truly masculine. Central to Willis's argument is the idea that a group's culture is a dynamic social phenomenon, reproduced through interaction with the social reality in which members live. One's lived culture serves as a prism through which life experiences are refracted and understood.

Willis argues that the ideological aspect of the lads' lived culture that rejects school actually penetrates the dominant ideology's claim that education leads to good jobs and social mobility—recall the staggering unemployment rate in northern England. But their rejection of school simultaneously condemns them to the working class because it eliminates any future possibility for upward mobility for the few who might have squeezed through the narrow aperture of opportunity.

Many of Willis's general theoretical propositions regarding class find their counterpart in John Ogbu's (1978, 1988) work on racial stratification and its relation to educational outcomes. He challenges research that attempts to connect family background, ability, and achievement, but fails to consider minorities' own notions of the meaning of schooling within the context of social reality as they themselves understand it. In order to understand school success and failure among minorities, Ogbu argues, it is necessary to understand minorities' perceptions, interpretations, and understandings of how the world works and the "actual" role of schooling in their world. Ogbu (1988) acknowledges that these beliefs constitute part of minority children's culture, but unlike neoconservatives, he makes clear that Blacks "develop their cultural model from collective historical experiences or collective problems and collective efforts to resolve such problems. The cultural model is sustained or modified by subsequent events or experiences in their universe" (p. 8).

Ogbu developed his concept of a cultural model of schooling from his field work among Blacks and Chicanos in Stockton, California as well as from an analysis of education in other racially stratified societies. His elegant and sweeping theories of minority achievement are too complex to summarize here. However, a key element of his theory is the distinction between immigrant and involuntary minorities. Immigrant minorities, while subjects of discrimination and racism, came to the United States voluntarily and often have an option of returning to their homeland. Asian immigrants fit this category. In contrast, involuntary minorities, such as Afro-Americans and American Indians, were encapsulated into U.S. society against their wills and lack significant choice about where to live. These conditions of incorporation into U.S. society and the subsequent racial stratification create a profound difference in immigrant and involuntary minorities' social realities and the cultural models of school success created by each (Ogbu, 1978, 1988).

The structural processes that produce inner-city social dislocations are very much a part of underclass Black youth's cultural model of society and schooling. The lives of parents, adult relatives, older siblings, and neighbors demonstrate the failure of education, per se, to bring good jobs or to end Black joblessness and poverty. "The result is that [underclass] children increasingly become disillusioned about their ability to succeed in an adult life through the mainstream strategy of schooling" (Ogbu, 1988, p. 22). Poor school performance and high rates of dropping out are directly linked to inner city Black adolescents' cultural model of schooling and society. Ogbu (1978) is worth quoting at length:

> Given the premise that what motivates Americans to maximize their
> achievement efforts in school is their belief that the better education one
> has, the more money and more status . . . , is it logical to expect Blacks
> and Whites to exert the same energy and perform alike in school when
> the (opportunity structure) consistently underutilizes Black talent and
> underrewards Blacks for their education? (p. 123)

Using the work of Willis and Ogbu as a starting point, Mickelson
(1984) surveyed 1200 Los Angeles students in nine comprehensive
high schools and found a significant relationship between school outcomes and expected returns to education from the occupational structure. Students, she found, simultaneously hold two different kinds of
attitudes toward education. The first, which she calls abstract, reflect
the dominant ideology's account of the relationship between education, opportunity, and social mobility. Race, gender, and class have little affect on abstract attitudes; they receive uniformly high support
throughout the sample, but do not predict high school grades.

The second kind of attitude, which she calls concrete, reflects the
students' lived culture, especially the race-, class-, and gender-
specific experiences that people have in the opportunity structure.
Table 5.1 shows the race and class differences by gender of her sample. The higher the concrete attitude score, the stronger and more
positive the respondent feels about education and opportunity. Not
surprisingly, people from working class and minority backgrounds
have concrete attitudes that are more cynical about education and
opportunity than are those of middle-class Whites. These differences are reflected in academic achievement. In a multiple regres-
sion analysis (not shown here) concrete attitudes were a significant
predictor of high school grades. In terms of the structural interpretation of poor school outcomes presented in this chapter, concrete attitudes are important in two ways: (a) The poorest Blacks have the
lowest concrete attitudes, and the most prosperous group, middle-
class Whites, have the highest; and (b) among both Blacks and
Whites, each considered separately, lower socioeconomic status is
linked to lower concrete attitude scores that predict lower academic
achievement. This second finding is reminiscent of Sampson's
(1987) demonstration of the parallel effects of family disruption on
Black and White crime rates and provides additional evidence that
there is nothing inherent in Black culture predisposing it to become
"pathological" as the culture of poverty theorists claim.

Table 5.1. Means of Concrete Attitudes by Race, Class, and Gender

	Black Male[a]	White Male	Black Female	White Female
Middle Class[b]	4.38	4.90	4.43	5.00
Working Class	4.19	4.54	4.19	4.81

[a]Race differences are significant at the $p < .0005$ level.
[b]Class differences are significant at the $p < .0001$ level.

The work of Mickelson, Willis, Ogbu, and the other ethnographers of inner-city education (Crichlow, 1986; Fordham & Ogbu, 1986; Fordham, 1988; MacLeod, 1987; Sleeter & Grant, 1986; Weis, 1983) undercuts the neoconservative argument that the underclass is the source of its own problems. That social dislocations as different as poor school outcomes and crime can be linked to structural variables reaffirms the analytic priority of structure. With this point in mind, we turn to policy implications.

Policy Implications

As the previous analysis indicates, if educational problems as well as most social dislocations plaguing many urban Blacks primarily reflect structural forces operating in the national and international political economy, there is little reason for optimism about finding policy solutions to these problems. Indeed, any policy recommendation that fails to take these structural forces into account virtually belies the analysis that purportedly demonstrates their existence.

In other words, from an analytic viewpoint it is certainly useful to show how intensified social problems in the ghetto primarily reflect structural forces such as movements of capital and government deficits. But having established such linkages, there is no point in making a policy recommendation calling for, say, a program of job creation unless this recommendation is accompanied by a political–economic strategy capable of affecting the structural forces that reproduce a political economy that accepts—some would say requires (Bonacich, 1972, 1976; Reich, 1981)—large-scale unemployment especially among minorities. Whether such changes entail a substantial redistribution of political power in this country is a subject best addressed elsewhere. But without such dramatic changes in the country's opportunity structure, any additional policy recommendations for improving educational outcomes for Black youth will, at best, help them run full speed just to stay in the same place.

To the extent that poor school outcomes (like most of the problems of the underclass) primarily reflect that interplay of various structural forces, only substantial changes in these forces can markedly affect school outcomes. For example, imagine a successful transformation of inner-city schools and students so that next June all inner-city seniors graduate from high school. How long will this trend last if the employment prospects for both Black high school and college graduates remain as bleak as they are today? There must be real incentives in the opportunity structure for students to do well in school.

These considerations make clear that one of the criteria for policy recommendations is that they facilitate the kind of structural change that will alleviate the broad problems of the underclass. A second criterion of policy is that it be feasible within the present constellation of structural forces. A third is that the policy have a direct and positive benefit on the quality of underclass life. Maximally satisfying all three criteria simultaneously is obviously impossible, but we offer four policies that satisfy each of them in some way.

First, we have shown the importance of employment opportunities to the young Black's view of social reality and how their vision of the future shapes their behavior in and out of school. Consequently, policies to improve school outcomes must start with the occupational opportunities in the central city. First among these is some form of comprehensive urban development and suburban growth policy to stem the tide of deindustrialization of central cities. Decisions by employers to move from inner cities to suburbs are rarely done in a social vacuum. Since municipal governments have some input into the deindustrialization of central cities and the reindustrialization of suburbs because of the tax incentives and infrastructural support (e.g., new roads, water, utilities) they offer, certain policies can be used to change this pattern as well.

Second, policies of city governments often times have unintended consequences that exacerbate the isolation and concentration of the underclass in the central city by facilitating the out-migration of working and middle-class Blacks to the suburbs (Wilson,

1988). For example, in the city where the authors live, there is a program designed to assist certain public-housing project residents, those with steady jobs and decent incomes, to move from the projects to other nonpublic housing. The waiting lists for public housing are long, and the city administrators feel that these successful, working-class and lower-middle-class residents are taking up space that could be better used by those without jobs. Municipalities must take into consideration the unintended consequence of their policies. In this case, the program to remove more financially able residents from public housing accelerates the isolation and concentration of the underclass in inner cities. Our point is not to suggest that upwardly mobile Blacks have an obligation to remain in the ghetto as role models, but simply that local policy makers should be aware of the latent consequences of their decisions.

Third, if a major source of underclass misery is the poverty of female-headed households, the women who do work need to be fairly compensated. The minimum wage must be raised to provide a decent family wage; comparable worth statutes must be instituted to ensure pay equity for the majority of women who work in the female occupational structure; and universal and affordable quality child care must be made available. That these proposals are already on some corporate and political agendas suggests the possibility of progress in these areas without sweeping structural changes referred to in the first part of this section.

Finally, inner-city schools themselves must be improved. Whether their education leads to a job or not, poor Black youth are entitled to a quality education. Inner-city schools have been the subject of expose since the 1960s (Kohl, 1967; Kozol, 1967; Levy, 1970). Recent work, however, moves beyond ethnographic accounts of the problems and identifies specific areas of instructional difference. For example, Dreeben and Gamoran (1986) show that Blacks in segregated minority schools in the Chicago area receive inferior instruction compared to White and Black students in integrated schools. The growing effective schools research offers some direction in this regard (Purkey & Smith, 1983; Rutter, Maughan, Mortimore, & Ouston, 1979; Shavelson & Berliner, 1988). Beyond improving the technology of instruction, the work of Dreeben and Gamoran also indicates the importance of school desegregation as a policy that is instrumental for improving the school achievement and graduation prospects of underclass youth.

Conclusions

It is a truism that schools mirror society. To understand schools and what goes on in them, we must first understand the society in which they are embedded. This essay has described the structural transformation of the inner cities and the effects of these on social organization of Black underclass life. This is the social reality in which the schools and students in central cities exists. We cannot blithely continue to recommend policies that focus attention only on school improvement (as professional educators often do), or primarily on underclass students and their families (as the neoconservatives do) and expect achievement to rise and drop-out rates to fall. The larger structure of opportunity must be transformed for underclass youth as well. Until then, we must ground our expectations for improved school outcomes in reality—the same social reality in which poor Black youth ground their educational attitudes and behaviors.

To paraphrase Duster (1987), we have a forced choice. As a society we can spend our taxes for more jails and criminal justice personnel, drug patrols and treatment centers for abusers, more police to match increasing crime rates, and numerous educational "band-aids" that attempt to arrest the hemorrhage of Black students who fail and drop out of school, "or we can choose to pay our taxes for public sector development of career employment. Since the story told herein leaves us with the conclusion the private sector cannot possibly absorb the emerging Black underclass, we are left only with *how* the public sector adjusts to the development. We don't get to not choose" (Duster, 1987, p. 314).

Note

1. Although the concept of the *underclass* is theoretically and empirically problematic, we use it as a bow to current academic practice as well as for rhetorical convenience. Similar considerations inform our use of the term *social dislocations,* of which we distinguish two kinds. The first are those, such as poverty, which no responsible commentator could find desirable. The second, female-headed households for example, are those to which, in our opinion, no moral judgment should be attached. It is not our place (nor that of the state) to dictate particular adult conjugal arrangements. A more useful response is the advocacy and implementation of policies that help impoverished female heads-of-house-

holds escape from poverty. As we indicate below, such measures include universally available, affordable, quality childcare and an increase in the minimum wage. For an incisive overview of the difficulties in the use of underclass and social dislocations, see Reed (1988).

REFERENCES

Auletta, K. (1982). *The underclass.* New York: Random House.

Baker, K. (1985). Research evidence of a school discipline problem. *Phi Delta Kappan, 9,* 482–487.

Bonacich, E. (1972). A theory of ethnic antagonism: The split labor market. *American Sociological Review, 37*(3), 541–559.

Bonacich, E. (1976). Advanced capitalism and Black/White race relations in the United States: A split labor market interpretation. *American Sociological Review, 41,* 34–51.

Children's Defense Fund. (1988). *Children's defense budget FY 1989.* Washington, DC: Author.

Cloward, R., & Ohlin, L. (1960). *Delinquency and opportunity: A theory of delinquent gangs.* New York: Free Press.

Coleman, J. S., Campbell, E., Hobson, D., McPartland, J., Mood, A., Weinfeld, F., & York, R. (1966). *Equality of educational opportunity.* Washington, DC: U.S. Government Printing Office.

Coleman, J. S., & Hoffer, T. (1987). *High school achievement. Public and private schools: The impact of communities.* New York: Basic Books.

Coleman, J. S., Hoffer, T., & Kilgore, S. (1982). *High school achievement: Public, private, Catholic, and other private schools compared.* New York: Basic Books.

Crichlow, W. (1986, April). *Responses of Afro-American students to processes of education in an urban high school.* Paper presented at the annual meeting of the American Educational Research Association, Washington, DC.

Curtis, L. (1975). *Violence, race, and culture.* Lexington, MA: D. C. Heath.

DiPrete, T. (1981). *Discipline and order in American high schools.* (Report to the National Center for Educational Statistics). Washington, DC: National Center for Educational Statistics.

Dreeben, R., & Gamoran, A. (1986). Race, instruction, and learning. *American Sociological Review, 51*(5), 660–669.

Duster, T. (1987). Crime, youth employment, and the Black urban underclass. *Crime and Delinquency, 33*(2), 300–316.

Ellwood, D., & Bane, M. (1984). *The impact of AFDC on family structure and living arrangements.* Working paper for U.S. Department of Health and Human Services (Grant No. 92A–82), Washington, DC.

Fine, M. (1988). Sexuality, schooling, and adolescent females: The missing discourse of desire. *Harvard Educational Review, 58*(1), 29–53.

Fordham, S. (1988). Racelessness as a factor in Black Students' school success: Programmatic strategy or pyrrhic victory? *Harvard Educational Review, 58*(1), 54–84.

Fordham, S., & Ogbu, J. U. (1986). Black students' school success: Coping with the burden of "acting White." *The Urban Review, 18,* 176–206.

Gilder, G. (1981). *Wealth and poverty.* New York: Basic Books.

Heyns, B., & Catsambis, S. (1986). Mother's employment and children's achievement: A critique. *Sociology of Education, 59*(3), 125–139.

Hollingshead, A. (1949). *Elmtown's Youth.* New York: John Wiley.

Joe, T. (1987). Economic inequality: The picture in Black and White. *Crime and Delinquency, 33*(2), 287–300.

Johnson, L. D., O'Malley, P., & Bachman, J. G. (1987). *National trends in drug use and related factors among American high school students and young adults.* Rockville, MD: National Institute on Drug Abuse.

Kohl, K. (1967). *Thirty-six children.* New York: New American Library.

Kozol, J. (1967). *Death at an early age.* New York: Bantam.

Lemann, N. (1986, June). The origins of the underclass. *Atlantic,* pp. 31–61.

Levy, G. (1970). *Ghetto school: Class warfare in an elementary school.* New York: Pegasus.

Lewis, O. (1966). The culture of poverty. *Scientific American, 215*(4), 19–25.

Lewis, O. (1968). The culture of poverty. In D. P. Moynihan (Ed.), *On understanding poverty: Reflections from the social sciences* (pp. 187–200). New York: Basic Books.

Lichter, D. L. (1988). Racial differences in underemployment in American cities. *American Journal of Sociology, 93*(4), 771–792.

Loury, G. C. (1985). The moral quandary of the Black community. *The Public Interest, 79,* 9–22.

MacLeod, J. (1987). *Ain't no makin' it. Leveled aspirations in a low income neighborhood.* Boulder, CO: Westview.

Matsueda, R., & Heimer, K. (1987). Race, family structure, and delinquency: A test of differential association and the social control theories. *American Sociological Review, 52*(6), 826–840.

Mensch, B. S., & Kandel, D. B. (1988). Dropping out of high school and drug involvement. *Sociology of Education, 61,* 95–113.

Mickelson, R. A. (1984). *Race, class, and gender differences in adolescent academic achievement attitudes and behaviors.* Unpublished doctoral dissertation, University of California, Los Angeles.

Milne, A., Myers, D., Rosenthal, A., & Ginsburg, A. (1986). Single parents, working mothers, and the educational achievement of school children. *Sociology of Education, 59*(3), 125–139.

Moynihan, D. P. (1965). *The Negro family: The case for national action.* Washington, DC: Office of Planning and Research, U.S. Department of Labor.

Murray, C. (1984). *Losing ground, American social policy 1950–1980.* New York: Basic Books.

Myers, D., Milne, A. M., Baker, K., & Ginsberg, A. (1987). Student discipline and high school performance. *Sociology of Education, 60*(1), 18–33.

National Academy of Science. (1987). *Risking the future.* Washington, DC: Author.

Ogbu, J. U. (1978). *Minority education and caste.* New York: Academic Press.

Ogbu, J. U. (1988, May). *Minority youth's school success.* Invited address, School/college collaboration: Advancing effective teaching for at-risk youth. Johns Hopkins University, Baltimore, MD.

Purkey, S. C., & Smith, M. S. (1983). Effective schools: A review. *Elementary School Journal, 83,* 427–450.

Reed, A., Jr. (1988, February). The liberal technocrat [Review of *The truly disadvantaged*]. *The Nation*, 167–170.

Reich, M. (1981). *Racial inequality. A political–economic analysis.* Princeton, NJ: Princeton University Press.

Rumberger, R. (1983). Dropping out of high school: The influence of race, sex, and family background. *American Educational Research Journal, 20,* 199–220.

Rumberger, R. (1987). High school drop outs: A review of issues and evidence. *Review of Educational Research, 57*(2), 101–121.

Rutter, M., Maughan, B., Mortimore, P., & Ouston, J. (1979). *Fifteen thousand hours.* Cambridge, MA: Harvard University Press.

Ryan, W. A. (1971). *Blaming the victim.* New York: Random House.

Sampson, R. J. (1987). Urban violence: The effects of male joblessness and family disruptions. *American Journal of Sociology, 93*(2), 348–382.

Shavelson, R. J., & Berliner, D. C. (1988). Erosion of the educational research infrastructure. *Educational Researcher, 17*(1), 9–12.

Sleeter, C. S., & Grant, C. A. (1986). *After the school bell rings.* Philadelphia: Temple University Press.

Valentine, C. A. (1968). *Culture and poverty: Critique and counterproposals.* Chicago: University of Chicago Press.

Viscusi, W. K. (1986). Market incentives for criminal behavior. In R. B. Freeman & H. J. Holzer (Eds.), *The Black youth unemployment crisis* (pp. 301–346). Chicago: University of Chicago Press.

Weis, L. (1983). *Between two worlds.* New York: Routledge & Kegan Paul.

Willis, P. (1977). *Learning to labor. How working class youth get working class jobs.* New York: Columbia University Press.

Wilson, W. J. (1988). *The truly disadvantaged. The inner city, the underclass, and public policy.* Chicago: University of Chicago Press.

Wilson, J. Q., & Herrnstein, R. (1985). *Crime and human nature.* New York: Simon & Schuster.

Wolfgang, M., & Ferracuti, F. (1967). *The subculture of violence.* London: Tavistock.

6

The Community and Academic Achievement

WILLIAM D. PARHAM and
THOMAS A. PARHAM

Introduction

The purpose of this chapter is to explore those factors (both internal and external) that are presumed to contribute (both positively and negatively) to the achievement aspirations of the African-American youngster.

Initially, the task of responding to the question, "How does the Afro-American community affect the academic achievement of the Afro-American youngster?" seemed fairly easy and straightforward. An immediate and almost instinctual response to the question that was posed was that the community positively influenced the achievement desires of its youth. Undoubtedly, this initial response was spawned from our own sense that we, as residents of a Black community, had fared well in the academic arena. As we began to ponder the question more seriously, however, it became clear that we were not really sure just what effect the community did have on our development and educational maturation.

In addressing the question of the influence of the Afro-American community on the academic achievement of Afro-American youngsters, it seemed important to first get a sense of the nature and structure of today's Afro-American community. What does it look like? What are the forces that shape its design? What are the conditions under which today's Afro-American child lives? It also seemed important to obtain a current academic achievement profile of Afro-American youth. How are they faring in today's academic arena?

Under what circumstances must they succeed? What follows is a brief synopsis of both. What follows thereafter will be an examination of the interrelationship between the two. Past and current writings that look at this interrelationship will be highlighted, and particular attention will be given to the degree and kind of influence that one has on the other.

Profile of the Afro-American Community

Afro-Americans, the largest ethnic minority group in the United States, constitute 12.1% of American's more than 200 million people (U.S. Department of Commerce, Bureau of the Census, 1987). This percentage is up slightly from the 11.5% figure that held constant for the last several years. An objective examination of the conditions under which most Afro-American adults and children live leads to one inescapable conclusion—that both live in conditions where the educational level of community residents is typically low and economic resources are extremely scarce. Substantial differences between Afro-Americans and Anglos in every area of American life continue to exist, and the differential is widening.

While there has been a slight increase in the number of Afro-Americans residing in the suburbs, still nearly 60% of them reside in the inner cities (U.S. Department of Health and Human Services, 1985). Approximately 85% of Afro-Americans rent versus own their place of residence, and an equally high proportion live in substandard housing. The percent of female-headed households within the Afro-American community is also high.

Economic resources continue to be a problem in the Afro-American community. The median income for African-Americans in 1986 was $14,819, which is $10,000 less than the median income for Anglos during the same year (U.S. Department of Commerce, Bureau of the Census, 1987). The 1986 African-American median income figures are slightly higher than the median income figures for Afro-Americans over the last three years, which averaged $13,500.

Communities within which many African-American children live also have major health-care problems, and the problems occur at every age level. For example, infant death rates for Afro-Americans

(21.1 per 1000) continue to be almost twice that of Anglos. Relatedly, deaths of African-American mothers at childbirth (19.8 per 1000) are almost three times that of the 6.7 per 1,000 figure for Anglo mothers. These data are not unrelated to the fact that Afro-American women are more likely to be teenage mothers who have out-of-wedlock births, and who receive either no prenatal care or begin that care in their third trimester (U.S. Department of Health and Human Services, 1985).

Differences in life expectancy between African-Americans and Anglos continue to exist. In 1985, the life expectancy for African-American males (65.3 years) continued to be lower than the rates for both Anglo males (71.8 years), females (78.7), and African-American females (73.7). The life expectancy for African-American women, while higher than both male groups, was lower than the rate for Anglo women (U.S. Department of Commerce, Bureau of the Census, 1987).

Academic Achievement Profile of African-American Youth

African-American children seem to start their educational lives with cognitive, sensory, and motor skills equal to their Anglo age mates, yet academic achievement levels for them seem to decrease with the length of time they stay in school. It would not be uncommon to find, for example, that African-American children have fallen from one to three grade levels behind their Anglo peers by the time they are in high school. Afro-American youngsters also seem 3.2 times more likely to be labeled as educable mentally retarded and to be enrolled in remedial education programs. They are also half as likely to be enrolled in programs for gifted students.

The illiteracy rate for Afro-Americans (44.0%) is more than 2.5 times that of Anglos. Their high school drop-out rates also continue to be high. Entrance rates into college for Afro-Americans have also decreased over the last several years. In the late 1970s, slightly more than 50% of Afro-American high school graduates entered college. By the early 1980s, the proportion of African-Americans entering college had dropped to 36% (Bureau of Labor Statistics, 1983).

It should also be pointed out that many African-American youngsters attend schools that are in "crisis." Several reports document a growing number of cases of violence (e.g., student–student, and student–teacher) and vandalism. Many of these same schools also have fewer experienced teachers, and less than adequate teaching equipment and facilities.

To say that the profiles of the Black community and of the educational attainment of African-American youngsters just presented paint rather dismal and discouraging pictures would be a gross understatement. The travesty of both situations is all too apparent and the prospects of any positive, substantive change occurring in the very near future appear remote. Yet, these are the precise social and educational conditions under which a large number of African-American children live and are educated. It seems to be the case that schools reflect what is going on in society, so predictably, troubled schools will mirror troubled environments.

Most profiles of the kind reported herein, however, need to be viewed with some caution. These kinds of statistical summaries, while useful, often fail to provide a balanced picture. For example, the academic achievement profile of African-American youngsters just presented says little about those youngsters who are in fact succeeding academically. Many of these youngsters are reared in the same environment within which the vast majority of their African-American peers are failing, yet some are succeeding at rates equal to, if not in excess of, their Anglo peers.

Correlates of Achievement

Identifying the correlates of positive and negative achievement for African-American youngsters has been the focus of several investigations. The list of factors that potentially correlate with (either positively or negatively) academic achievement is almost endless. Yet several factors are more consistently identified as contributing to or inhibiting academic achievement in Black youngsters. Included among the list are family composition, socioeconomic status, teacher expectation, values, parental expectations, and self-concept, among others. This nonexhaustive review will briefly discuss four of these factors.

Historically, many social scientists have attempted to answer the question of academic achievement and the Black community by assuming that the environment negatively impacted the child. That is, it was assumed that low achievement was related to an absence of supportive attributes external to the child him- or herself. The chief scapegoat in these studies appears to have been the family.

Family Background as a Correlate

As early as the 1930s, research sought to document the consequences of poverty on the perceived instability, weakness, and disintegration of the family (Frazier, 1957). Not surprisingly, much of the research that followed attempted to validate these prior assumptions about the "pathological Black family" (Moynihan, 1965). Moynihan (1965), for example, characterizes the family as "tangled and a web of pathology."

By and large, the family variables that were identified as culprits included low socioeconomic status (SES), a matriarchal family structure, and a lack of educational resources (Clark, 1983). Assuming these factors are absolutely essential in promoting academic achievement in some youngsters, perceived low achievement by Blacks came as no surprise.

Explaining positive achievement of Black youth who are nurtured in a supportive environment has been a recent, albeit seldom, focus in the literature. For one thing, crediting the Black family (supportive or not) with helping to develop and promote achievement ideals occurs on too few fronts.

Images of the "pathological" and "disorganized" family have begun to change over the past decade, however. In some respects, the formation of positive family images has been assisted by researchers who understood that previous characterizations of the unhealthy Black family were in part influenced by biased assumptions and conclusions of the previous researchers themselves. Not surprisingly then, these latest studies (Billingsley, 1968; Hill, 1971; Ladner, 1971; Stack, 1974) have served as a reaction to previous Black family research by criticizing previous research efforts, and by attempting to explain family dynamics and composition in a way that highlights strengths of the family. For example, Billingsley (1968) cautions researchers against classifying the Black family as a single entity, rather than recognizing that, indeed, there is not one description that accurately characterizes the Black family of today. Similarly, Hill (1971) presented strengths or factors that have helped Black families to sustain themselves under less than ideal circumstances. These include strong orientations to work, religion, achievement, kinship bonds, and role flexibility by family members.

Recent studies on the Black family have continued to substantiate the work by Billingsley, Hill, and Ladner by isolating those factors that help modern-day Black family members in meeting their needs (McAdoo, 1981; Nobles, 1986). While these studies have been successful in characterizing the Black family as a vehicle that presumably helps to foster academic achievement in Black youth, they have been limited in their ability to explain exactly how achievement is supported and encouraged. The most important study to emerge in the literature that attempts to explain this phenomenon was conducted by Clark (1983). Clark attempted to answer the question of "Why poor Black children succeed or fail" in his book on *Family Life and School Achievement.* Essentially, he compares and contrasts five high-achieving students with five low-achieving students, and identifies parenting and child development strategies used by each family. He concludes that parents' dispositions and interpersonal relationships with the child are the main contributors to a child's success in school. Perhaps the most profound statement made in Clark's research effort is that communication and quality of interaction are more important than sociodemographic variables (i.e., family composition, income status) in predicting high achievement in Black youngsters. It is our contention, however, that while quality of interaction between parent and child is an important component in school achievement, we cannot overlook a youngster's willingness and motivation to respond to supportive environmental cues. Indeed, motivation is a characteristic that emerges from within the child herself.

Black Self-Concept as a Correlate

Another variable that undoubtedly influences the achievement aspirations of Black youngsters is self-concept. Yet, exactly how self-concept impacts achievement aspirations yields a debatable answer. Psychologists and sociologists have argued that the concept of self is found to be in direct relation to how a person thinks others perceive him (Mead, 1934; Rogers, 1961). Thus, a person in our society validates his identity through the evaluations of significant others. If the notion of necessary external validation is accurate, it seems reasonable to assume that achievement aspirations of Black youngsters would be influenced by evaluations by significant others in the child's life.

While such an assertion might be reasonable, researchers have had difficulty agreeing on where the child's source of validation is derived. Some research suggests that validation and approval is derived from the Black community (Banks 1972; Barnes, 1972; Norton, 1983). Unfortunately, the larger body of research suggests that approval is sought from the dominant culture (Kardiner & Ovessey, 1951), and because of the negative attitudes perpetuated by the larger White society, positive achievement by Blacks was not an expected outcome.

In contrast to the low self-concept/low-achievement-oriented studies of the past, more contemporary research cites evidence that African-American children do have positive racial self-concepts (Powell & Fuller, 1970; Soares & Soares, 1969). In fact, Powell (1983) concludes that the concept of low self-esteem in Black children should be disregarded in light of several extensive literature reviews by Wylie (1978), Rosenberg (1979), and Weinberg (1977) that revealed (a) little or no differences in self-concept between Black and White children, and (b) higher self-esteem scores in Black children.

The low self-concept conclusion of the past has also been questioned by challenging the notion that Black children agree with and internalize the negative evaluations of them promoted by the larger society. On the contrary, several studies have indicated that African-American children do not believe or agree with negative stereotypes about themselves or that they are inferior (Brigham, 1974; Campbell, 1976; Rosenberg, 1979). "What has been overlooked . . . is the minimization of the role of the oppressor (in influencing self-images), and more specifically, the adaptive strengths of the Afro-American (child)" (Gurin & Epps, 1975). Consequently, social scientists, teachers, and students themselves must come to grips with the fact that positive academic achievement among Black children is not only a possibility but a realistic expectation.

While the debate over the disposition of the Black child's self-concept may be temporarily suspended, the notion that a child's sense of self influences his or her academic achievement appears to be unanimous. If such is the case, how can the community contribute to the development of a healthy self-image? Parents and immediate family must provide reinforcement for a child's self-image by instilling a sense of pride, and by acting as a filter for the negative images to which a child is exposed. Parents and schools must play a role in communicating both expectations and encouragement for achievement, and constant praise and reinforcement for a child's mastery of various developmental and educational tasks. Children must also be assisted in identifying and participating in positive peer relationships and group activities that reinforce a positive sense of self. Each of these influences, together with other community resources (churches, parks and recreation, business leaders) must collaborate to reinforce for the Afro-American child principles of self-affirmation and self-determination. Other suggestions for enhancing self-concept were provided by Powell (1983) in her study on the effects of school desegregation on the self-concepts of Black children. Her investigation concluded that in order for self-concept of children in various schools to develop in a normal pattern, several criteria seem to be necessary. Those factors included (a) maximum participation by parents and teachers; (b) mores and values of the home reinforced in the immediate community and school; (c) Black culture and life-styles reflected in the educational curriculum; and (d) academic achievement being encouraged regardless of social class.

Value Orientation as a Correlate

Thomas (1967) defines values as a normative, conceptual standard of desired behavior that influences individuals in choosing among personally perceived alternatives of behavior. Values are believed to influence ways in which people think, feel, and behave (Kluckjohn & Strodtbeck, 1961). As such, values may also influence academic achievement of Black youngsters. Much of what Black youngsters come to value positively and negatively in the world is influenced by what significant others in their life value as well. Typically, values of specific ethnic groups are transmitted from generation to generation in ways that allow cultural traditions to continue and self-actualizing behavior to flourish. Occasionally, however, perceptions that culture-specific values are less functional than values of other cultures force many Black youngsters to abandon traditional African-American values in favor of Eurocentric ones. One consequence of this phenomenon is the adoption of many behaviors that are perceived as functional, but ultimately prove to be self-destructive to the individual and the community. Nobles (1980, 1986) helps to clarify the relationships between personal values and academic achievement by suggesting that ideas are the substance of behavior. Essentially, Nobles implies that the development of a strong desire to achieve academically, and behavior directed toward that goal attainment, are facilitated by a conceptual grounding in the philosophies of African culture.

The notion that education is a necessity for survival and advancement of one's people and oneself is a value that must be promoted by significant others in the child's life. Academic achievement in Black youngsters occurs when achievement is encouraged and supported by the community at large. Families, schools, churches, community organizations, and peer groups must come together in a collective voice and support efforts toward excellence. In absence of a unanimous consent for this idea, there must be enough support from particular significant others in the child's life, in order for that value to be internalized and practiced by the youngster.

Kunjufu (1986) suggests that values are the foundation for motivation, which in turn influences one's behavior. He further asserts that values are developed and nurtured through exposure to information. If Kunjufu's assertion is at all correct (and we suspect it is), then some analysis of the types of information Black children are receiving (or not receiving) is in order, and may help to crystalize how incorporation of values influences achievement of Black youngsters.

Exposure to television on a daily basis has been identified as one of the prime socializers of African-American youngsters. In subtle and some not-so-subtle ways, Black children's value systems are being influenced and shaped by what they visually and auditorily absorb from that medium (Berry, 1982). This realization is compounded by the notion that Black children devote a disproportionately high amount of time to television viewing (as high as six hours per day), and like other children, are likely to believe that television accurately reflects life as it really is or should be (Greenberg & Dervin, 1970).

Children are being exposed to images and role models that depict the Black community in very negative ways. Images of street-smart children and adults who will do whatever it takes to "get over" (lie, cheat, steal, murder, sell narcotics) are very inappropriate. Images of Blacks being confined to low-status jobs and being prevented from exploring a wider variety of career options are also inappropriate, and may be especially damaging to a child's achievement aspirations. Scenarios that promote money, status, material possessions, and sexual exploits as measures of manhood and womanhood are extremely destructive.

In many cases, the Black community has reacted strongly to these negative portrayals of Blacks on television by calling for a change of venue. Yet, the very community that demands that television images change fails to realize that the validation for Black children adopting these negative stereotypes and portrayals is being provided in and by the community itself.

If exposure to information is to remain as a prominent influence on values, and values in turn influence behavior, then manipulating the type, amount, and quality of information Black children receive will help them to develop a value system that is more consistent with their African culture. Such values might include, for example, the principles of *Nguzo Saba* (Karenga, 1976). These include *umoja* (unity), *kujichagulia* (self-determination), *ujima* (collective work and responsibility), *nia* (purpose), *kuumba* (creativity), and *imani* (faith). Presentation of, and teaching about, Africentric value systems may be an important strategy in helping Black children to develop the will and intent to achieve.

Teacher Expectations as a Correlate

Teacher expectations is yet another correlate of academic achievement that spawned wide-scale interest among researchers. The bulk of the studies suggesting that teacher attitudes and expectations affect a child's school performance began to appear in the late 1960s and early 1970s when Rosenthal and Jacobson (1968) published their now-classic study, *Pygmalion in the Classroom.*

At the heart of the Rosenthal and Jacobson experiment was a belief that teacher's expectations would significantly affect the learning of a group of socially and racially mixed elementary school children whose teachers were told possessed special intellectual talents. The teachers were also told that these "talented" children would show marked intellectual improvement by the end of the first few months of the experiment. The results confirmed the experimenters' prediction in that these intellectually talented students scored significantly higher than the control group on measures of the intelligence quotient (I.Q.).

In explaining their results, Rosenthal and Jacobson (1968) speculated that teachers are especially attentive to students who are expected to show intellectual promise. These students are often treated in a more encouraging manner, and teachers tend to show increased tolerance and patience with the child's learning process. The converse is true for students perceived to be less intellectually gifted. When students are not expected to make significant educational gains, less attention and encouragement is given to them.

The Rubovitz and Maehr (1973) investigation took a slightly different slant in that differential teacher expectations with respect to student's race and learning ability were of interest. A group of four, mixed-ability eighth-grade students (two Afro-American and two Anglos) were assigned to one of 66 women teachers (creating 66 teacher–student groupings), and two of the four students in each group (one Afro-American and one Anglo) were randomly given high I.Q. scores. The experimenters found differential teacher expectancy effects in predicted and unpredicted directions, and the student's race proved to be a very salient factor. Afro-Americans, both "gifted" and "nongifted," received less favorable treatment than "gifted" and "nongifted" Anglos. In rank order, increased attention and encouragement were given to "gifted" Anglos, "nongifted" Anglos, "nongifted" Afro-Americans, and "gifted" Afro-Americans. In essence, Afro-American "giftedness" was penalized with less attention and praise whereas Anglo "giftedness" was rewarded.

Reframing the Question

In reviewing the issues of achievement, nonachievement, positive influences, and negative influences, two variables emerged as most salient in our literature review and subsequent discussion; they were *outcome* and *environment*. As such, these variables were used to construct a model by which factors contributing to and inhibiting academic achievement could be appropriately identified, labeled, and classified.

Figure 6.1 is a model with the horizontal and vertical axes represented by the *environment* and *outcome* variables respectively. The outcome axis has a positive (top) and a negative (bottom) pole, while the environment axis has a supportive (left) and unsupportive (right) pole. In essence, each axis is a continuum that represents the range of possibilities between each end point. The intersecting axes form four quadrants that help up to frame our discussion into four outcome/environment possibilities. They are (1) supportive environment/positive outcome; (2) supportive environment/negative outcome; (3) unsupportive environment/positive outcome; and (4) unsupportive environment/negative outcome.

Table 6.1 illustrates that the internal dimension is subdivided into three components that represent the possible responses any individual can make in a given situation. For example, he or she can either think (cognitive), feel (affective), and/or do (behavioral) something in response to environmental stimuli. Each component, thus, has a positive and a negative set of options that he or she chooses.

Table 6.2 illustrates the external dimension that has three components representing the evaluative nature of environmental stimuli (positive, negative, neutral). Environmental realities that Afro-American youngsters must confront on a daily basis interact with components of the internal dimension of the model to create life circumstances or outcomes, some of which are positive and some of which are negative.

The two-dimensional aspect of our model is also designed as a reminder to researchers that outcomes (life circumstances) are influenced and determined by both environmental conditions *and* individual decisions to respond to environmental stimuli. Personal choices to accept some options and restrict others are important factors to consider in any discussion of outcome/environment possibilities. A further utility of the model lies in the categorization of those community resources that serve as primary socializing agents to Black youth (e.g., home/family, school, church, immediate community, society at large). We are suggesting that in order to identify and isolate the factors that contribute to and/or impede academic performance, researchers must learn more about (a) how a child fails to achieve academically despite a healthy, supportive environment, and (b) how a child manages to achieve or even excel in spite of an

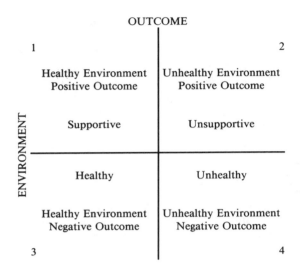

Figure 6.1 Personal Choice—Life Circumstances Model

Table 6.1.   Internal Dimension

Cognitive		Affective		Behavioral	
Positive Self-Statements	Negative Self-Statements	Positive Feelings	Negative Feelings	Self-Actualizing Responses	Non-Self-Actualizing Responses
Past/ Present/ Future oriented	Present centered only	High self-esteem	Low self-esteem	Social constructive pursuits	Criminal activity
Ability to dream	Inability to dream	Ethnic pride	Ethnic deroga-tion	Social clubs	Gang participation
Self-pride	Self-devaluation	Self-love	Self-hate hate	High educational achievement	Low educational achievement
No fear of failure	Fear of failure	Motiva-tion	Apathy	Church attendance	No church attendance
High frustration	Low frustration	Con-fidence	Helpless-ness	Sports	Drug/ substance abuse

Table 6.2. External Dimension

Community Resources		
Positive	*Neutral*	*Negative*
Education valued		Education not valued
Strong communication		Lack of communication
Mother and father in	Home/Family	Little emotional
home		nurturance
Constant emotional		
nurturance		
Strong leadership		No cultural curriculum
Effective counseling		Uninterested/
Career development	School	incompetent/negative
Cultural curriculum		teachers
Interested/caring/		Inadequate resources
competent teachers		
Progressive church		
education valued	Church	
Education valued		Negative role models
Employment		Unemployment/
Positive peer group		underemployment
Positive role models	Black Community	Gangs
Job training		Crime/vice
Recreation clubs		Negative peer groups
Cultural awareness		
programs		
Opportunities for		Racism and
participation	Larger Society	discrimination
Positive Black media		Negative Black media
images		images

unhealthy, unsupportive environment. For example, how does the author of "Brothers" (Monroe & Goldman, 1988) manage to obtain a Harvard degree along the way to becoming a *Newsweek* reporter and author, despite growing up in a Southside Chicago ghetto? Perhaps researchers may also want to follow Clark's (1983) lead by examining ethnographically how differential outcomes can be achieved under environmentally similar circumstances.

Reframing the question requires that we (researchers, parents, community) acknowledge each child's personal responsibility for his or her academic achievement and communicate these expectations to him or her. Children who interact in their environments without feeling a personal sense of control are usually quick to develop feelings of helplessness and apathy about their lives and life conditions. Such feelings, if internalized, ultimately prove destructive to African-American children's achievement aspirations because they confront even the smallest of obstacles to their achievement believing that they are powerless to influence the outcome. The issue of helping a child to acknowledge and accept some of the responsibility for his academic achievement is not meant to project blame or deny the community's (parents, schools, peers, etc.) responsibility in supporting achievement in African-American youngsters. Indeed, our intention is not to blame the victim. However, fostering academic achievement in Black youngsters begins with instilling in them the belief that personal effort, determination, and perseverance can lead to mastery over the subject matter. In addition, a child's ability to cultivate and receive emotional nourishment, support, and encouragement from parents (and significant others), and the ability to "dream" (set goals) beyond one's current life circumstances, seem to be factors related to academic achievement (Monroe & Goldman, 1988).

Conclusions

The intent of this chapter has been to address the Afro-American community's influence on the academic achievement of the Afro-American youngster. A nonexhaustive review of the literature on selected factors within the Afro-American community that purportedly influence the academic achievement of Afro-American youth has been presented and specific attention has been given to the inferences drawn from these types of investigations.

There appears to be several implications for how the community (schools, parents) can interact with the child in positively influencing academic achievement. White (1984) suggests that learning is best when it is additive in nature. He implies that learning is facilitated when new concepts and techniques are built on a foundation of strengths that a child brings to the learning environment. Accordingly, recognizing how an African-American child normally processes information and adapting learning exercises to correspond to that style seems a logical first step. Also, teaching exercises that help a child to master and add the information processing skills (analytical, sequential, and object-oriented reasoning) necessary to effectively compete in school to their existing repetoire of skills should be encouraged. Furthermore, using interpersonal relationships rather than or in conjunction with advanced technology as a means of supporting and promoting academic achievement should be encouraged. Finally, exhibiting congruence between verbal and nonverbal messages given to Black children is an important step in assisting Black youth in internalizing positive expectations for achievement.

Continued research in this area is necessary and future researchers may find it useful to assume a person–environment interaction perspective. This perspective acknowledges the interrelationship between an individual and the environment, and it assumes that several outcomes (e.g., life choices) are possible. By attempting to study those positive and negative factors that can influence academic achievement, it is possible to generate several questions, each serving as a point of departure for future research.

1. What internal factors contribute to an Afro-American child perceiving his environment as supportive, and in what ways does this perception influence the pursuit of positive life options?

2. What internal factors contribute to an Afro-American child perceiving his environment as supportive and in what ways is this perception altered so that less positive life options are pursued?

3. What internal factors contribute to an Afro-American perceiving his environment as unsupportive and in what ways does this perception influence the pursuit of life options that are less positive?

4. What internal factors contribute to an Afro-American child perceiving his or her environment as unsupportive and in what ways is this perception altered so that positive life options are pursued?

5. How does the Afro-American child allow cultural, societal, and familial expectations and experiences to influence his or her decision-making process?

6. How does the Afro-American child incorporate prior experiences into his or her present makeup?

7. What allows the Afro-American child to perceive a situation as challenging versus an impediment to a future goal?

This manuscript began by asking a series of questions about what effect the Black community has on the achievement aspirations of

Black youngsters. An analysis of the literature reveals that the community is impacting Black youth in both positive and negative ways. Our brief review has also provided us with some insights into what specific ways the community influences academic achievement in many youngsters.

REFERENCES

Ames, R. (1950). Protest and irony in Negro folksong. *Social Science, 14,* 193–213.
Banks, J. (1972). Racial prejudice and the Black self-concept. In J. Banks & J. Grambs *Black self-concept.* New York: McGraw-Hill.
Barnes, E. J. (1972). The Black community as the source of positive self-concept for Black children: A theoretical prespective. In R. L. Jones (Ed.), *Black psychology* (pp. 66–76). New York: Harper & Row.
Berry, G. (1982). Television, self-esteem, and the Afro-American child: Some implications for mental health professionals. In B. A. Bass, G. E. Wyatt, & G. J. Powell (Eds.), *The Afro-American family: Assessment, treatment, and research issues* (pp. 317–332). New York: Grune & Stratton.
Billingsley, A. (1968). *Black families in White America.* New York: Prentice-Hall.
Brigham, J. C. (1974). Views of Black and White children concerning the distribution of personality characteristics. *Journal of Personality, 42,* 144–158.
Bureau of Labor Statistics (1983). Youth labor force marked turning point in 1982. *Monthly Labor Review* (August).
Campbell, D. T. (1976). Stereotypes and the perception of group differences. *American Psychologists, 22,* 817–829.
Clark, R. (1983). *Family life and school achievement.* Chicago: University of Chicago Press.
Frazier, E. F. (1957). *Black bourgeoisie.* Glencoe, IL: Free Press.
Greenberg, B., & Dervin, B. (1970). Mass communication among the urban poor. *Public Opinion Quarterly, 34,* 224–235.
Gurin, P., & Epps, E. (1975). *Black consciousness, identity, and achievement: A study of students in historically Black colleges.* New York: John Wiley.
Hill, R. (1971). *Strengths of the Black family.* Report by National Urban League.
Kardiner, A., & Ovessey, S. (1951). *Mark of oppression.* New York: Norton.
Karenga, M. (1976). *Kwanzaa, origin, concepts, practice.* Los Angeles: Kawaida Publications.
Kluckjohn, F. R., & Strodtbeck, F. L. (1961). *Variations in value orientations.* Evanston, IL: Row, Peterson.
Kunjufu, J. (1986). *Motivating and preparing Black youth to work.* Chicago: African American Images.
Ladner, J. (1971). *Tomorrow's tomorrow: Black women.* Garden City, NY: Doubleday.
McAdoo, H. P. (Ed.) (1981). *Black families.* Beverly Hills, CA: Sage.
Mead, G. (1934). *Mind, self, & society.* Chicago: University of Chicago Press.
Monroe, S. & Goldman, P. (1988). *Brothers: Black and poor. A true story of courage and survival.* New York: William Morrow.

Moynihan, D. P. (1965). *The Negro family: The case for national action.* Washington, DC: U.S. Government Printing Office.

Nobles, W. (1980). *African philosophy: Foundations for Black psychology.* In Jones, R. L. (Ed.), *Black psychology* (pp. 18–32). New York: Harper & Row.

Nobles, W. (1986). *African psychology.* Oakland: Black Family Institute.

Norton, D. G. (1983). Black family life patterns, the development of self and cognitive development of Black children. In G. Powell, J. Yamamoto, & E. Morales (Eds.), *The psychosocial development of minority group children* (pp. 181–193). New York: Brunner & Muzel.

Powell, G. J. (1983). Self-concept in White and Black children. In C. V. Willie, B. M. Kramer, & B. S. Brown (Eds.), *Racism and Mental Health* (pp. 299–318). Pittsburgh: University of Pittsburgh Press.

Powell, G. J., & Fuller, M. (1970). Self-concept and school desegregation. *American Journal of Orthopsychiatry, 40,* 303.

Rainwater. (1970). *Behind ghetto walls: Black family life in a federal slum.* Chicago: Aldine.

Rogers, C. (1961). *On becoming a person.* Boston: Houghton Mifflin.

Rosenberg, M. (1979). *Conceiving of self.* New York: Basic Books.

Rosenthal, R., & Jacobson, L. (1968). *Pygmalion in the classroom.* New York: Holt, Rinehart & Winston.

Rubovitz, P. C., & Maehr, M. L. (1973). Pygmalion Black and White. *Journal of Personality and Social Psychology, 25*(2), 210–218.

Soares, A. T., & Soares, L. H. (1969). Self-perception of culturally disadvantaged children. *American Educational Research Journal, 6,* 31–45.

Stack, C. (1974). *All our kin: Strategies for survival in the Black community.* New York: Harper & Row.

Thomas, W. (1967). *The Thomas self-concept values test: For children ages 3–9.* Grand Rapids, MI: Educational Service.

U.S. Department of Health and Human Services (1985, August). *Report of the secretary's task force on Black and minority health,* Vol. 1, Executive Summary.

U.S. Department of Commerce, Bureau of the Census. (1987). *Statistical abstracts of the United States* (107th).

Weinberg, M. (1977). *Minority students: A research appraisal.* Washington, DC: National Institute of Education.

White, J. (1984). *The psychology of Blacks.* Englewood Cliffs, NJ: Prentice-Hall.

Wylie, R. (1978). *The self-concept: Revised edition* (Vol. 2: Theory and research on selected topics). Lincoln: University of Nebraska Press.

7

The Black Family and Academic Achievement

LOUIS E. JENKINS

The majority of critiques and discussions of the Afro-American family have generally portrayed it as a social system that is disorganized, matriarchally dominated, single-family directed, and subnuclear arranged (Bianchi & Farley, 1979; Elkins, 1968; Moynihan, 1965; Rainwater, 1970). This view of the Black family has served as the bedrock for examining issues of achievement, both academic and educational, motivation, self-concept, and self-esteem. A consequence of this viewpoint has been the deficit-deficiency model of the Black family as the explanatory paradigm (White, 1984). It has been precisely this posture taken by observers that has served to proliferate spurious information about Black families, to eclipse the relevant social factors essential for producing economic and political changes favorable to Black family life in America, and to encourage insensitive and ineffective institutional responses to the academic achievement of the family.

Black family research has studied, for the most part, the family as if it were isolated from its environmental context. Any explication of the Black family, and its subsequent role and impact on academic achievement of its members, must acknowledge the fact that the family is embedded within a larger social system, that is, a system with reciprocal interactions and relationships that often do not enhance its best interest. To ignore the embeddedness of the Black family within the larger social system and the complexity of the reciprocal relationships serves not only to confound research findings and create unwarranted perturbations but also to blame the victim for his condition. Halpern (1973) illuminates the latter thought well:

Basic to culture (American way of life) are such concepts as universal education, equal opportunities, the importance of achieving, and the emphasis on "getting ahead." Implicit in all this is the assumption that,
afforded the blessings and opportunities provided by a democracy, failure to attain success must be regarded as indicative of some inherent de-
fect, some lack of intelligence or character. . . . Failure to achieve must be
the fault of the individual not the system. (p. 28)

A debilitating aspect of Black family research has been its insistence on comparing Black families with White families. The under-
pinnings of such an approach assumes that there is equality of
opportunity and equivalency of life space between Black and White
families. It also flagrantly implies that "White" is the standard.
"Still deeply ingrained is the assumption that the proper approach
to the study of a minority people is to compare them to White"
(Korchin, 1980, p. 263). This is the violence of research that inter-
feres with arriving at more accurate and suitable explanations of the
phenomena under study; this viewpoint is further underscored by
Nobles (1979) and by what Triandis, Malpass, and Davidson (1973)
(cited in Draguns, 1981), relative to empirical research, have called
the "pseudoetic orientation": the assumption that the observer's
own culturally bound experience is an adequate guide to what is humanly universal. This belief is applicable to all observers regardless
of cultural/ethnic origin. Specifically, however, this belief has, relative to research on Black families, led to a highlighting and preoccupation with the weaknesses of the family with little or no focus on its
strengths. Hill (1972) and Nobles (1974) have contributed much to
the understanding of Afro-American families' strengths. Their emphasis has permitted a fruitful examination of the contextual arrangements of the family and the social organization within the
family that impacts the academic achievement of its members.
    The Black family is like any other family in that it wants the best
that life has to offer educationally, financially, spiritually, politically,
and socially for its members. Simultaneously, it is unlike any other
family due to its unique status imposed by the deep structure (warf
and woof of racism) of the American social system. From a historical perspective, Black families have not been entirely free to manipulate the essential components of life to the same degree as have
their White counterparts. The amazing thing about the Black family
has been its ability to design a family structure that has contributed

to the accomplishments and survival of its members in spite of the social system; that is, the family has demonstrated an unparalleled resiliency in the face of all the obstacles strewn in its pathway.

For the interested reader, much has been written about the Black family that is both negative and positive, and that discusses the family in detail. Therefore, this chapter will not focus on the Black family per se, but will confine itself to the task of identifying those factors that impact the successful and unsuccessful academic achievement of Afro-Americans.

Successful Achievement

Successful academic achievement appears to be greatly influenced by good parenting skills and positive parental involvement. A longitudinal study of 62 low-income Black mother–child pairs investigated mother–child interaction and child intellectual development. The children were observed and tested every six months beginning at age 2 months and ending at age 36 months. Research results indicated that mother–child interactions, especially from birth to 24 months, were strong determinants of the child's intellectual abilities. The findings appeared to be consistent with a number of studies cited in the study (Blumenthal, 1985). Norman-Jackson (1982) studied the effects of family interactions on language development and primary reading achievement of Black children in families of low income. Results indicated that successful readers received more verbal stimulation and encouragement than unsuccessful readers who received significantly more parental discouragement.

Reading activities and reading proficiency among Hispanic, Black, and White students were investigated by Ortiz (1986). It was found that parents' educational level, reading activities, and behaviors on the part of family and child had a direct effect on reading proficiency. A lack of these activities was found to be important in explaining lower achievement of Black and Hispanic children. A similar study was conducted by Shields and Dupree (1983) on the influence of parent practices upon reading achievement of good and poor readers. The findings indicated that parental responses were significantly related to successful reading achievement: lavish praise, teaching responsibility, and buying trade books. The study also indicated that successful learning of school-related subjects requires a high level of parental involvement.

Lee (1984) identified eight psychosocial family variables that contributed to the academic success of rural Black adolescents: (a) closely knit family structure, (b) high degree of parental control, (c) moderate to high degree of family openness, (d) high degree of educational encouragement, (e) strong family values, (f) good relationships with sibling role models, (g) extended family members, and (h) sense of responsibility fostered by required chores. An extensive study by Clark (1983) of academic achievement of 10 low-income Black families with 10 high school seniors (5 high achievers and 5 low achievers who were classified into one of four distinct family groups: two-parent families/one high-achieving senior; one-parent families/one high-achieving senior; two-parent families/one low-achieving senior; and one-parent families/one low-achieving senior) identified 17 comparisons of the quality of success-producing patterns in the homes of high achievers and low achievers. The patterns for the high achievers were as follows: (a) there was frequent school contact initiated by the parent(s), (b) the students had some stimulating and supportive teachers, (c) parents were psychologically and emotionally calm with students, (d) students were psychologically and emotionally calm with parents, (e) parents were expected to play a major role in the children's schooling, (f) parents expected their children to play a major role in schooling, (g) parents expected their children to get postsecondary training, (h) parents had explicit achievement-centered rules and norms, (i) students showed long-term acceptance of norms as legitimate, (j) parents established clear, specific role boundaries and status structures with parents as dominant authority, (k) siblings interacted as an organized subgroup, (l) conflict between family members was infrequent, (m) parents frequently engaged in deliberate achievement training, (n) parents frequently engaged in implicit achievement-training activities, (o) parents exercised firm, consistent monitoring and role enforcement, (p) parents provided liberal nurturance and support, and (q) parents deferred to child's knowledge in intellectual matters. These home patterns were the opposite for the low achievers.

Matthews-Juarez (1982) studied 100 Black families for the purpose of determining the effects of family background on the educational outcome of 97 Black teenagers. The research results showed that 77 of the 97 students graduated from high school with 20 dropping out. The reasons given for successful completion of high school relative to the family were parents' interest, parents' awareness, family finances, and positive family image. Findings of the study also showed that 41 of the 77 students were from two-parent households and 36 were from other than two-parent homes. Results of the study also indicated that the high aspirations and expectations of the parents appeared to highly influence graduation from high school, that is, achievement motivation of the family.

The results of the studies reviewed strongly support the premise that successful academic achievement was a function of good parenting skills, positive parent involvement in the student's educative process, and other associated psychosocial variables.

Unsuccessful Achievement

Economics, in all its variations, impacts greatly upon the Afro-American family system. While this factor may not impact every Black family to the same degree, its influence may be generalized in such a manner as to act as a "perceptual mediator" of those involved directly in the achievement process. White (1984) points out that since there is little assurance of a payoff in the end, it does not make sense to Black children to expend the time or effort to achieve. They witness on a daily basis Black high school and college graduates who are either underemployed or unemployed and rarely see those Blacks who have been successful achievers, due to minimal visibility, in areas of employment that command decision making and have status in society.

The U.S. Department of Labor (1988) indicates that among various ethnic groups Blacks have the highest rates in every major aspect of unemployment. The same document showed that of those individuals not in the labor force who desire work, 51% could not find work and 45% think that jobs are not available. When a lack of payoff, limited visibility of successful Blacks, and the realities of underemployment and unemployment are combined, it is not difficult to understand how these conditions alter one's perceptions to the extent of adversely influencing the pursuit of academic achievement. In spite of the positive achievement orientation the family may embrace, the perceptions are so internalized as not to be overridden by alternative viewpoints that encourage academic achievement.

Much has been written about the single-parent household. The literature has tended to be pejorative in presentation, that is, single-parent families are judged to be inherently inferior and the cause for society's ills. Due to factors such as death of a spouse, divorce, separation, children born out of wedlock, and choice not to marry, the single-parent family is an ever-increasing phenomenon. Single-parent households are usually compared with the traditional nuclear family, which is seen as the standard of stability. Arrangements other than those of a nuclear family are seen as a sign of instability (Bianchi & Farley, 1979). Single-parent families appear to be shackled with the burden of contributing to substandard scholastic achievement, poor self-concept, and delinquency (Sciara, 1975; Austin, 1978; Farmer, 1979). There seems to be a gap in the literature in identifying the strengths of single-parent homes that are stable. Some studies have attempted to address the issue although their particular focus was not on academic achievement; for example, Carter (1975), Wilkinson & O'Connor (1977), and Fields (1981) examined self-concept development of Black children. Results of these studies indicated that female-headed households can function effectively as family units and do not necessarily produce problems of poverty, delinquency, and mental health. Another shortcoming in the single-parent literature has been the failure to examine the factors, for example, limited resources and support networks, that impinge significantly on the single parent. These factors, rather than single parenthood itself, need to be the focus of attention. Smith and Smith (1986) have examined many of the factors and issues of single parents in the Black community. The study identifies the concerns and the need for reasonable social support in order for these homes to be viable and resourceful.

That many single-parent homes adversely influence academic achievement cannot be denied. A literature review by Dawson (1981) of 23 documents showed that the one-parent family has an adverse effect on academic achievement of children as well as other emotional and behavioral areas. Brown (1980) showed in his extensive study that children from single-parent homes demonstrated lower achievement and also evidenced a host of other related problems compared with children from two-parent homes. A related area of the literature has been the effect of father absence from the home. Carter (1980) found that the absence of the father had less influence on academic achievement and had its greatest effect on interpersonal distancing. This finding seems consistent with reported studies that place greater emphasis on the influence of the mother rather than the father on academic achievement (Dawson, 1981; Smith & Smith, 1986).

Unsuccessful academic achievement has also been impacted by the behavior of the home and the school relative to expectations and support. Rosenthal and Jacobson (1968) demonstrated dramatically the effect of diminished teacher expectation and support on classroom learning. For the Black child in this situation, which is one of diminished teacher expectation and support, a similar situation may be encountered at home. Bridges (1986) found that low-level school performers received little encouragement from family members. A study by McAdoo (1979) highlights the importance of the home and school working together as a means of assisting Black children.

Incompatibilities between the culture of the home and school are contributing factors to unsuccessful academic achievement. Behaviors and styles of learning endorsed by the home are often not acceptable to the school. A study by Hale (1980) focused on the role of cultural variables: learning styles of Black students, emotional expressions, orientation toward people rather than objects, interpersonal relationships, and proficiency in nonverbal communications in contrast to the learning styles and behaviors expected by the school setting. Findings of the study indicated that these differences between student behaviors and school expectations generate misconceptions and misperceptions that in turn impede academic achievement and portray Black students as disruptive and academically inferior.

A mixed group of 99 Black and 44 White high-risk college freshmen were studied relative to cultural factors. An investigation found discontinuities between the culture of students and the culture of the university. It was recognized that the cultural demands of the university could not be met appropriately by the high-risk freshmen because they lacked the necessary behavioral repertoire that would facilitate adjustment and positive academic achievement. Results of the study demonstrated that in order for the students to meet the cultural demands of the university, the necessary behavioral repertoire could be acquired through behavioral rehearsal, and that acquisition of the extended behavioral repertoire contributed to a higher level of academic success. Without such a repertoire, they would continue to be unsuccessful (Jenkins & Guthrie, 1976).

Incompatibilities relative to cognitive styles of Blacks and that required by the school have been studied and found to negatively affect academic achievement. Results of these studies have shown that students who have not developed the analytic cognitive style required by the school are poor achievers early in school and will do poorer as they progress to higher grade levels (Cohen, 1969; Ward, 1973).

Poor physical and mental health exacts a deleterious toll on Afro-Americans. In almost every major health category, Blacks have the highest rates of ill health and continue to be at highest risk (Hamburg, Elliot, & Parton, 1982). The effects of poor health are represented in different ways within families. Vaughn and Leff's (1976a; 1976b) study on types of expressed emotion found that the manner in which families handle illness has a profound effect on the family. A study by Gray (1985) indicated that support systems within families may be sources of stress that in turn aggravate interactions between the person who is ill and family members. Turkat and Buzzell (1983) indicated that family burnout due to dealing with major health problems within the family can have very negative consequences. The literature related to Black health punctuates the seriousness of physical and mental health problems. It seems reasonable to assume that poor health will seriously affect every aspect of a family and individual; therefore, academic achievement, either directly or indirectly by the trickle-down effect, may also be negatively compromised.

Methodological and Conceptual Limitations of the Research

The research studies investigating the influence of the Afro-American family on successful and unsuccessful academic achievement have examined such factors as one-parent versus two-parent households, parent involvement, economics, home and school expectations, and a number of related psychosocial factors. These studies have provided useful information and a forum for generating additional research questions. However, a weakness in the approach to the studies has been the treatment of the various factors in an isolated manner, that is, as if they existed separately and apart from each other. Families are embedded in a complex of reciprocal relationships. They do not function in a vacuum. Therefore, the variables under scrutiny must be probed within this contextual arrangement. To ignore the interrelationships of the reciprocal interactions contributes to conflicting and inconclusive results.

Another limitation of the research appears to be in the choice of families to be studied. The majority of the studies selected low-income or poor families. Conceptually, this choice infers that the model of the Black family is low-income or poor. It also suggests an implicit attachment to the deficit-deficiency hypothesis. Afro-American families, like other families, cut across all levels of socio-economic status, and to "freeze" the family at one level conceptually is limiting. In addition, this approach eclipses the fact that even at the same SES level, families are qualitatively different in the manner in which they function and impact academic achievement. This writer acknowledges the methodological and conceptual difficulties inherent in conducting this kind of research; and while there are no simple and sovereign answers to this complex task, a way to minimize the limitations will be to recognize the contextual arrangements of the variables under study and apply a combined objective–phenomenological method of analysis and explication. Additionally, this approach will serve to mediate the observer's own culturally bound experience as a guide to what is humanly universal relative to the Black family and its impact on academic achievement.

The Quest For Successful Academic Achievement

In spite of conflicting and inconclusive research findings, identifiable variables have been uncovered that merit further study and understanding relative to their influence on successful academic achievement. Of all the studies reviewed, the extensive research by Clark (1983) provides the focus for ongoing research endeavors. Clark (1983) concludes that "the form and substance of the family psycho-social patterns are the most significant components for understanding the educational effects of high achievers' families and low achievers' families, not their race or social class background per se" (p. 199). He says that "family processes and culture, not structural and demographic variables, determine achievement orientation in children" (p. 203). The emphasis placed on the quality of family life seems to be the key that will open the door to greater understanding of the issues involved. In the foreword of the study, it is pointed out that "differences in the quality of life are not explained by such family composition variables as marital status of parents, income, or amount of parents' formal education" (Clark, 1983, p. ix). This finding appears to support the writer's contention that when variables are examined in isolation, they seem to qualify as causes. However, when considered within a complex of reciprocal relationships, a more reasonable explanation emerges. In this case, the quality of family life is the significant variable. Assuming this to be true, the question arises as to what mechanisms will contribute to the enhancement of quality family life and patterns of conducive interactions and influence successful academic achievements? Five mechanisms are suggested: research, social policy, home–school relationships, family, and an existential perspective.

Research on Afro-American families and academic achievement needs to redirect its agenda to the significant psychosocial patterns of family life that facilitate and maintain successful achievement. The research enterprise would do well to relinquish its preoccupation with the weaknesses of Black families and focus on the variables that make successful families function maximally. Moving the research agenda in this direction will develop a useful data base for educational planning and reform, and inform the process for the development of meaningful and viable social policy that impacts Black families. To continue research endeavors in the present direction only serves to compound existing misconceptions and contribute to the birth of new ones.

Given that social policy is often influenced by research findings, an accurate data base is needed in order to inform social policy process. Black Americans have experienced the outcomes of social policy ill informed; for example, see Moynihan (1965). Social policy endeavors should be directed toward using the strengths of Afro-American families to ensure that the political and social institutions are responsive in a manner that is redemptive in terms of empowering Black families to greater viability and self-determination. It appears that this response could be accomplished by policies that would remove the obstacles and interferences that are strewn in the pathway of Black families, for example, debilitating social and racial practices. Although Black families have flourished in spite of the system, good social policy would allow the energies that are siphoned off to deal with social issues to be redirected positively for home use.

Another mechanism for enhancing and facilitating quality family life is the home–school relationship. Based on the writer's years of experience in public school education, it seems that the relationship between home and school was primarily adversarial in content and quality. In order to ensure successful academic achievement, the two bodies must work in concert. A greater portion of the responsibility must be placed on the school for interpreting to Black families the nature of the education process and their expected role in it. By the same token, the Black family must recognize that the student's first school is the home, that it must be responsible for the learning that takes place, interpret for the school what has taken place in terms of the student's growth and development, and work cooperatively with the school to build upon prior learning. Each institution needs to know what the expectations are and the role each plays in meeting them. Both must work for a balance between them that will ensure successful school achievement.

Since the quality of life within the home has been identified as the significant influence on academic achievement, it is imperative that ways be developed in communities that would enable parents from homes that are successful to assist families that have not reached that same level of successful functioning. In the same manner in which communities have developed the supraordinate goal of "community watch" for their protection, the same families could develop the supraordinate goal of "parent effectiveness." Often families want to do what is best, but many lack the knowledge or skills to make life work effectively. This approach is not new. It is simply reawakening the spirit that many Blacks grew up under, that is, every adult on the street was one's guardian/parent. This approach assisted in instilling confidence and competence toward coping with life effectively. Everyone on the block was his brothers' keeper, thus helping to improve the quality of family life and its subsequent outcomes.

The vicissitudes of life are often harsh, unjust, and difficult to cope with effectively. Nonetheless, that is the reality of life and it must be dealt with in a way that maximizes individual and group potential. The mechanism of facilitation is the "existential imperative." The writer defines this as the recognition that people cannot always control situations, but they can control or choose how they want to respond to them, that is, a person must accept the responsibility for the quality of his or her life. It is a responsibility that many may deny; however, it still cannot be avoided. For Blacks in American society, the added burden of racism, discrimination, and oppression influence this imperative. Of critical importance are the attributions that persons connect to their situations that have immobilizing effects in terms of productive actions. This is a function of repeated experience of the noncontingency of their responses and the uncontrollability of events due to the person's attributions to explain causes that foster a kind of learned helplessness (Thomas, 1986). Therefore, it is vitally important for the individual to maintain that sense of choice relative to choosing how to respond. That form of control may be all that the person possesses at a given point in time.

It is important for Afro-Americans to realize that they will never reach a higher standard than they themselves set. It must be ingrained in the psyche that fate has not woven its meshes about any human being so completely that the person need remain helpless and in uncertainty. It needs to be understood that opposing circumstances should create a firm determination to overcome them, and to let nothing hinder that process. Joseph White (1984) echoes similar thoughts in his description of psychologically healthy Afro-Americans: They accept as a given that unavoidable pain, struggle, disappointment, and tragedy are necessary for personal growth; this is simply how things are. They are resourceful, inventive, imaginative, and enterprising in their approach to life. They are not immobilized or devastated by the realities of oppression in American life. They have learned through the course of a lifetime that if they are going to have an equal range of options they have to depend on their own resources to create them. They are not afraid of being destroyed by racism and are proud to be Black. They have established a workable balance between the Afro-American and Euro-American value systems in their internal space. It is important that the existential imperative be communicated boldly in all Black families, communities, and classrooms.

A consequence of this imperative for the achievement of academic success is that Black families and Black students fully understand that learning is not an option—it is a mandate. They must come to understand that even though underemployment and unemployment rates are highest for Blacks, that Blacks are underrepresented in higher educational attainment, and that obstacles in society are plentiful, without successful academic achievement the options of life are near zero. With an education, one's options are increased.

Howard and Hammond (1985) point out that one of the reasons Blacks do not perform well academically is because they have internalized the larger society's projections of Black genetic intellectual inferiority. As a result, they avoid intellectual competition, and lean more toward competition in athletics and entertainment, and forget the opportunity for intellectual development. Howard and Hammond (1985) conclude that Blacks must hold themselves accountable and recognize their own responsibility. Clearly, both of the assumptions from these researchers are open to further questions and debate.

Black researchers, behavioral and social scientist, must be careful of the emphasis they place on the psychosocial realities. It sometimes appears that the emphasis "on how terrible it is" serves to explain away or psychologize away personal responsibility. That is not to say that the realities of life are to be denied; it is to say that their existence cannot be used as excuses for not doing what one knows needs to be done. Black history has countless accounts of individuals who faced incredible situations and made it. While the victim must not be blamed, personal responsibility for academic achievement and attainment primarily rests with the family and individual student. It is a responsibility that cannot be avoided. This message must be heralded in all quarters of Black life. The family, in its many forms, is the focal point.

REFERENCES

Austin, R. (1978). Race, father-absence, and female delinquency. *Criminology,* *15,* 487–504.

Bianchi, S. (1980). Racial differences in per capita income, 1960–76: The importance of household size, leadership, and labor force participation. *Demography,* *17* (2), 129–142.

Bianchi, S., & Farley, R. (1979). Racial differences in family living arrangements and economic well-being: An analysis of recent trends. *Journal of Marriage and the Family, 41*(3), 537–551.

Blumenthal, J. B. (1985). *Mother–child interaction and child cognitive development in low-income Black children: A longitudinal study.* Paper presented at the biannual meeting of the Society for Research in Child Development, Toronto, Canada. (ERIC Document Reproduction Service No. ED 262 892)

Bridges, R. E. (1986). *Black male child development: A broken model.* Paper presented at the Annual Conference of the National Black Child Development Institute, Miami, Florida, (ERIC Document Reproduction Service No. ED 276 502)

Brown, F. B. (1980). A study of the school needs of children from one-parent families. *Phi Delta Kappan, 61,* 537.

Carter, C. (1975). An investigation of self-acceptance and the perception of the mother–offspring relationship of Black educable mentally retarded and nonretarded offspring. *Dissertation Abstracts International, 35*(7-A), 4880.

Carter, D. E. (1980). Father absence and the Black child: A multivariate analysis. *Journal of Negro Education, 49*(2), 134–143.

Clark, R. (1983). *Family life and school achievement: Why poor Black children succeed or fail.* Chicago: University of Chicago Press.

Cohen, R. (1969). Conceptual styles, culture conflict, and nonverbal tests of intelligence. *American Anthropologist, 71,* 828–856.

Dawson, P. (1981). *The effect of the single-parent family on academic achievement: A review of related literature.* (ERIC Document Reproduction Service No. ED 241–604)

Draguns, J. G. (1981). Counseling across cultures: Common themes and distinct approaches. In P. B. Pedersen, J. G. Draguns, W. J. Lonner, & J. E. Trimble (Eds.), *Counseling across cultures* (p. 5). Hawaii: University of Hawaii Press.

Elkins, S. (1968). *Slavery: A problem in American institutional and intellectual life.* Chicago: University of Chicago Press.

Farmer, B. (1979). Black family structure and its effects on adolescents. *Dissertation Abstracts International, 40*(2), 1102-A.

Fields, A. (1981). Perceived parent behavior and the self-evaluations of lower-class Black male and female children. *Adolescence, 16,* 919–934.

Gray, B. A. (1985). *The relationship between stress and social support systems of Black female professionals.* Unpublished doctoral dissertation, Lincoln Medical and Mental Health Center, New York.

Hale, J. (1980). *A matter of culture: The educative styles of Afro-American children.* (ERIC Document Reproduction Service No. ED 197–856)

Halpern, F. (1973). *Survival: Black/White.* New York: Pergamon.

Hamburg, D., Elliot, G., & Parton, D. (Eds.) (1982). *Health behavior: Frontiers of research in the biobehavioral sciences.* Washington, DC: National Academic Press.

Hill, R. (1972). *The strengths of Black families.* New York: Emerson Hall.

Howard, J., & Hammond, R. (1985). Rumors of inferiority. *The New Republic* (pp. 17–21).

Jenkins, L., & Guthrie, G. (1976). Behavior rehearsal for high-risk freshmen. *Journal of Psychology, 92,* 147–154.

Korchin, S. J. (1980). Clinical psychology and minority problems. *American Psychologist, 35*(3), 262–269.

Lee, C. C. (1984). An investigation of psychosocial variables related to academic success for rural Black adolescents. *Journal of Negro Education, 53*(4), 424–433.

Matthews-Juarez, P. (1982). *The effect of family backgrounds on the educational out-*

come of Black teenagers in Worcester, Massachusetts. University Microfilms International, Ann Arbor, Michigan.

McAdoo, J. (1979). Father–child interaction patterns and self-esteem in Black preschool children. *Young Children, 34,* 46–53.

Moynihan, D. D. (1965). *The Negro family: The case for national action.* Washington, DC: U.S. Government Printing Office.

Nobles, W. (1974). Africanity: Its role in Black families. *Black Scholar, 5,* 10–17.

Nobles, W. (1979). The Black family and its children: The survival of humaneness. *Black Books Bulletin, 6,* 7–14.

Norman-Jackson, J. (1982). Family interactions, language development, and primary reading achievement of Black children in families of low income. *Child Development, 53,* 349–358.

Ortiz, V. (1986). Reading activities and reading proficiency among Hispanic, Black, and White students. *American Journal of Education, 95,* 58–76.

Rainwater, L. (1970). *Behind ghetto walls.* Chicago: Aldine.

Rosenthal, R., & Jacobson, L. (1968). *Pygmalion in the classroom: Teacher expectation and pupils' intellectual development.* New York: Holt, Rinehart & Winston.

Sciara, F. (1975). Effects of father absence on the educational achievement of urban Black children. *Child Study Journal, 5*(1), 45–55.

Shields, P. H., & Dupree, D. (1983). Influence of parent practices upon the reading achievement of good and poor readers. *Journal of Negro Education, 52*(4), 436–445.

Smith, E. J., & Smith, P. M. (1986). The Black female single-parent family condition. *Journal of Black Studies, 17*(1), 125–134.

Thomas, M. B. (1986). The use of expectancy theory and theory of learned helplessness in building upon strengths of ethnic minorities: The Black experience in the United States. *International Journal for the Advancement of Counseling, 9,* 371–379.

Turkat, D., & Buzzell, V. (1983). The relationship between family violence and hospital recidivism. *Hospital and Community Psychiatry, 34*(6).

U.S. Department of Labor (1988). *Employment and Earnings.* Washington, DC: U.S. Government Printing Office.

Vaughn, C. E., & Leff, J. P. (1976a). The measurement of expressed emotion in the families of psychiatric patients. *British Journal of Psychiatry, 15,* 157–165.

Vaughn, C. E., & Leff, J. P. (1976b) The influence of family and social factors on the course of psychiatric illness. *British Journal of Psychiatry, 129,* 125–137.

Ward, T. (1973). Cognitive processes and learning: Reflections on a comparative study of cognitive style in fourteen African societies. *Comparative Education Review, 17,* 1–10.

White, J. L. (1984). *The psychology of Blacks: An Afro-American perspective.* Englewood Cliffs, NJ: Prentice-Hall.

Wilkinson, C. S., & O'Connor, W. (1977). Growing up male in a Black single-parent family. *Psychiatric Annals, 7*(7), 50–59.

8

Academic Success and the School Dropout: A Minority Perspective

ROMERIA TIDWELL

For decades members of minority groups have viewed education as a vehicle to gain entry into the mainstream of American life. Formal schooling and education have long been considered the ways through which all could partake of the American dream. Even when other opportunities are unavailable because of class, racial, or economic barriers, formal schooling has continued to be one avenue to success that many minority group members perceive as accessible to all.

Afro-Americans provide an excellent example of a minority group's conviction that formal education provides the means to achieve social status and financial security. The history of the United States is darkened by the blatant injustices suffered by Afro-Americans. Nevertheless, Afro-Americans have held on to the belief that education is a way out even when they have had to endure the most dire of circumstances. Despite the conditions under which many that been forced to live, Afro-Americans remain committed to the belief that education is a means of advancement for their children (Billingsley, 1974; Oyemade, 1985) and that school is a place for learning that prepares children for life (Mookini & Tidwell, 1989).

Although Afro-Americans perceive the educational process as a means to achieve economic and social success, increased attention has focused on the Afro-American drop-out problem. Many Afro-American youngsters leave school early without a high school diploma. The incidence of dropping out among minorities, including Afro-Americans, remains an increasing problem in the public

153

schools (Census Bureau, 1987; Department of Defense, 1982; Rumberger, 1983). For example, recent data from a 1984–1985 California study reported that nearly half of all Black high school students in the Los Angeles Unified School District will drop out before graduation (Black Dropout, 1987).

If Afro-Americans still believe education is one of the surest ways to make it in American society, why are the drop-out rates for this group's youth increasing? What happens to these students when they leave school prematurely? What factors impact on the drop-out rate of Afro-Americans? What are the effects of dropping out on the individual, the group, and society? Finally, what can be done to prevent drop-out activity among Afro-American youngsters? A discussion of these and other questions is presented from a minority researcher's point of view.

Prevalence of the Drop-Out Problem

One way to better understand the drop-out phenomenon among Afro-American youth is to recognize the prevalence of dropping out among Afro-Americans and to compare that group's drop-out rate with those of other ethnic and racial groups. Statistics on school drop-out rates shed some light on the general drop-out problem and the specific drop-out problem for Afro-Americans.

The annual drop-out rate for the nation's high school students significantly declined from the 1970s into the 1980s. During the late 1970s, 11% of the high school population dropped out before obtaining their high school diplomas. Ten percent of White high school students dropped out, but the minority rates were substantially higher: 15% for Blacks and 23% for Hispanics. When the drop-out population is broken down by race and sex, White males and females have the lowest drop-out percentage nationwide, 10% and 9% respectively; Black males and females have the next lowest, 17% and 14% respectively; and Hispanic males and females have the highest rates, 22% and 24% respectively (Rumberger, 1983).

For the 1982 academic year, about 535,000 students prematurely left grades 10, 11, or 12, amounting to only 5.2 percent of the total high school population. The drop-out rate for Afro-American students also showed a decline, falling from 12% in 1973 to 7% in 1982, but remaining slightly higher than the percentage for the total high school group (Census Bureau, 1987). More recent data from the General Accounting Office (GAO) indicate that in 1985 4.3 million young people between the ages of 16 and 24 dropped out of school— 13% of the age group. Of these, 3.5 million were White, 700,000 were Afro-Americans, and 100,000 were from other racial groups. In addition, male drop-outs outnumbered female dropouts: Approximately 16% of males between the ages of 18 and 19 were dropouts, while only 12% of females in the same age group had dropped out (Hahn, 1987).

The Consequences of Dropping Out

Most available research supports the widely held view that leaving school without a diploma in hand has several negative economic, social, and personal consequences, in addition to affecting the social integration of the dropout.

Economic Consequences

It is important to study the economic consequences of dropping out because they affect the individual dropout as well as the society in which that person lives. The costs of dropping out include difficulty in finding employment, being relegated to a low-paying job, and having less opportunity for economic advancement than high school graduates. Dropouts have lower life-time earnings, and are more likely to be the recipients of welfare payments than are high school graduates (Beck & Muia, 1980; Catterall, 1986). Statistics from California indicate, for example, that of those who drop out of Los Angeles schools, 72% of this group will end up receiving public monetary assistance (California State Department of Education, 1981).

Timberlake (1982) believes dropouts cannot cope with the increasing competition for education and jobs, and consequently are alienated from mainstream America. Because of their limited education and training, dropouts, especially minority group members and women, experience higher unemployment rates and lower earnings than do other workers. Dropping out, therefore, has deleterious economic consequences for Afro-American students and other minority group members, since it contributes to the unemployment rate and an income that is already low.

Social Consequences

Dropping out also exerts an impact on society that is closely related to the economic consequences already mentioned. For example, because many school dropouts are also unemployed, they must cope with idleness—how best to spend the many hours that were once taken up with school-related activities. Few inexpensive opportunities for recreation are available to adolescents in the United States compared with other countries; therefore, school dropouts in the States are more likely to engage in antisocial behavior than are their counterparts in other countries (Biddle, Bank, Anderson, Keats, & Keats, 1981).

Dropouts become a social burden since they often require public assistance or engage in criminal behavior to alleviate their financial woes. An increase in criminal behavior among dropouts has consequences for their families of origin as well as for their own children. For example, a drop-out father involved in criminal behavior puts his family at risk of even greater poverty if he is caught and sent to jail. Single, drop-out mothers engaged in criminal behavior risk losing their children to institutions and foster homes. In addition to socioeconomic status, Steinberg, Blinde, and Chan (1984) report that several family variables have been implicated in premature school leaving. Dropouts are more likely to come from families with many children, single-parent homes, homes with few possessions, and homes with limited reading material.

Rates of delinquency are far higher among dropouts than among those who remain in school (Bachman, Green, & Wirtanen, 1972). Kaplan and Luck (1977) found that one fourth of all the dropouts in their study had been suspended from school at least once, and that an additional one fifth had been determined by their teachers to be "classroom problem students."

Children from homes where only a single parent is present are least likely to remain in the formal school setting until graduation, possibly because of financial difficulties rather than because of the structure of the home environment per se (Shaw, 1982). Family size, housing conditions, and geographic location (Hill, 1979; Mare, 1980), as well as early marriage and pregnancy, are strongly linked with early school leaving (Marini, 1978; Howell & Frese, 1982; Rumberger, 1983; Waite & Moore, 1978).

Students from low socioeconomic status (SES) backgrounds are more likely to leave school prematurely than are students from high SES backgrounds (Rumberger, 1983). The more highly educated the parents, the more likely they are to serve as positive role models. Such parents positively influence their children's aspiration for advanced schooling; they spend more "quality time" with their children; they actively increase the academic abilities and opportunities of their children. Because higher SES families usually live in more affluent communities with better-financed schools, the children from these families are likely to have supportive, rewarding educational experiences. Further, children from poorer families may find it necessary to seek employment to supplement their family's income, as many Hispanic dropouts have indicated (Borus, Crowley, Rumberger, Santos, & Shapiro 1980).

There is also a concern that dropouts literally create more dropouts. Rumberger (1983) found that family background strongly influences the propensity to drop out of school and accounts for virtually all the racial differences in drop-out rates. Aspects of the family background factor include the education level of both parents, income, family size, and living conditions. As we can see, then, the factors connected with dropping out are closely interrelated—so closely, that it is difficult to draw generalizations about their causal relation to one another.

Personal Consequences

Two opposing views are reflected in the literature on the relationship between dropping out and personality structure. Some believe that the problem belongs to the individual "dropout," an individual with low motivation, low self-esteem, and low intelligence. Others advocate the position that dropping out is a natural reaction to one's environment, low teacher expectations, discrimination, racial or ethnic group prejudice, and so on. Regardless of which position is correct, drop-out behavior does correlate with certain personal traits. For example, Steinberg, Blinde, and Chan (1984) found that, as a group, dropouts are more impulsive, less mature, and less sociable than their non-dropout counterparts.

Dropouts face additional problems because they are often judged negatively by others as well as by themselves. Several studies have demonstrated that dropping out of high school is related to low self-esteem and depression. Students who leave school early are more likely to experience racial discrimination, to receive disapproval from parents, friends, and society, and to devalue themselves because of their decision to leave school (Steinberg, Blinde, & Chan, 1984). Timberlake (1982) found that a significant number of dropouts participate in organized activities outside of school, suggesting they are searching for a positive experience to compensate for their limited success in school.

Social Integration and Early Adulthood

Although many of the factors related to school drop-out activity are interrelated and in one way or another interact and depend on each other, the social integration of a young student, especially the Afro-American youth, deserves some attention. The variable most often studied in this category is the self-esteem of the youngster especially as it is reflected in academic achievement and school-related matters. Researchers believe that the potential dropout's self-esteem suffers because of his or her poor social integration. Potential dropouts, it is claimed, typically have not made friends easily and if they do have friends they are more susceptible to losing them, because of being held back or because of being ostracized by teachers and other students. Looking retrospectively, those who eventually drop out score lower on measures of self-esteem than do those who eventually graduate (Steinberg, Blinde, & Chan, 1984).

It has been said that a child not only values his or her identity but will engage in activities designed to protect or enhance it. Children will often decide to leave a disagreeable situation in school where they are devalued and join friends who validate their worth. The potential for accepting dropping out as a solution to school-related problems is maximized when the individual has numerous contacts with persons who have dropped out, such as friends, parents, and siblings. Thus the syndrome continues.

Probably the most widely researched element in the relationship of dropping out to the transitions of early adulthood is pregnancy. Simply put, pregnant adolescents are more likely to drop out of school than their nonpregnant peers (Steinberg, Blinde, & Chan,

1984). Even in this age of relative sexual freedom, adolescents who get pregnant and have babies are virtually forced out of school, if not by the ostracization of teachers and peers, then by the demands of taking care of a baby. Also, early pregnancy is highly correlated with low socioeconomic status and minority group status. (Once again, it is difficult to isolate the causal factors in dropping out of school.)

Employment during high school may lead to a decline in school involvement and performance in students who work more than 15 hours per week. Specifically, Steinberg and Pickney (1982) have shown that when a student works in excess of 15 hours a week, his or her school attendance drops, the amount of time the student spends on homework declines, participation in extracurricular activities diminishes, and reported enjoyment of school declines. Not surprisingly, a decline in school involvement is usually followed by a decline in school performance. The truth of these findings is only too obvious in the Afro-American community. Too often, for example, employment draws poor youngsters away from school, especially if the work involves a substantial number of hours per week. An Afro-American male high school student who wants to own a car may decide that he must work in order to maintain the vehicle; therefore, he prefers working to attending school because the immediate rewards are greater.

Academic Performance and Dropping Out

It appears that the attitudes students have toward school and the degree of students' social integration in the school environment are related to early school departure. In a recent study conducted by the Center of Human Resource Research at Ohio State University (1980), large numbers of American male youth of all ethnic groups reported leaving school because they "disliked" it. Dropouts nearly always experience alienation (restlessness, hopelessness, and estrangement) from their schools, homes, neighborhoods, and from society in general. Such perceptions are grounded in the youths' belief that they have suffered great injustices because of their race, language, culture, or religion. Potential dropouts typically have inferior social and communication skills, and such students seldom, if ever, participate in extracurricular activities (Cervantes, 1965).

Poor school achievement is predictive of early school leaving

(Bachman et al. 1971; Howell & Frese, 1982). Most important are patterns of achievement; students who are required to repeat grades or classes are especially at risk to drop out before completing high school. Half of the school dropouts in a Maryland study had been held back or had repeated classes at least once (Kaplan & Luck, 1977). Dropouts have been held back four times more often than those students who eventually graduate (Curley, 1971). Repeating grades even as far back as the primary level is also predictive of dropping out (Howell & Frese, 1982; Stroup & Robins, 1972). The social isolation that being held back involves has already been mentioned. In itself, it is also discouraging.

Ability has been widely investigated as a factor in dropping out of school. It is possible that high school dropouts have lower average intelligence quotients (IQ's) than those who stay in school (Sewell, Palmo, & Manni, 1981; Hill, 1979). Although IQ has intuitive appeal as an explanation of early school leaving, IQ differences fail to account for the many school dropouts who are intellectually capable and who were performing at an average or above-average level academically before they left high school (Sewell et al., 1981).

The IQ question, it hardly needs saying, is especially relevant to a discussion of the educational experience of Afro-American students. Just as schools are structured to dovetail well with the home life of White, middle-class society, the standardized tests that measure school achievement and determine class placement embody the value system and experiences of the largely White, middle-class people who design them. Hence, it is not unusual for such tests to underestimate the abilities and experiences of Afro-American youngsters if only because they do not measure, by and large, many of the things Black youngsters routinely learn (Tidwell, 1981).

Culture and Social Class

Many researchers believe that dropping out is a response to a certain status deprivation that some minority students or lower-class majority group youngsters experience in competition with middle-class students. Middle-class values emphasize order and discipline. In contrast, lower-class values emphasize avoidance of trouble with authorities, development of physical prowess, and independence from external control. Although their socialization prepares middle-class youth to compete successfully in school, lower-class children are not socialized to conform to the social requirements of school, which are, of course, aligned with middle-class values. The lower-class child, not prepared from an early age to be studious, obedient, and docile, comes into conflict with the middle-class teacher. "Poor social adjustment" impairs his or her chances for academic success.

Culture and social class interact in complex ways to produce the drop-out problem among Afro-Americans. To say this is to suggest that certain elements of the relationship between culture and class are unique to Afro-Americans. When those elements operate within other racial/ethnic groups, they operate in systematically different ways.

It is most important to recognize that, as a group, Afro-Americans have had to struggle continuously to maintain their cultural identity as a people. That is what the Black Consciousness and Black Power movements are all about. Even when other immigrant groups have lost connection with their families in the Old Country, they maintain much of their cultural identity. Afro-Americans, on the other hand, because of slavery, lost their cultural identity nearly totally. Consequently, they have had to invent and reinvent, discover and rediscover their identity.

Given their tenuous sociohistorical identity, social status assumes a large role in Afro-Americans' sense of themselves. Social class, therefore, predominates in determining Afro-Americans' ability to "make it" in the educational environment. In some places and on some terms, Blacks' long-held values about education do affect their educational experience, but the effect of those values is strongly mediated by social class—more strongly than for most other ethnic groups.

Cultural Factors

The cultural influences on a young student can have a significant impact on his or her decision to drop out. These cultural factors are usually manifest in maladaptive attitudes toward education and toward the educational system in general. Many Latin cultures, for example, place a large emphasis on the obligation of women to stay at home and take care of children. Thus, the importance of schooling for females is sometimes minimized by cultural values. Members of some ethnic groups who have recently come to the United States consider education a luxury that neither they nor their children can afford. In many Third World countries only the rich are educated and the rest of the population's concern is with survival. Therefore, parents who have been raised in such an environment, while they *value* education, often do not *do* the things necessary to keep their children in school at the expense of earning money the entire family desperately needs.

Cultural factors are heavily intertwined with other factors such as the language spoken in the student's home, parental attitudes toward education, and the family's socioeconomic status. Studies that control for all of these factors in order to isolate purely cultural influences do not exist. For one thing, a "cultural influence" remains very much in the eye of the beholder.

Sometimes, it is arguable that attitudes toward education reflect deeply held cultural values (among Jewish Americans and many, if not most, Chinese, for example). In those instances, in line with what was said above, culture predominates over social class in determining the structure of attitudes about education and in determining the value of education. For other groups, educational achievement may more strongly reflect social status: One suspects that many of the Vietnamese immigrants who do so well in school, despite their apparently low socioeconomic status, actually come from high-status families driven into temporary poverty. In such instances, their "true" social class predominates over their present social status in structuring the educational experiences of their children.

If correct, this relationship between culture and class, between values and social status, is the answer to the question with which we began: If Afro-Americans value education so highly, why do so many drop out of school? The intergenerational poverty of so many Afro-Americans buries, among other things, parents' ability to act upon their culturally ingrained beliefs about education and it prevents children from internalizing those beliefs in ways that translate into action. The regard for learning is there, but the mechanisms for facilitating its actual attainment are insufficiently ingrained to withstand the other imperatives of poverty. For middle-class Afro-Americans, on the other hand, a number of factors come into play that permit social class to provide the matrix in which Blacks' historical high regard for education is given some scope for action. The picture is not a simple one. Both social class and sociohistorical factors play a part in the educational or material well-being of virtually any individual. For Afro-Americans the weight of socioeconomic factors is relatively great.

The relationship between culture and class, moreover, operates in a number of ways to produce unsatisfactory educational experiences for Blacks and unsatisfactory educational outcomes. First, class differences between poor Blacks and middle-class children of any race emphasize the nonalignment of some Blacks with the value structure of the school. Second, class differences encourage the identification of lower-class children with groups completely outside the school. Third, factors that tend to discourage an interest in education among poor Black children are particularly deleterious to their educational futures, because neither the schools nor the society from which such children come provide many avenues for correcting negative attitudes toward school.

An increasing feeling of alienation from school among poor Afro-American children manifests in their eventual turning away from an interest in the educational experience. Many Whites are already, for cultural as well as socioeconomic reasons, aligned with the values entrenched in the public schools. Alienating experiences initiate and, ultimately, reinforce poor Black children's nonalignment with the value structure of the schools.

Even for the motivated, career-oriented youngster, adolescence is a time of upheaval during which school gives way to other preoccupations. A child who has never had a strong connection with school in the first place can become, in high school, a teenager who easily drifts away from school, intellectually, emotionally, and even physically. The pull away from school can be particularly strong for the poor minority group adolescent who frequently needs to work in order to provide things for him or herself or even for other family members. In any case, by high school, the illusion of their identity and alignment with the middle-class value structure of the school has been completely dispelled for many poor Black youngsters. They have not so much turned away from school, but have developed shared interests with others that have little to do with school.

There is little to counterbalance the forces that drive poor Blacks out of school. Furthermore, poor Black parents are often uninvolved in their children's education from the very beginning, and teachers are generally insensitive to the needs of poor children, particularly to the needs of poor Black children. At present, public schools are not designed to meet the needs of disadvantaged youngsters, especially those from distinct ethnic minorities. Until schools provide an inviting social climate to poor Black youngsters, and until the educational experience of poor Black youngsters involves their parents, dropping out of school will remain a substantial problem among poor Blacks.

It is important to emphasize again how the situation of the poor Afro-American adolescent differs from that of the middle-class Afro-American adolescent. The middle-class Black can find social support and social reinforcement for remaining anchored in the educational system: His or her parents, other relatives, or other significant others provide role models for success; he or she has long been attuned to school and his or her parents provide continuing pressure to perform, as middle-class parents, regardless of their race, generally do. That is, for the middle-class Afro-American social class interacts positively with the high cultural valuation of education at least compensating for the lack of cultural facilitation of educational attainment. Although poor Blacks regard education highly, they find themselves, both as children and later as parents, without the social mechanisms to turn their goals into realities.

Conclusions

Despite the existence of many valuable programs aimed at improving academic functioning (Veritz, Fortune, & Hutson, 1985), individual social variables (New York State Education Department, 1984), and social skills (Gallagher, 1985), widespread implementation of drop-out prevention programs is not in evidence. Various recommendations have been made regarding prevention programs, notably from the National Committee for Children and Youth (1961). Long ago the National Committee for Children and Youth recommended that special programs be developed for the gifted as well as remedial classes for slow learners and speech therapy for those needing it. It was stressed that schools too small to provide such services should be consolidated with other small schools. It was also suggested that high schools should provide multitrack curricula and achievement groupings. Work study was deemed a must to be coordinated with an expanded community program.

School counseling was also stressed throughout all grade levels, rendering a ratio of no more than 600 to 1 at the elementary school level and no more than 250 to 1 at the high school level. Vocational and education planning were deemed a necessary function of school counselors and it was recommended that these services be available year-round to serve students' needs.

Weidman and Freidman (1984) further recommend that the school counselor maintain strong ties between family and employment. Gadwa and Griggs (1985) support this recommendation by maintaining that counselors should influence the parents' values to support education. Furthermore, case conferences should be held with teachers, support groups established, and small group projects developed. Svec (1986) stresses the role of the teacher as an advocate and recommends follow-up and tracking of dropouts.

Perhaps the most comprehensive guidelines for setting up a drop-out prevention program were developed by the National Advisory Council on Supplementary Centers and Services (1975). Their report on drop-out prevention begins with explaining how to manage a drop-out prevention project, and subsequently covers how to choose staff, suggests a timeline for the first year, discusses federal monies available, and discusses prior programs exhibiting success. Furthermore, the report stresses the importance of summer learning, alternate learning, school within a school programs, alternative school for those already dropped out, and involvement of teachers in implementing prevention.

Thus, drop-out prevention remains a major issue in education today. The need for solutions will not go away, as exhibited by the nationwide drop-out rate of 30% and in some large cities 50%. However, if recommendations for programs and existing strategies that have proven effective are implemented, the gains shown by various individual school districts may someday be enjoyed by the nation at large.

The form of programs to prevent dropping out depends on a number of factors. First of all, and quite simply, to be effective a program must address an actual need connected with the drop-out phenomenon. The Job Corps, for example, is an excellent program that serves teenagers *after* they have left the traditional school, in many cases; the truly effective program would reach youngsters *before* they have dropped out. Second, a program must constitute a real solution to the problem. The concept of "separate but equal" schools has found favor with both Whites and Blacks at various

times, the justification being that Blacks would be better off in
schools attuned to their needs and governed by personnel committed to the Black cause and Black youngsters. For practical as well as
ethical, moral, and legal reasons such an approach is untenable; it is
a nonsolution because it means creating new problems rather than
confronting the ones that already exist. Third, a program is most effective when it is undertaken in full consciousness of where and how
it is addressing the dropout problem. That is, it must be abundantly
clear where the program is focused: at the "top" or "bottom" of the
educational system, in the family, in the school, in the community.
Knowing what a program is really designed to do and where it is designed to do it can help in determining if it is aimed at a real solution
and if it addresses real problems.

One of the claims made here is that, relative to other groups, the
low social status of poor Afro-Americans is especially destructive
of their educational advancement. It follows that changes in the
overall composition of the Black work force involving an increase
in the number of professionals and skilled workers will reduce
Blacks' contribution to the drop-out figures. Unfortunately, probably the quickest way to effect such a change is *through* the educational apparatus already in place, which brings us where we began.
The point is that we must not make the mistake, just because everything is connected to everything else, of supposing we have an anti-
drop-out program when what we really have is, say, a public works
project. Prevention programs that more or less directly address the
drop-out problem are of two basic types: those that focus on the
children and those that focus on the schools. The child-focused
programs can be further subdivided into those for young children
who have recently entered the educational system or are about to
enter it, and those for older children and adolescents. Likewise,
school-focused programs fall into two basic subcategories: those
aimed at teachers and teaching and those aimed at the structure of
the educational system at the level of the individual school or
higher. I do not mean to suggest through this classification that
programs in one category cannot also fall partly into others or be
intimately related to programs in other categories.

The reason that programs for students are divided into those directed toward young children and those directed toward older children is that the former are ideally aimed at eliminating the
underlying sources of the drop-out problem whereas the latter are

designed to manage the problem as it actually appears. Keeping students in high school when they are already deeply disaffected with the educational system that is supposed to deliver education is a tough assignment.

The design of early intervention programs depends on how we conceive their goals. In some sense, a problem in educating poor Afro-Americans and other disadvantaged groups is connected with early development, which suggests that intervention to attack the drop-out problem should begin very early. It is possible, however, that the usual arguments advanced in favor of such early intervention programs overvalue the "modeling" of literacy skills and exposure to what are perceived as middle-class values. Instead, I think we should look to the success of Head Start and other similar programs in increasing parent involvement in disadvantaged children's education. Parents' involvement in education has diminished across the socioeconomic spectrum and there is every reason to believe that lack of such involvement hurts lower-class children the most (Coleman, 1987). Because a main value of preschool programs for the poor is parent involvement, their actual dollar costs can be minimized by encouraging parents to work as volunteers in such programs.

The effectiveness of program interventions aimed at preventing dropping out among older children depends at least partly on what is meant by the term *older children*. Must we begin fighting to keep children in the schools before they leave elementary school? In junior high school? Or only during their later high school years? Beyond that, there is the question of whether such programs are most effective when they concentrate on academic skills or on the social skills that help children and adolescents adapt well to the school environment. My background in counseling leads me to favor programs that emphasize the latter.

Along those same lines, programs to reduce the drop-out problem can be aimed at teachers, not as much on what they know as on their sensitivity to the needs and problems of poor children and minority children. Teachers who recognize that they can either encourage an identification with the educational process or discourage it through their behavior in the classroom are going to be more effective in keeping minority children, especially poor minority children, in meaningful contact with school. The work of increasing teacher sensitivity can go on within the schools, but it also is a job for education departments and teacher education programs of the educational establishment.

Likewise, schools are going to have to adapt themselves to the varied "clientele" they serve (Tidwell, 1988). The curriculum, from elementary school through high school, must reflect the interests of minority students. Furthermore, school districts must alter time-honored policies of placing inexperienced and inept teachers in urban schools. Instead, they must aggressively pursue policies that place quality teachers where they can do the most good—providing challenging instruction to those who need it most.

REFERENCES

Bachman, J., Green, S., & Wirtanen, I. (1972). Dropping out is a symptom. *Education Digest, 37,* 1–5.

Beck, L., & Muia, J. (1980). A portrait of tragedy: Research findings on dropouts. *High School Journal, 64,* 65–72.

Biddle, B., Bank, B., Anderson, D., Keats, J., & Keats, D. (1981). The structure of idleness: In-school and dropout adolescent activities in the United States and Australia. *Sociology of Education, 54,* 106–119.

Billingsley, A. (1974). *Black families and the struggle for survival.* New York: Friendship Press.

Black dropout rate alarms LAUSD officials. (1987, December). *Los Angeles Sentinel,* p. A–4.

Borus, M., Crowley, J., Rumberger, R., Santos, R., & Shapiro, D. (1980). *Findings of the national longitudinal survey of young Americans, 1979* (Youth Knowledge Development Report 2.7). Washington, DC: U.S. Government Printing Office

California State Department of Education (1981). Statewide summary of pupil performance on school district proficiency assessments. Sacramento: Author

Catterall, J. S. (1986). *On the social costs of dropping out of school* (Report No. SEPI-86-3). Stanford, CA: Stanford Educational Policy Institute

Census Bureau finds lower dropout rates. (1987, July). *Guidepost,* pp. 1, 3

Center for Human Resource Research (1980). *The national longitudinal surveys handbook.* Columbus: Ohio State University, Center for Human Resource Research

Cervantes, L. (1965). *The dropout: Causes and cures.* Ann Arbor: University of Michigan Press

Coleman, J. S. (1987). Families and schools. *Educational Researcher, 16,* 32–38

Curley, T. (1971). *The social system: Contributor or inhibitor to the school dropout.* U.S. Educational Resources Information Center. (ERIC Document Reproduction Service No. ED 049 344)

Department of Defense. (1982). *Profile of American youth.* Washington, DC: Department of Defense, Office of Assistant Secretary of Defense, Manpower, Reserve Affairs, & Logistics.

Gadwa, K., & Griggs, S. A. (1985). The school dropout: Implications for counselors. *The School Counselor, 33,* 9–15.

Gallagher, V. (1985). The dropout: A new challenge to Catholic education. *Momentum, 16,* 40–41.

Hahn, A. (1987, December). Reaching out to America's dropouts: What to do? *Phi Delta Kappan,* pp. 256–263.

Hill, C. (1979). Capacities, opportunities, and educational investments: The case of the high school dropout. *Reviewing Economics and Statistics, 61,* 9–20.

Howell, F., & Frese, W. (1982). Early transition into adult roles: Some antecedants and outcomes. *American Educational Research Journal, 19,* 51–73.

Kaplan, J., & Luck, E. (1977). The dropout phenomenon as a social problem. *Educational Forum, 42,* 41–56.

Mare, R. (1980). Social background and school continuation decisions. *Journals of the American Statistical Association, 75,* 295–305.

Marini, M. (1978). The transition to adulthood: Sex differences in educational attainment and age at marriage. *American Sociological Review, 43,* 199–220.

Mookini, M., & Tidwell, R. (1989). A qualitative paradigm for exploring parent education in inner-city parent education programs. Manuscript submitted for publication.

National Advisory Council on Supplementary Centers and Services (1975). *Dropout prevention.* Washington, DC: Author.

National Committee for Children and Youth (1961). *Guidelines for consideration of the dropout and unemployment problems of youth.* Prepared conference on unemployed out of school in urban areas. Washington, DC: Author.

New York State Education Department (1984). *Operation success: Sponsored by the New York State Education Department. A co-operative program of federation employment and guidance service, the New York City Board of Education and the United Federation of Teachers, evaluation report, year ending June 30, 1983* (Report No. QPX62775). New York State Education Department Albany. (ERIC Document Reproduction Service No. ED 257 889)

Oyemade, V. J. (1985). The rationale for Head Start as a vehicle for the upward mobility of minority families: A minority perspective. *American Journal of Orthopsychiatry, 55,* 591–602.

Rumberger, R. W. (1983). Dropping out of high school: The influence of race, sex, and family background. *American Educational Research Journal, 20,* 199–220.

Sewell, T., Palmo, A., & Manni, J. (1981). High school dropout: Psychological, academic, and vocational factors. *Urban Education, 16,* 65–76.

Shaw, L. (1982). High school completion for young women: Effects of low income and living with a single parent. *Journal of Family Issues, 3,* 147–163.

Steinberg, L., Blinde, P., & Chan, K. (1984). Dropping out among language minority youth. *Review of Educational Research, 54,* 113–132.

Steinberg, L., & Pickney, J. D. (1982). Dropouts and the structure of opportunities. *Adolescence, 17,* 214–257.

Stroup, A., & Robins, L. (1972). Elementary school predictors of high school dropout among Black males. *Sociology of Education, 45,* 212–222.

Svec, H. (1986). School discrimination and the case for the high school dropout: A case for adolescent advocacy. *Adolescence, 21,* 449–452.

Tidwell, R. (1981). A psycho-educational profile of gifted minority group students identified without reliance on aptitude tests. *Journal of Non-White Concerns, 9,* 77–86.

Tidwell, R. (1988). The high school dropout: A consumer poorly served. *The High School Journal, 71,* 116–119.

Timberlake, C. (1982). Demographic factors and personal resources that Black female students identified as being supportive in attaining their high school diplomas. *Adolescence, 17,* 107–115.

Veritz, V., Fortune, J., & Hutson, B. (1985). Teacher leadership styles as they relate to academic gain for unsuccessful students. *Journal of Research and Development in Education, 16,* 25–42.

Waite, L., & Moore, K. (1978). The impact of an early first birth in young women's educational attainment. *Social Forces, 56,* 845–865.

Weidman, J. C., & Freidmann, R. R. (1984). The school-to-work transition for high school dropouts. *The Urban Review, 16,* 25–42.

PART III

Personal Adjustment and Programmatic Factors In Higher Education

9

Race Consciousness Among African-American College Students

MARCIA L. HALL and WALTER R. ALLEN

The history of Black people in this country reveals contradictions regarding the ideals that form the society's core. While the Declaration of Independence explicitly affirms the equality of all men, the Constitution implicitly defined an enslaved Black as three fifths of a man (Harding, 1981). From the very beginning, then, Blacks were defined as nonpersons without constitutional rights. As a result, African-Americans have been forced to continuously struggle to not only obtain basic constitutional rights (i.e., liberty, justice, and equality) but to regain and define their personhood as well.

The African-American community has historically looked to its educated members to assume the mantle of leadership in this struggle (Marable, 1983). This is particularly true of those with college educations. DuBois was one of the first to articulate this idea with his notion of a "Talented Tenth" (DuBois, 1970). Ideally, a college education developed the manual, mental, and related skills of the individual, while a concern for the race (i.e., race consciousness) motivated the person to use these skills to improve the group's status, thereby serving the community. Because a college degree also enabled one to improve his or her individual status, the question for Blacks has always been whether to use these skills to benefit both themselves and the group.

Because the Afro-American community was until recently excluded from predominantly White colleges and universities, most of

---

AUTHORS' NOTE: Funding for this project was provided by the Joyce Foundation.

its leaders have been graduates of the historically Black schools. Today, however, a majority of Black students attend mostly White institutions. One theory suggests that Blacks attending predominently White institutions are socialized into the value system of White society. As a result, they would be less willing to use their individual skills for the greater good of Black people. While Carter G. Woodson (1933) made this argument about the "miseducation" of Negroes 50 years ago, it has contemporary proponents. Gaines-Carter (1985) and Jordan and Cleveland (1986) point to students' ignorance of their own history, lack of political activism, and apparent overriding concern with material comfort as evidence of low race consciousness. There has been little research addressing the issue, however, leaving it an open question.

The current situation in Black America brings a sense of urgency to the issue. The Civil Rights Movement has brought about unprecedented opportunities for positive change in the lives of African-Americans. Some Afro-Americans have been able to take advantage of opportunities for educational and occupational advancement, thereby moving into and thus expanding the ranks of the Black middle class. Yet, many Black Americans have experienced little, if any, positive change in their individual lives, and several theorists argue that there really has been little change in the collective status of Black Americans (Farley & Allen, 1987). In fact, there are those who contend that given the current rates of unemployment, school attrition, drug abuse, violent crime, and related problems, the Black community faces an unprecedented crisis.

Lincoln (1979) and Wilson (1987) contend that progress for some has the potential to exacerbate this crisis. Desegregation has allowed the expanding Black middle class to move away from the spatial confines of American Black communities. Both authors suggest that these moves may lead to a loosening of the emotional ties to the community as well. Severance of these bonds, coupled with the continued dismantling of social welfare programs and the decline in unskilled jobs, would further devastate the Afro-American community.

Here, then, is the crux of the matter: Will the current generation of college students and graduates step forward as leaders in the ongoing Afro-American struggle for liberty, justice, and equality? Will they ignore the needs of the Black community and concentrate on their own individual upward mobility? Will they try to combine both goals? Historically, there have always been African-Americans who have used their individual achievements to provide needed services and leadership to further the collective mobility of the race (Ballard, 1973). There have also been those who used their individual achievements selfishly, opting for self-advancement and aggrandizement over collective gains. We are interested in whether contemporary Black college students most personify the norms and values of the "Talented Tenth" or of the "Me Generation."

Consequently, we propose to explore this issue through a study of race consciousness in African-American students attending universities with a predominantly White student body. More specifically, we will be examining the levels of race consciousness in a sample of Black students from the University of Michigan (Ann Arbor) and the University of North Carolina (Chapel Hill).

Black Students on White Campuses

One cannot adequately understand the phenomenon of Black students on White campuses without placing it in the proper historical context. The African-American community has always highly valued education, viewing it as the key to upward mobility in American society (Anderson, 1984; Ballard, 1973; Thompson, 1986). Since Black Americans have been systematically denied the right to acquire an education, attempts to gain access to educational institutions have always been a central part of the Afro-American struggle. In the postemancipation period this striving for education was initially met by the establishment of separate schools, from the elementary to postsecondary levels. Once the "separate but equal" doctrine began to result in separate and unequal facilities, however, the struggle turned to legal challenges to gain access to the better-equipped, predominantly White schools (Anderson, 1984). These legal challenges culminated in the 1954 Supreme Court decision that initiated the formal desegregation process. Other scholars such as Blackwell (1982), Edwards (1970), Harding (1970), and Peterson et al. (1978) emphasize the role Black students played to increase their number at White institutions. As a result, by 1975, more than 75% of all African-American college students attended mostly White schools (Blackwell, 1982).

This shift in enrollment patterns heightened interest in the experiences of Black American students at Anglo-American colleges and universities. The question of access was still an issue, especially with the controversy over open admissions. Morris (1981) and Blackwell (1982), among others, argue that the more elite institutions used standardized tests as gatekeepers against those who might detract from the quality of these institutions. Researchers also began to expand the definition of access beyond exclusion from the educational system to distribution across and within institutions as well as disciplines. In this respect, as of the mid 1970s, Black students tended to be "marginal students, enrolled in marginal programs, in marginal institutions" (Morris, 1979, p. 40). Ironically, this marginality was occurring at the same time that Black enrollment was at its peak. Further examination of the data reveal that while Black enrollment was high, persistence and retention were low. Abramowitz (1976) notes that although Afro-Americans comprised 6% to 7% of all undergraduates between 1969 and 1970, less than 3% of the bachelor's degrees granted in 1974 were awarded to Black students. Astin (1982) estimates college completion rates for Blacks were about one third that for Whites in 1979. As a result, scholars again broadened the scope of research to focus on the factors contributing to race differences in drop-out rates.

Thus far, researchers have concluded that there has been a "lack of fit" between African-American students and White American colleges (Allen, 1986). White colleges and universities most often constitute vastly different environments from prior home and school experiences. In comparison to their White peers, Black students tend to have lower family incomes and parents with lower educational attainment. Their high school grades and scores on standardized tests are also likely to be lower (Astin, 1982; Centra, 1970). In addition, their basic cultural orientation differs from that of Whites (Ballard, 1973). As a result, Afro-American students are usually academically and psychologically unprepared for the "dog-eat-dog" competitiveness they often encounter in predominantly White universities (Allen, 1982; Smith, 1980). Furthermore, as reflections of the larger social order, White colleges sustain and promote the values of the dominant group that not only differ from but denigrate those of dominated groups (Cave & Chesler, 1974).

These economic, educational, and cultural differences produce adjustment problems, for both the students and universities

(Peterson et al., 1978). As the less powerful member of this institutional relationship, however, the adjustment has a more negative impact on Black students. Studies by Allen (1981, 1982, 1986) and Willie and McCord (1972) point to the isolation and alienation, as well as depressed academic aspirations and achievement experienced by Afro-Americans on White campuses. Gibbs (1974) and Fleming's (1984) work in particular indicate the high physical and emotional stress that the students undergo in trying to sustain themselves in such hostile, alien environments. Not surprisingly, the result for some is poor academic performance and even dropout. For those who do stay on, academic success is often gained at the expense of psychosocial development (Fleming, 1984).

Race Consciousness Literature

Since race consciousness relates to intraracial attitudes and behavior, it fits under the rubric of "psychological development," suggesting, then, that predominantly White universities have a negative impact on race consciousness. Yet there has been little research that really examines the issue. The study of race consciousness itself dates back only to the 1920s and 1930s. Scholars such as Robert Park did content analysis of Black newspapers and poems in an attempt to define what they perceived as a new, more "militant," Negro mood. They called this new mood *race consciousness,* defining it as a collective sentiment that expressed identification and solidarity with Blacks, feelings of oppression, and a desire to change their oppressive state (Brown, 1931a, 1931b; Ferguson, 1938; Standing, 1938). These writers saw race consciousness as a reaction to and reflection of group conflict (Park, 1923). Most of this work was theoretical, however, and based on observations of Blacks throughout the whole of America and South African society, not just Black students on White campuses. After World War II, moreover, the research focus shifted from the study of group conflict to the nature of prejudice in individuals (Pitts, 1974). Studies of interracial relations dominated the 1940s and 1950s.

Scholars in the 1970s and 1980s began to make more use of the term *race consciousness* in their attempts to describe and define Afro-American political activity. Most of this new work, both theoretical and empirical, focused on Black college students because of their prominence in the struggle. As foot-soldiers in the Civil Rights Movement, they had actively participated in sit-ins, voter registration drives, and other demonstrations for equal rights (Edwards, 1970; Gurin & Epps, 1975; Harding, 1970). They carried the ideology of the Black Power Movement back to their campuses and led demonstrations for Black studies and increased Black representation at White colleges. Researchers who studied the race consciousness of these students found their participation in the Civil Rights and Black Power Movements had heightened their identification with and pride in Blackness and Black people (Edwards, 1970; Gurin & Epps, 1975; Pitts, 1975). Gurin and Epps (1975) argue further that once the students were confronted with seemingly immovable obstacles to economic justice, they tended to reevaluate their beliefs about the legitimacy of the American political–economic system. This reappraisal most often moved them away from blaming African-Americans for their lack of progress to blaming a racist political–economic system. Many often geared their career plans to ensure continued involvement in the Afro-American struggle.

There has been both empirical and theoretical work in the 1980s that uses the concepts of group or race consciousness. The Gurin, Miller, and Gurin (1980) work is theoretically useful in its efforts to more accurately conceptualize race consciousness. The authors contend that identification is not the same as race consciousness, a problem with the work of Orum and Cohen (1973). Their definition clearly encompasses earlier theorists' notions about group conflict and struggle to rectify group disadvantages. This is in contrast to work in the 1970s by Banks (1970), and Stanford (1971), who either do not define the term at all or define it so vaguely and in such a rhetorical manner that its usefulness as an organizing framework for study is lost. On the empirical side, Gurin, Miller, and Gurin (1980) found Blacks in their national sample to have higher levels of group consciousness, identification, and commitment to collective action than women, working men, older people, middle-class persons, and Whites. However, the sample deliberately excludes students. Work by Pitts (1975) does examine race consciousness in students on White campuses. This study was conducted during the 1970s, however, at a time when Black race consciousness was generally high (Schuman & Hatchett, 1974).

Consequently, it does not address the issue of race consciousness in today's Black college students, who have come of age during a more politically conservative time. It is also specific to one campus, which raises questions of generalizability.

Hall and Allen (1982) and Allen (1984) do attempt to address this issue. Both analyze data from Black students on White campuses in the 1980s. Hall and Allen (1982) found that males and students from northern schools were less race conscious. Allen (1984), on the other hand, compares race consciousness in Black students at Black and White campuses. He found that while race consciousness was higher in Black students at Black versus White universities, it was lower overall than for the students studied by Gurin and Epps in 1970.

How can this study add to these two bodies of research? Most important, the research is an examination of race consciousness itself. Most of the work identified above uses race consciousness as an intervening variable, for the purpose of explaining or predicting another dependent variable. This work, then, directly addresses the question of the amount of race consciousness that exists. Because we are studying a group of students attending White schools in the 1980s, this work is more relevant for the current generation of college students and its particular set of life circumstances. The aim, then, is to expand the scope of the Black student/White college literature beyond its current focus on attrition and retention to an equal emphasis on issues of psychological development.

Problem Statements

Our interest lies in examining the race consciousness of Black college students at predominantly White universities. This topic can be summarized as two research questions:

1. How race conscious are Black students at predominantly White universities? In other words, what are their levels of race consciousness?
2. What factors are associated with these current levels of race consciousness?

Our definition of race consciousness draws on the literature previously discussed, particularly the Gurin, Miller, and Gurin (1980) and Pitts (1974) research. While the Gurin, Miller, and Gurin (1980) approach has an attitudinally based definition, it restricts action to collective behavior only. Here we tend to agree with Pitts (1974), with his emphasis on a range of manifestations of race consciousness. Nonetheless, whereas Pitts (1974) restricts his definition of race consciousness to behavior only, we argue for a more broadly-based definition that includes attitudes. Rokeach (1969) defines an attitude as "a relatively enduring organization of interrelated beliefs that describe, evaluate, and advocate action with respect to an object or situation, with each belief having cognitive, affective and behavioral components" (p. 457). A definition of race consciousness, then, incorporates beliefs and feelings that guide a person's behavior toward the race. We define race consciousness as a set of political attitudes that address a person's relationship to or feelings about his race, an understanding of his race's status in the social structure, and his orientation or tendency to act given the understanding of the group's position. This definition has three major components:

1. *Race identification*—a sense of shared ideas, feelings, and interests with other members of one's race.
2. *System blame*—a belief that racial discrimination or racism is embedded in the social structure or "system" rather than solely in individuals. Racial discrimination or racism is viewed as the reason for the lack or slowed progress of Black Americans.
3. *Action orientation*—the type of action espoused or undertaken (i.e., individual vs. collective).

Miller, Gurin, Gurin, and Malanchuk (1981) employ a fourth dimension, polar affect, which is positive affect for one's group or negative regard for other group(s). We do not agree with and do not use this dimension. McCullough (1982) notes this assumption underlies much of the research on reference group orientation. Recent work by Cross (1985), however, suggests that Black parents present both Black and White worlds to their children, resulting in a "dual reference group orientation." Thus, positive affect for one's group does not automatically mean negative regard for the outgroup. Indeed, Miller et al.'s (1981) and McCullough's (1982) own research do not support the use of polar affect as a fourth dimension of race consciousness.

Conceptual Model

The conceptual model is adapted from educational studies of college impact. This model examines the separate and joint effects of a student's precollegiate characteristics (also known as "input" variables) and the characteristics of the college (or environmental variables) on some outcome or "output" variable(s). Race consciousness, rather than attrition or achievement, is the "output" or outcome variable of interest.

Because the definition of race consciousness is attitudinally based, we have turned to the literature on attitude and attitude change in order to develop the empirical framework. Fishbein and Azjen (1974) assert one of the basic features of an attitude is that it is learned. Freedman, Carlsmith, and Sears (1978) argue attitudes are learned through "the basic processes of association, reinforcement, and limitation" (p. 371). The first part of the model, then, focuses on variables that shape and influence students' precollegiate associations and reinforcement of these associations. The precollegiate variables examined in this study are gender, religiosity, socioeconomic status (SES), urbanism, and intraracial contact. The collegiate variables examined in this study are dominant climate, academic discipline, level of involvement in campus social life, participation in Black organizations on campus, and the frequency/quality of interpersonal contacts with White and Blacks on campus.

Data and Methods of Study

Questionnaire data were used from the 1982 National Study of Black College Students (NSBCS). This study collected data on Black students at eight predominantly White public institutions: the University of Michigan, Ann Arbor; the University of North Carolina, Chapel Hill; the University of California, Los Angeles; Memphis State University; Arizona State University; the State University of New York–Stony Brook; Eastern Michigan University; the University of Wisconsin, Madison. A simple random sample of all first-year students was drawn from a list of students provided by the registrar's office at each school. A 19-page questionnaire consisting mainly of closed-ended questions was mailed to the students. Our study was limited to the Universities of Michigan (UM) and North

Carolina (UNC) due to historical differences in race relations and constraints on time and money. The response rates were 38% (n = 82) for UM and 52% (n = 188) for UNC.

Analysis of the sample proceeded in two distinct stages. The first stage was primarily descriptive, relating the composition and key characteristics of the overall sample (both the Michigan and North Carolina students). The most important question to be answered at this level of analysis was "What were the levels of race consciousness among the students in 1982?" Frequency distributions were used to answer this and other descriptive questions. The second stage was an examination of the bivariate relationships, that is, relationships between sets of two variables. Contingency tables were used to uncover relationships between each precollegiate factor, collegiate factor, and race consciousness. Chi-square was the statistic used to test for the existence of these relationships, with a probability level of 0.05 or less indicating a statistically significant relationship.

Results

Descriptive analyses reveal that in 1982 women students comprised three quarters of the combined Michigan/North Carolina sample. The sample was nearly split in terms of their religious feelings, with 54% saying they were religious to very religious. Fifty-seven percent spent most of their lives in places that had 10,000 or fewer inhabitants. The high schools that these students attended were neither predominantly White nor all Black, but somewhere in the middle. Twenty-nine percent attended high schools that were 21% to 40% Black, while another 30% attended high schools that were 41% to 60% Black. These students tended to come from fairly well-educated families. Forty-five percent of the fathers and 50% of the mothers had more than a high school diploma. Family incomes were fairly high as well. Only 13% had family incomes of less than $8,000, while 41% had family incomes of $25,000 or more. An examination of their fathers' occupational prestige scores reveals that 39% fell into such categories as laborers and service workers, 23% were craftsmen and kindred workers, and 38% had more highly ranked jobs, such as managers and other professional workers. Overall, then, these students had backgrounds of middle to high SES.

In terms of their collegiate experience, more than two thirds of the sample were students at the University of North Carolina. Most (58%) were seeking careers in the professions such as business and engineering, with the rest scattered amongst the humanities (4%), social and behavioral sciences (13%), natural and physical sciences (14%), and undecided (12%). Given the difficulties noted in the literature, one might predict a difficult social adjustment for Black students at a predominantly White university. Yet, just more than half the sample stated that they felt somewhat to a considerable part of campus life, with 70% saying that the extracurricular activities on campus reflected their interests somewhat to a considerable extent. Perhaps their participation in activities sponsored by Black organizations facilitated this adjustment, for less than a quarter of the sample said they hardly ever participated in these activities. A large majority of the students in the sample (88%) interacted with other Black students at least once to several times a day.

Yet, things change when we look at the frequency of their interactions with Black faculty and staff: 63% and 57% said they interacted with these two groups less than once a week. Not surprisingly, an overwhelming majority of the students said there were not enough Black faculty (99%) on campus. The relative absence of contact, however, did not seem to affect the quality of their interactions. Ninety-five percent, 69%, and 79% had good to excellent relations with Black students, faculty, and staff. There was a significant difference in the percentage of students having high-quality relations with Black faculty (69%) as opposed to students (95%) or staff (79%). Yet, it was still more than two thirds of the sample in each case, and if we look at the distribution, we see that students were more likely to say that they had no contact with Black faculty (22%) as opposed to students (.4%) or staff (11%).

The picture of their interactions with Whites reflects the reality of their environment. Black students comprised only 5% of the student body at the University of Michigan and 9% of the student body at the University of North Carolina. More than three quarters of the sample said they interacted with White students at least once to several times a day. Just more than half (59%) interacted with White faculty at least once to several times a day, whereas 34% had similarly frequent interactions with White staff. Nearly a quarter of the sample interacted with White staff members only once a week.

These interactions seem to be quite positive. More than three quarters of the sample said they had good to excellent relations with

White students (91%), faculty (90%), and staff (85%). Perhaps the high quality of these relations can be attributed to the students having attended schools with Whites. In other words, the skills they gained from their high school interactions carried over to the college setting. Still, there was a clear difference in the quality of interracial relations for Blacks as individuals versus as a group. While the majority of the students reported positive interracial relations at the group level, a sizable number did perceive a qualitative difference in the response of Whites to themselves as individuals as opposed to the overall group. Nearly a third of the sample characterized overall Black student relations with White students, faculty, and staff as poor to very poor (37%, 30%, and 28%, respectively).

How race conscious were the students? They were divided in terms of their feelings toward system blame. Just more than half argued that a Black person will still meet serious discrimination regardless of the propriety of his or her behavior. At the same time, however, two thirds felt that many Blacks had only themselves to blame for not getting ahead in life. Moreover, a majority agreed that being better trained and qualified rather than applying pressure and advocating social action is the best way to overcome discrimination. Given these results, our inclination is to place these students in the middle of a race-consciousness continuum. They do not have the system blame and collective action orientation expressed by Gurin and Epps' 1970 students. Yet, they do not attribute blame solely to individuals, as did many of Gurin and Epps' students in 1964, or to their individualistic achievers in 1970.

Michigan Versus North Carolina

What were some of the precollegiate characteristics at each school in 1982? At the University of Michigan we found the sample was 70% female. Fifty-nine percent grew up in large cities, that is, more than 300,000 inhabitants. Just more than half reported being somewhat to not at all religious. These students came from families that had high socioeconomic status. Fifty-nine percent of the fathers and 73% of the mothers had more than a high school education. The occupational status of these fathers was high, with just more than half (51%) falling into the professional, technical, and managerial categories. Family incomes were high as well: 54% came from families making $30,000 or more annually. These figures suggest students materially prepared for the elite environment of the University of Michigan. But what about their preparation in terms of racial environment? Barely one fifth attended high schools that approximated the situation at UM (i.e., less that 10% Black). Most attended high schools that were more than 40% Black.

The transition from high school to college does not seem to have affected these students socially. Despite having attended high schools that were predominantly Black, 56% stated they felt somewhat to considerably a part of general campus life. Two thirds said that the extracurricular activities reflected their interests. This seemingly tranquil social adjustment to a predominantly White environment was also reflected in their relations with Whites on campus. More than 80% of the students had very positive relations with White students, faculty, and staff. Due to the very nature of the environment, their contact with Whites was high: Around half interacted with White faculty and staff at least once a day and three quarters interacted with White students several times a day.

Yet, what about their relations with Blacks on campus? They interacted with Black students regularly: 72% reported several times a day. A large majority participated in activities sponsored by Black students organizations. More than three quarters stated their relations with Black students as being good to excellent. But the reality of being on a White campus is more apparent as we look at their interaction with Black faculty and staff. Most of the sample interacted with Black faculty and staff less than once a week. The lack of contact was reflected in their relations with Black faculty and staff: While over half reported positive relations, nearly one third said they had no contact with Black faculty.

Finally, let us look at the race consciousness of these UM students. Fifty-three percent argued "proper" behavior does pay off, while over three quarters believed Blacks would do better in life if they tried harder. More than half felt that discrimination can best be overcome by the efforts of highly qualified Black individuals. In the initial stages of their collegiate career, then, the University of Michigan sample could be labeled "Individualistic Achievers." They seemed to downplay the significance of discrimination and racism by emphasizing the ability of the individual to overcome such obstacles to success. The socialization they have received has stressed individual achievement and each success, whether good grades in school or enrollment at a prestigious university, reinforces that drive. Their positive contacts with Whites may also indicate to them greater possibilities for succeeding in the predominantly White professions they plan to enter. This positive contact is another success at the individual level, thereby reinforcing the notion that there are few obstacles they cannot overcome.

How did the University of North Carolina students compare on these same characteristics? The Carolina sample is also predominantly female (74%). In contrast to the UM students, however, more than half of the UNC students grew up in places that had fewer than 55,000 inhabitants. This is not surprising, given that North Carolina is a more rural state than Michigan. There is also a slight difference in religiosity: A majority of UNC students reported being religious to very religious. In comparison to their Michigan colleagues, most students attended high schools that were less than or equal to 40% Black and thus had experienced minority status before college.

An examination of family background characteristics shows clear differences between the two samples. At UNC, 61% of the fathers and 60% of the mothers did not go beyond high school. Nearly half of the fathers had occupations that fell into the lowest ranges such as laborers and service workers (49%), while just more than a quarter (30%) fell into the professional and managerial categories. Nearly one third of these students came from families where the annual income is less than $13,000, and almost half of the sample (49%) makes less than $20,000 annually. Thus, Carolina students came from more economically disadvantaged backgrounds than their Michigan counterparts.

What did the University of North Carolina students look like at the collegiate level? UNC students seemed to be making the social adjustments as well as the students at Michigan. As at UM, most stated they felt somewhat to considerably a part of general campus life (57%). More than two thirds reported that extracurricular activities reflected their interests. They also had good relations with White students (93%), faculty (90%), and staff (86%). Nevertheless, there were some differences here in level of contact not seen at Michigan. Their interaction with White students was high: More than two thirds interact with White professors at least once a day. Yet, there was much less contact with White staff members. Just more than a quarter interacted with them on a daily basis, whereas a larger percentage (30%) did not have contact with White staff on a weekly basis.

And what about their relations with Blacks? While 81% reported contact several times a day with Black students, fewer than half (46%) often participated in activities sponsored by Black organizations. At the same time, however, nearly everyone reported very positive relations with Black students. Perhaps the larger density of Black students at UNC decreased the need for frequent participation in Black organizational activities. The low level of interaction with Black faculty and staff noted at UM was seen also at Carolina: 61% of the students had contact with Black faculty less than once a week. Yet, the relations were very positive, with more than two thirds reporting positive relations with Black faculty and Black staff. Only 19% reported no contact with Black faculty.

Carolina students also appeared slightly more ambivalent than Michigan students in terms of their race consciousness. Sixty-three percent of the UNC students believed "proper" behavior does not pay off for Blacks, whereas 53% of the UM students believe "proper" behavior does pay off ($\chi^2[1, N = 256] = 5.8, p < 0.05$). Yet, this is the only item on which the samples differed. More than two thirds of the North Carolina students felt Blacks would do better in life if they tried harder and discrimination is best overcome by the efforts of highly qualified Black individuals.

Why the differences between the two samples? We attribute it to the regional differences between the states of Michigan and North Carolina. Michigan is a more urbanized and highly industrialized state. There were never any legal barriers keeping Afro-Americans from matriculating at the state's predominantly White postsecondary institutions. Moreover, Blacks were able to break down the barriers to participation in the unionized labor market and political arena. Thus was born the middle class of Michigan's urban areas, particularly Detroit, the city from which most of University of Michigan's Black student population is drawn. The parents of Michigan students have apparently socialized their children to work hard to take advantage of the greater educational and vocational opportunities opened by the Civil Rights Movement. The prominence of African-Americans on the professional as well as the political scene in such cities as Detroit serves to fuel the drive for individual success and achievement. It can be done because it has been done.

On the other hand, North Carolina is a more rural state, with low levels of industrialization and unionization. As part of the South, North Carolina openly circumscribed the rights of its Black residents through legal (Jim Crow) and extralegal (lynching) means. "Proper" behavior for Blacks meant accepting one's place as an inferior person with little status. There has been some movement toward unifying and desegregating the dual system of higher education. But for the most part, Black North Carolinians have not made the same economic and political gains as their Michigan counterparts. As a result, the parents of North Carolina students have seemingly socialized their children to the continuing reality of racism and its impact on their lives. While the students believe that it's possible to succeed through hard work, they also acknowledge that racism will place obstacles in their way.

Contingency Table Analysis

A contingency table is a joint frequency distribution of two or more categorical variables. Different measures of association or tests of statistical significance are computed to help summarize the relationship shown in the table (Nie, Hill, Jerkins, Steinbrenner, & Bert, 1975). In this case, we used chi-square (χ^2) as the test of statistical significance in order to determine whether a relationship exists between the independent and independent variable. Here all the variables except academic discipline and religiosity have been recoded or collapsed to two or three categories.

Urbanism had a significant negative relationship with group efficacy ($\chi^2[2, N = 264] = 6.6, p < 0.05$). Students from more urbanized areas tended to have less of a belief in group efficacy. Gurin and Epps (1975) suggest that people raised in an urbanized environment are more likely to be exposed and socialized to more "sophisticated" political beliefs and attitudes. McCullough (1982) suggests, however, that urbanized settings are more heterogeneous than rural ones. As such, they provide greater opportunities for more interracial contact, which could dampen group consciousness; maybe this is what occurred with the sample. Students who attended predominantly White high schools were also less likely to favor group efficacy. Although this relationship was not statistically significant, the presence of this trend gives more support to the idea of a constraining effect of interracial contact on race consciousness.

Students with highly educated mothers and fathers with high occupational status were also oriented away from group toward individual efficacy (χ^2[2, N = 259] = 9.5 and χ^2[2, N = 219] = 10.4, respectively, with $p < .05$). Although not statistically significant, students from high-income families (over \$30,000) also had low race consciousness. Contrary to previous research, SES does have an effect on race consciousness as operationalized here, suggesting that high SES Black families are socializing their children to think and perhaps even act in terms of individual rather than collective achievement and success. Of the last two precollegiate variables, religiosity showed a nonstatistically significant relationship with race consciousness. Students who were somewhat to very religious were less likely to favor group efficacy. This finding is consistent with Mathis (1971) and Allen (1984), and indicates that for these students, religion is a conservatizing influence. Gender had no relationship to group efficacy. Men were no more likely than women to have high or low group efficacy. Despite the prevalence of women in the sample, this finding is consistent with much of the previous research, suggesting that the absence of a privileged position for Black women vis-à-vis Black men leads to socialization of similar political attitudes.

Since precollegiate interracial contact appeared to moderate advocacy of group efficacy, it is not surprising that students with a high frequency of collegiate interracial contact as well as those with good-quality collegiate interracial contact were less likely to be oriented toward group efficacy. These relationships (χ^2[2, N = 265] = 7.5 and χ^2[2, N = 261] = 15.9) were significant at the 0.05 and 0.001 levels, respectively. Positive interactions with Whites that are reinforced by frequency seem to lead Black students to believe they have less of a need for the group. As far as they can tell, they are doing just fine by themselves. Thus, interracial contact continues to have the predicted negative effect on race consciousness at the collegiate level.

Other aspects of the college experience show trends toward having a positive impact on race consciousness. It was the students who had not decided on a major as well as those who were majoring in the professions who were more likely to favor group efficacy. Findings from research on Black and White student activists tend to show social science majors as politically active. However, academic discipline was not related to Black nationalism ideology for Gurin and Epps' 1970 sample. Moreover, many of their committed activists were students who planned careers in the professions, at that time mainly law or medicine. Black students in the 1980s perceive a wider range of occupations available to them. Thus, race consciousness attitudes, if not behavior, may no longer be limited to social science majors.

There was a trend for North Carolina students to favor group efficacy, which can probably be explained by the fact that since North Carolina is a more rural state, students were more likely to be raised in rural or at least distinctly less urbanized settings. Because the less urbanized students were more likely to favor group efficacy, and the North Carolina students were from rural backgrounds, it follows that the North Carolina sample would also favor group efficacy. But it may also be that the dominant climate of overt hostility in the South heightens race consciousness. Perhaps the inability of the state's Afro-American population to translate its size into political power has sensitized the UNC students to the need for working together as a group. On the other hand, maybe the relatively long history of political power exercised by Michigan Blacks at the national and local levels is something the UM students take for granted. Group efficacy, in this sense, is a given. As a result, there is more stress on the individual.

Other students showing trends toward high group efficacy were those feeling most connected to general campus networks as well as those most active in Black organizational activities. While Gurin and Epps' Committed Activists were involved in all kinds of campus activities, and thus well integrated into their environments, we did not expect Black students feeling connected to predominantly White networks to have high race consciousness. Indeed, it seems to run counter to the findings that interracial contact depressed advocacy of group efficacy.

Perhaps these students feel so much a part of general campus life because of the opportunities in which they participate. As first-year students much of their life revolves around the residence halls. At the University of Michigan, the Black dorm organizations are approved by and thus part of the institutional structure. An example of their institutional status is their receipt of funds from dormitory treasuries. At the University of North Carolina, the Black Student Movement puts on most of the activities for the Black student population there. Although the funding is not automatic (a budget must be submitted to and approved by the student government), it too receives funding. In seeing these organizations, Black students do feel a part of general campus life. And because the activities sponsored by these organizations are generally intended to enhance the Black presence on campus, they heighten race consciousness.

If this is the case, then why is intraracial interaction unrelated to group efficacy? After all, participation in activities sponsored by Black organizations led to high group efficacy. Perhaps it was because these interactions took place between and among a fairly homogeneous group of students. In this case, homogeneity is defined in terms of the same or a presumed similarity of cultural values and attitudes. That is, these students may come to their interactions with other Blacks on campus assuming similarities based on skin color. While Black students may get along very well with campus Whites, other Blacks are more like family, like home. There is no need to be Black or race conscious with other Blacks. Intrafamily squabbles, that is, between Blacks, do not have the same implications as interracial disagreements. As McCullough (1982) notes, interracial contact sharpens the boundaries or the differences between groups; intraracial interaction does not.

Discussion

African-Americans have historically viewed education as the way to success in this society. Due to the exclusionary nature of Black existence in America, much of the early Black college student literature focuses on the struggle for access to educational institutions. Although the struggle for access continues, high rates of attrition led to an expansion of the research problem. In other words, researchers now ask two basic questions: (a) How many Afro-Americans are attending predominantly White colleges? (b) Why are Afro-Americans experiencing disproportionate rates in attrition and achievement? Thus far, they have concluded that the answer to the second question lies in the economic, educational, and cultural differences between the students and their environments. This "lack of fit" has resulted in poor academic and social adjustments, leading many to leave or be pushed out.

This exclusive attention to the underachievers has led to a relative neglect of the achievers, those who do go on to successfully complete college. When researchers do study Black college graduates, it is often to simply compare their rates of success with their White counterparts. Consequently, they have virtually ignored the other half of education's importance for Black people: the notion that education should provide leaders and service providers for the advancement of the community. Theoretically, that was and continues to be the *raison d'etre* of Black colleges. But there have been few studies that examine the impact of a White collegiate environment on Black students' willingness or desire to "return" to their communities.

The purpose of this study was to explore the phenomenon of race consciousness in the "Talented Tenth" of the 1980s. In other words, we wanted to understand whether the current generation of Black college students and graduates was willing to assume its role as leaders in the ongoing Afro-American struggle. DuBois' notion was that African-Americans would actively use the skills acquired through the educational process to improve the status of the race. Since educational training also enhances one's potential for individual mobility, the choice for Black Americans has always been self-actualization alone or self and group actualization. DuBois (1969) referred to it as double consciousness.

As DuBois so eloquently pointed out, this dual consciousness has been part and parcel of African-American history. This history is replete with examples of educated women and men such as DuBois himself, Ida B. Wells, Martin Luther King, Jr., and Angela Davis, who stepped forward to challenge and change the status quo. The Civil Rights Movement was fueled by the actions of young Black college students, who initiated the sit-ins at public facilities and engineered the takeovers of campus buildings. At the same time, E. Franklin Frazier (1957) argued many, if not most, middle-class Blacks wanted to sever their ties with the poor Black masses, preferring to concentrate on the acquisition of material wealth. Indeed, Lincoln (1979) and Wilson (1987) maintain that the expanded opportunities created as a result of the Civil Rights Movement have increased the likelihood for greater class rather than race consciousness. Some observers have already alluded to the small amount of protest on college campuses in the early 1980s as evidence of such low race consciousness.

Where do our students stand in terms of this dilemma? Our results indicate it depends on the student's socioeconomic status as well as the region of the country in which the university is located. The Michigan students, who came from middle- to upper-class African-American families, were more likely to agree "proper" behavior does pay off for Blacks and Blacks have only themselves to blame for not doing better in life. They have grown up in a state that offers considerable educational and vocational opportunities to Afro-Americans, largely in response to the Civil Rights Movement. The SES of their families suggests their parents have been able to take advantage of such opportunities. North Carolina Blacks, in contrast, have not made similar gains in the economic and political sectors, which can be clearly seen in the lower SES of the UNC students.

Overall, however, the greater difference is between the entire Michigan/North Carolina sample and their counterparts of the 1960s. The students of the 1960s went to college at a time when the life chances of African-Americans were still severely constrained. Many of them participated in the Civil Rights Movement in order to open up the system to Black people. It was widely believed that the civil rights reforms would significantly upgrade the status of Black America. However, as Gurin and Epps (1975) point out, the students' own movement participation brought them face-to-face with the limits of reform, given the extent of institutional racism. This knowledge led to system blame, which culminated in a widespread adoption of the Black nationalism ideology. Due to its pervasiveness and persuasiveness, Black nationalism became the ideological framework of much of campus-based protest in the late 1960s and early 1970s. The struggle was still very much a part of the lives of these students.

In contrast, there was no prominent national struggle with an alternative ideology and opportunity for participation when our UM and UNC students went to college (the Free South Africa movement intensified after this study was completed). As a result, these students were more concerned with taking advantage of the expanded opportunities brought about by the Civil Rights Movement. They were now able to attend prestigious universities that could enable them to maximize their potential for individual success. They were also able to elect Blacks to public office who could improve the status of the group. The advent of such opportunities signaled the opening of a system previously closed to them. It is no wonder, then, our students attribute little blame to a system now viewed as accessible. Individual flaws, the root of institutionalized racism, cannot be addressed by collective action. In the absence of a countervailing ideology, along with a national mass movement, the ideology of the American Dream, with its emphasis on individualism, has reasserted itself.

There should be little surprise at the individual orientation of our students. Levine (1980) argues American college students of the 1980s are in general more egocentric and materialistic. The "Me Generation," with its young, upwardly mobile professionals (usually shortened to "yuppies"), has been one of the most dominant topics of the decade. Their seemingly obsessive materialism has been deplored by social commentators, yet encouraged by manufacturers. Evidence of a similar attitude among our students indicates this phenomenon transcends racial boundaries. Furthermore, the major thrust of the Civil Rights Movement was to gain entry to the educational and vocational as well as the political arenas. Thus, Black students in the 1980s have been socialized and groomed to take advantage of the expanded opportunities for their benefit.

Postscript: A Plan for Action

What about the future of the Afro-American community? The explosion of campus protests in the late 1980s may indicate Black students are once again willing to stand up and be counted as active participants in the Afro-American struggle. We are not sure this is the case. The nation has witnessed a resurgence in Black student protest activity on predominantly White campuses since 1987. This revival had roots in the anti-apartheid movement and was sparked by a sizable increase in the number of public threats and assaults upon African-American students. The university administration's slow or negligible responses to what were no longer viewed as "isolated incidents" were interpreted as signs of institutional racism, which was also linked to racism and imperialism at the national and international levels. More important, the inadequate responses were no longer tolerated. Hence, a Black student movement evolved, at the University of Michigan and nationwide, with collective action (i.e., mass protest) as its modus operandi.

Embarrassed by the demonstrations, universities across the country have begun to take concrete steps to deal with the problem of racism on campus. Michigan in particular has instituted several measures to demonstrate its commitment to diversity and pluralism, which include the appointment of a vice-provost with responsibility for minority affairs, permanent funding for the Black Student Union, the establishment of a grievance procedure for racial harassment, and budget support for attracting and retaining Black faculty. While a few measures have met with student disfavor (a code regulating nonacademic conduct with academic sanctions, for example), many if not most African-American students at UM feel satisfied with the University's efforts. Whether in response to these initiatives or not, overt threats and actions have diminished (or are "invisible" to the public eye). Consequently, fewer students currently participate in the revived movement. So again, the perception of a more open system has resulted in a shift of priorities, with individual goals (i.e., school work and social life) becoming preeminent.

How, then, can stronger commitments to the collective progress of Black people be fostered and maintained? The parents of our students emphasized individual success against the odds, and our respondents planned similar socialization messages. While this is clearly important for the children of an oppressed people, they must also understand the importance of actively participating in the group struggle. We believe it is incumbent upon all able and willing African-Americans to spread this message, by word and deed, to all Black youngsters. What must be stressed is that there is no one way, and all have a significant role to play. College students, for example, currently have skills that they do not need money and power to use. *Now* they can give advice and information to junior high and high school students in their churches, neighborhoods, and schools. *Now* they can help improve the concrete skills of poorly achieving elementary school youngsters by tutoring them in math, reading, and other subjects. *Now* they can build a network of speakers, tutors, and yes, even role models, by recruiting other volunteers through their professional, sororal, and fraternal organizations. Colleges and universities can help, too, by encouraging students to volunteer their time, ensuring Black male and female students are able to take advantage of leadership opportunities, and providing more Afro-American men and women faculty, administrators, and other staff for support, guidance, and encouragement.

We acknowledge our suggestions are neither comprehensive nor innovative. In and of themselves, they are too simplistic to solve the varied and complex problems that are wreaking havoc in the Black community. The point is to offer ways in which these students, as well as other African-Americans, can actively contribute to the life of the community, in the present as well as in the future. One possibility is that more active involvement could generate new and creative ideas to address the problems. Or it could lead to an understanding of the systematic root of the problems and the limits of the system's willingness to solve them. With the second possibility there is the potential for a real challenge of the status quo.

Our goal is to create and nurture socially responsible African-Americans. We believe this process ought to start with socialization messages and activities in childhood and continue throughout the life-style. In this way, we (Black social scientists, teachers, preachers, counselors, college professors, parents, and all others who are willing and able) may challenge others, and be challenged ourselves, to step forward as leaders to carry on the struggle for freedom, justice, and equality.

REFERENCES

Abramowitz, E. (1976). *Equal educational opportunity for Blacks in U.S. higher education: An assessment.* Washington, DC: Howard University Press.

Allen, W. R. (1981). Correlates of Black student adjustment, achievement, and aspirations at a predominantly White southern university. In G. Thomas (Ed.), *Black students in higher education: Conditions and experiences in the 1970s* (pp. 126–141). Westport, CT: Greenwood Press.

Allen, W. R. (1982). Black and blue: Black students at the University of Michigan, Ann Arbor. *LS&A Magazine, 6*(1), 13–17.

Allen, W. R. (1984). Race consciousness and collective commitments among Black students on White campuses. *Western Journal of Black Studies, 8*(3), 156–166.

Allen, W. R. (1986). *Gender and campus race differences in Black student academic performance, racial attitudes, and college satisfaction.* Atlanta: Southern Education Foundation.

Anderson, J. D. (1984). The schooling and achievement of Black children: Before and after *Brown v. Topeka*, 1900–1980. In D. E. Bartz & M. L. Maehr (Eds.), *Advances in motivation and achievement* (pp. 103–122). Greenwich, CT: JAI.

Astin, A. (1982). *Minorities in American higher education: Recent trends, current prospects, and recommendations.* San Francisco: Jossey-Bass.

Ballard, A. B. (1973). *The education of Black folk: The Afro-American struggle for knowledge in White America.* New York: Harper & Row.

Banks, H. A. (1970). *Summary of Black consciousness: A student survey. Black Scholar, 1,* 44–51.

Blackwell, J. E. (1982). Demographics of desegregation. In R. Wilson (Ed.), *Race and equity in higher education* (pp. 28–70). Washington, DC: American Council on Education.

Brown, W. O. (1931a). The nature of race consciousness. *Social Forces, 10,* 90–97.

Brown, W. O. (1931b). Emergence of race consciousness. *Sociology and Social Research, 15,* 428–436.

Cave, W. M., & Chesler, M. A. (1974). *Sociology of education: An anthology of issues and problems.* New York: Macmillan.

Centra, J. A. (1970). Black students at predominantly White colleges: A research description. *Sociology of Education, 43,* 325–339.

Cross, W. E., Jr. (1985). Black identity: Rediscovering the distinction between personal identity and reference group orientation. In M. B. Spencer, G. K. Brookins, & W. R. Allen (Eds.), *Beginnings: The social and affective development of Black children* (pp. 155–472). Hillsdale, NJ: Lawrence Erlbaum.

Dubois, W. E. B. (1970). The talented tenth. In H. Storing (Ed.), *What country have I? Political writings by Black Americans* (pp. 102–104). New York: St. Martin's.

Edwards, H. (1970). *Black students.* New York: New American Library.

Farley, R., & Allen, W. R. (1987). *The color line and the quality of life in America.* New York: Russell Sage Foundation.

Ferguson, E. A. (1938). Race consciousness among American Negroes. *Journal of Negro Education, 7,* 32–40.

Fishbein, M., & Azjen, I. (1974). *Belief, attitudes, intentions, and behavior.* Reading, MA: Addison-Wesley.

Fleming, J. (1984). *Blacks in college: A comparative study of students' success in Black and White institutions.* San Francisco: Jossey-Bass.

Frazier, E. F. (1957). *Black bourgeoisie: The rise of a new middle class in the United States.* London: Collier-MacMillan.

Freedman, J. L., Carlsmith, J. M., & Sears, D. O. (1978). *Social psychology* (2nd ed.). Englewood Cliffs, NJ: Prentice-Hall.

Gaines-Carter, P. (1985, September). Speaking out: Is my post-integration daughter Black enough? *Ebony,* pp. 54–56.

Gibbs, J. T. (1974). Patterns of adaption among Black students at a predominantly White university: Selected case studies. *American Journal of Orthopsychiatry, 44*(5), 728–740.

Gurin, P., Miller, A. H., & Gurin, G. (1980). Stratum identification and consciousness. *Social Psychology Quarterly, 43*(1), 30–47.

Gurin, P., & Epps, E. G. (1975). *Black consciousness, identity, and achievement: A study of students in historically Black colleges.* New York: John Wiley.

Hall, M., & Allen, W. R. (1982). Race consciousness and achievement: Two issues in the study of Black graduate/professional students. *Integrated Education, 20*(1–2), 56–61.

Harding, V. (1970). Black students and the impossible revolution. *Journal of Black Studies, 1*(1), 75–100.

Harding, V. (1981). *There is a river: The Black struggle for freedom in America.* New York: Random House.

Jordan, J., & Cleveland, L. (1986, May). Where I'm coming from. *Essence,* pp. 86–88, 150.

Levine, A. (1980). *When dreams and heroes died: A portrait of today's college student.* San Francisco: Jossey-Bass.

Lincoln, C. E. (1979). The new Black estate: The coming of age in Black America. In M. V. Namorato (Ed.), *Have we overcome? Race relations since Brown* (pp. 3–30). Jackson: University Press of Mississippi.

Marable, M. (1983). *How capitalism underdeveloped the Black community.* Boston: South End Press.

Mathis, A. L. (1971). *Social and psychological characteristics of the Black liberation movement: A colonial analogy.* Unpublished doctoral dissertation, University of Michigan, Ann Arbor.

McCullough, W. (1982). *The development of group identification in Black Americans.* Unpublished doctoral dissertation, University of Michigan, Ann Arbor.

Miller, A. H., Gurin, P., Gurin, G., & Malanchuk, O. (1981). Group consciousness and political participation. *American Journal of Political Science, 25*(3), 494–511.

Morris, L. (1979). *Elusive equality: The status of Black Americans in U.S. higher education.* Washington, DC: Howard University Press.

Morris, L. (1981). The role of testing in institutional selectivity and Black access to higher education. In G. Thomas (Ed.), *Black students in higher education: Conditions and experiences in the 1970s* (pp. 64–75). Westport, CT: Greenwood Press.

Nie, N. H., Hill, C. H., Jerkins, J. G., Steinbrenner, K., & Bert, D. H. (1975). *SPSS: Statistical packaging for the social sciences.* New York: McGraw-Hill.

Orum, A. M., & Cohen, R. S. (1973). The development of political orientations among Black and White children. *American Sociological Review, 38,* 62–74.

Park, R. (1923). Negro race consciousness as reflected in race literature. *American Review, 1*(5), 505–517.

Peterson, M., Blackburn, R. T., Gamson, Z. F., Arce, C. H., Davenport, R. W., & Mingle, J. R. (1978). *Black students on White campuses: The impacts of increased Black enrollments.* Ann Arbor: Institute for Social Research, University of Michigan.

Pitts, J. P. (1974). The study of race consciousness: Comments on new directions. *American Journal of Sociology, 80*(3), 665–687.

Pitts, J. P. (1975). The politicization of Black students. *Journal of Black Studies, 5*(3), 277–319.

Rokeach, M. (1969). The nature of attitudes. In Sills, D. L. (Ed.), *The international encyclopedia of the social sciences* (pp. 449–459). New York: Macmillan and Free Press.

Schuman, H., & Hatchett, S. J. (1974). *Black racial attitudes: Trends and complexities.* Ann Arbor, MI: Institute for Social Research.

Smith, D. H. (1980). Admission and retention problems of Black students at seven predominantly White universities. *METAS, 1*(2), 22–46.

Standing, T. G. (1938). Race consciousness as reflected in the Negro press. *Southwestern Social Science Quarterly, 19,* 269–280.

Stanford, M. (1971). Black nationalism and the Afro-American student. *Black Scholar, 2*(10), 27–31.

Thompson, D. C. (1986). *A Black elite: A profile of graduates of UNCF colleges.* New York: Greenwood Press.

Willie, C. V., & McCord, S. A. (1972). *Black students at White colleges.* New York: Praeger.

Wilson, W. J. (1987). *The truly disadvantaged: The inner city, the underclass, and public policy.* Chicago: University of Chicago Press.

Woodson, C. G. (1983). *The miseducation of the Negro.* Washington, DC: Associated Publishers.

10

Stress, Well-Being, and Academic Achievement in College

SHELLY L. PRILLERMAN, HECTOR F. MYERS, and BRIAN D. SMEDLEY

Introduction

At the beginning of World War II, one in ten (10%) of the approximately 45,000 Afro-American university students was attending a predominantly White institution (Mingle, 1981). Until the advent of the Civil Rights Movement, traditionally Black colleges and universities in the South were almost exclusively responsible for the higher education of Afro-Americans (Fleming, 1981). However, by 1978, more than one million Afro-American students were attending college and seven out of ten (70%) were attending predominantly White institutions (Mingle, 1981). By 1984, four out of five Black students (80%) were enrolled in predominantly White colleges and universities (Evans, 1986).

This shift of many of the best and brightest Afro-Americans to White universities means that the majority of educated Afro-Americans now obtain their college educations at institutions in

AUTHORS' NOTE: For purposes of simplicity, the term Black will be used interchangeably with Afro-American to refer to U.S. born students of African descent. We acknowledge, of course, that the designation "Black" is most appropriately used to refer to racial background, while "Afro-American" is more appropriate in designating ethnicity (i.e., race, nationality, and culture). This research was made possible, in part, by a grant from the center for Afro-American Studies, University of California, Los Angeles, and by support from the Academic Advancement Program and the Office for Student Development at UCLA.

which they are in the minority, where their personal and cultural needs may not be recognized or meaningfully addressed, and where interracial tensions and conflicts are commonplace in the social milieu. This shift also means that the economic and social future of Afro-Americans is being determined largely by the success and failure of these students at White colleges and universities.

Research on the relative success of Afro-American students at these institutions indicates that Black students typically have lower grade-point averages, higher attrition rates, and lower enrollments in postgraduate programs than White students (Thomas, 1981; Lunneborg and Lunneborg, 1986; Nettles, 1988), and show a decrease in achievement motivation during college compared to their counterparts at Black colleges (Fleming, 1984).

There is considerable debate over what factors account for these outcomes. Studies have implicated several factors in this problem. These include system factors such as university admissions and retention practices (Smith, 1981; Spaights, Dixon, and Nickolai, 1985) and the availability of financial aid (Thomas, 1981), academic preparation (Thomas, 1981), and psychosocial factors such as social integration and satisfaction (Gunnings, 1982; Fleming, 1984; Allen, 1985, 1988; Nettles, 1988). Unfortunately, no integrative theory has emerged to account for how these factors interact to predict the outcomes observed among Afro-American college students.

The purpose of this chapter, therefore, is to present a conceptual model that depicts the hypothesized interplay of sociocultural and psychological processes in Black college student adjustment and achievement. This model was developed by conceptualizing the reported experiences of Afro-American students at White universities from a stress, coping, and adaptation perspective. Preliminary results from a year-long study of a multiethnic sample of freshmen at a large, predominantly White university are also presented and discussed, and suggestions for future research and interventions are made.

Afro-American Students at Predominantly White Universities

The preponderance of the evidence indicates that the academic performance and well-being of Afro-American students at predominantly White universities suffer as a result of the peculiar psychological and social adjustments required by these high-demand and often nonsupportive environments (Gunnings, 1982; Fleming, 1984; Allen, 1985). A major premise in this research is that the academic success and retention of Black students are determined by the person–environment transactions and related sociocultural processes in the institution rather than by the traditional intellective and academic factors (e.g., aptitude test scores, high school preparation) that are usually considered.

Evidence in support of this argument is provided by Lunneborg and Lunneborg (1986) who found that freshman-year grades for Black students were lower than those predicted for Whites with comparable high school preparation. Thus, either the high school grades of Black students are less reliable indicators of their actual academic preparation than those of Whites, or other factors affect the Black academic performance but have little effect on Whites (i.e., minority-status stresses). Tracey and Sedlacek (1985) also found that noncognitive, personal, and contextual factors such as positive self-concept, an understanding of racism, and the availability of supportive people at the university were more predictive of Black student retention than academic ability. However, these factors were not important predictors of attrition for White students. These authors suggest that "a different process is involved in academic achievement for Black and White students" (Tracey and Sedlacek, 1985, p. 409).

What then is the process involved in Afro-American student academic achievement and adjustment at the university? Studies have identified four important process variables implicated in the pathways to success or failure for Black students. These include perceived supportiveness of the environment, degree of alienation, unique status-related pressures or problems, and the relative effect of using different adaptational strategies to cope with these pressures. Several recent studies have also investigated the effects of several of these factors in a more integrative fashion.

One consistent theme in this research is the degree to which Afro-American students perceive their university campuses as supportive versus hostile. Most studies have found that Black and other ethnic minority students perceive the university climate more negatively than their White counterparts (Pfeifer and Schneider, 1974; Keller, Piotrowski, and Sherry, 1982) and that Black students hold different and more negative perceptions than do even Hispanic students (Patterson, Sedlacek, and Perry, 1984; Oliver, Rodriguez, and Mickelson, 1985).

Not surprisingly, studies that investigated the related issue of alienation have found convergent evidence that feelings of alienation are prevalent among Black students and that this is an important predictor of Black student adjustment at White universities (Allen, 1981; Suen, 1983). Unfortunately, it is not possible to determine whether the feelings of alienation cause academic difficulties or are a consequence of these difficulties. We can only conclude that both interact to increase the risk for early college attrition.

A third body of research has pursued the hypothesis that Afro-American students face unique status-related pressures at White universities that are beyond those pressures common to all college students (e.g., difficult classes, roommate conflicts, financial problems, etc.). These problems may be unique (i.e., few available dating partners of one's race) or reflect an exacerbation of the problems of being a student (i.e., greater academic concerns). Gibbs (1973) and Lee (1982) noted that among these problems particularly relevant to Black students were the need to establish a meaningful identity as a Black person, achieving a desired level of academic performance, pressures from male–female relationships, the need for increased Black unity, and developing meaningful long-range career plans.

Investigators have also begun to study the role coping plays in mediating the stresses that Afro-American students face in college. In the frequently cited Gurin and Epps (1975) study, several styles of coping were identified and linked to academic performance and adjustment of Black students at Black colleges. They found that adjustment styles that combined a commitment to both personal and racial group objectives were most adaptive. The results of Allen's (1984) recent national study of Black students supports the applicability of these findings to non-Black colleges.

In a small descriptive study of Black students who sought counseling, Gibbs (1974) also identified four patterns of adaptation, all of which were associated with high psychological distress, but different levels of academic performance. These patterns are assimilation, withdrawal, separation, and self/group affirmation. The identification of these adaptational styles offers an opportunity to gain an understanding of how students cope with the demands of the university in terms of their relationship to Blacks and to Whites, and how these efforts to cope contribute to different adjustment and achievement outcomes.

The recent works by Fleming (1984), Nettles (1988) and Allen (1985, 1988) have investigated Afro-American student adjustment and achievement in a more multivariate and integrative manner. All of these studies found that nonintellective, psychosocial, and contextual factors (e.g., self-concept, ethnic ideology, relationships with faculty, feelings and experiences of racism and discrimination, and feelings of social isolation) were among the strongest predictors of negative outcomes for Black students.

It is evident from this review that the differences in outcomes between Black and other students who attend predominantly White universities are not predictable simply from differences in academic preparation. Instead, the interaction between personal attributes and background, experiences with overt and covert racism in their interactions with faculty and peers, and the development of maladaptive coping styles all confer an additional risk for early attrition, poor academic performance, and psychological distress in a large percentage of Black students.

Stress and Coping

There is a common theme in the studies of Afro-American college student adjustment and achievement. Namely, there is a problematic person–environment fit between Black students and the social/academic milieu at predominantly White universities. Theories of stress, coping, and adaptation as articulated by Lazarus and others (i.e., Lazarus and Folkman, 1984) offer a useful conceptual perspective from which to investigate the issue of higher relative vulnerability of Blacks in White settings. There are several complex models of stress that we can draw upon to guide our analysis (Lazarus and Launier, 1978; Pearlin, Menaghan, Lieberman, and Mullan, 1981; Cronkite and Moos, 1984), including models that have been specifically articulated for use in research with Afro-Americans (Myers, 1982; Barbarin, 1983). These models typically include consideration of personal background factors, different types and sources of stress, and various factors that serve as mediators of stress to predict functional and health outcomes. The multiple predictors are thought to interact dynamically over time to impact these outcomes.

There has been a great deal of empirical attention to generic models of stress in the prediction of individual functioning. Background factors measured have included such demographic variables as socioeconomic status, gender, and race (Neighbors, Jackson, Bowman, and Gurin, 1983). Several sources of stress have been hypothesized to impact outcomes, including acute life change events (Rabkin and Struening, 1976), chronic role strains (Pearlin et al., 1981), daily hassles (Kanner, Coyne, Schaefer, and Lazarus, 1981), and transitional events (Connell and Furman, 1984). Coping behaviors (Lazarus and Folkman, 1984), social support (Cohen and Willis, 1985), locus of control (Johnson and Sarason, 1978), and self-esteem (Pearlin et al., 1981) have all been suggested as important mediators of stressful experiences. Finally, the psychosocial stresses and mediators have been linked etiologically to many psychological, physical, and functional outcomes. The predominance of the evidence indicates that the impact of stressful environments are mediated by personal vulnerabilities and strengths, as well as by social resources and obstacles.

The problem of greater Black student distress and attrition at White universities, however, is not simply a problem of failed individual efforts to cope with stress. In fact, several theorists have argued against conceptualizing the dynamics of stress and coping in individualistic terms. They argue that stress should be understood as a product of transactions occurring in a broader social context (Lazarus and Launier, 1978; Pearlin, 1982).

Contextual factors are also believed to play a role in shaping coping behavior. Mechanic (1974) argues that "it is a myth that adaptation is dependent [simply] on the ability of individuals to develop personal mastery over their environment" (p. 34). He maintains that coping also involves the extent to which environmental demands influence personal and social adaptation. Kessler (1979) also notes that social status position impacts *access* to coping resources. This observation suggests, therefore, that the university milieu can either foster effective coping and adaptation in Afro-American students or it can interfere with and stifle coping. Previous studies seem to indicate that traditional southern Black colleges were more effective in fostering healthy coping in their Black students than were modern White universities (Fleming, 1984; Allen, 1984, 1988).

Several theorists have argued that a key factor in the transactions between ethnic minorities and White institutions is the issue of minority status (Dohrenwend and Dohrenwend, 1970; Myers, 1982; Moritsugu and Sue, 1983). Many of the stresses that ethnic minorities face, and the coping options and resources that may be used, are influenced by the perceived lower status of ethnic minority groups in our society. Therefore, whether persons from low-status groups, such as Blacks, are able to cope successfully in high-status university settings would appear to depend not only on their personal attributes and resources but also on whether appropriate resources exist for them at the university and whether they have effective access to and can use the resources of the university. We suspect that Black students have achieved greater academic success and report greater feelings of well-being at Black colleges specifically because their low-status differential is effectively mediated by Black faculty and administrators, and by the close link between the Black colleges and the adjoining Black communities.

In summary, multidimensional models of stress, coping, and adaptation offer useful conceptual tools with which to investigate the problem of Black academic performance and well-being at predominantly White universities. Their attention to how personal and contextual factors can serve as precursors or mediators of stress-related outcomes, and their emphasis on the process of adaptation over time, makes it possible to disentangle the factors that are likely to be involved in these undesirable outcomes.

The model also affords the opportunity to study functionally successful and healthy Black students. As several Black scholars have noted, there is an unfortunate historical tendency to focus our attention only on "What is wrong with Blacks?" (Gary, 1980). What is needed is more research on how Afro-Americans have survived and succeeded in often oppressive environments (Nobles and Goddard, 1977; Barbarin, 1983). Specifically, as Allen (1985) noted, we need to define what is meant by "success" (e.g., grade point average vs. social involvement) among Black college students and investigate the determinants of success outcomes of Black students. Finally, stress and coping models may also identify different points of the adaptation process and different aspects of the problem as targets for meaningful corrective and preventive interventions. As such, the same paradigm can be used to elucidate the factors causally implicated in the problem as well as to suggest the appropriate corrective actions.

Stress and Coping at White Universities

The literature we have reviewed on Afro-American student functioning at predominantly White universities suggests that their relative success or failure at the university is related to a number of factors. These can be conceptualized in terms of stress and coping processes. For example, sources of stress may include few Black classmates, racial discrimination, and conflicted or distant relationships with faculty. The perceived deficits in social supports, the modes of adaptation identified by Gibbs (1974), and other nonintellective factors such as self-concept and perceived control can be thought of as potential mediators of stress that can affect how well Afro-American students ultimately function in college.

Figure 10.1 depicts a conceptual model that was developed and initially tested in a study of stress and coping processes among ethnic minority college freshmen (Prillerman, 1988). It identifies seven factors that are believed to influence adaptational outcomes. They include *sociodemographic factors* (1) that consist of variables such as race, gender, socioeconomic status (SES), and degree of previous exposure to other racial groups. *Individual predisposing factors* (2) include the traditional predictors of college preparation (i.e., SAT scores, high school GPA). The third factor is the *developmental period* (3) of the student. Issues such as identity formation, establishing peer and romantic relationships, and developing autonomy from one's family are primary developmental tasks during late adolescence and early adulthood. All three of these factors are considered important background factors, or precursors, and are thought to influence the stressful experiences of college students.

The model includes a "generic" pathway by which stress is hypothesized to effect outcomes (A→B→C), linking life stresses, coping processes, and outcomes as defined in most traditional models of stress. *General acute and chronic stressors* (4) include those sources of stress that many college students face (e.g., dormitory living, academic pressures, financial pressures, etc.). *Coping processes* (5) include specific coping behaviors; the availability, use, and satisfaction with social supports; and the cognitive appraisals students

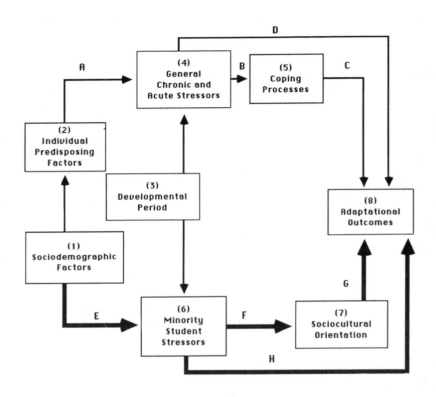

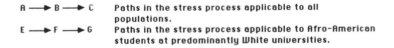

A ⟶ B ⟶ C   Paths in the stress process applicable to all
             populations.
E ⟶ F ⟶ G   Paths in the stress process applicable to Afro-American
             students at predominantly White universities.

Figure 10.1 Model of Stress and Coping Processes of Afro-American Students at Predominantly White Universities

make of the stresses they face. This set of variables is conceptualized as mediating the impact of stress on outcomes, such that how a student perceives a stressor or copes with it can buffer or exacerbate the effects of stress. Prior research also indicates that stress can have direct effects on outcomes, independent of coping and other mediators, depicted in the figure as pathway D.

The model also identifies an additional and parallel pathway, which can be considered a minority-status pathway, in the stress process that reflects the unique experiences of Afro-American students at White universities (E→F→G). This pathway includes *minority student stressors* (6), which are stressful occurrences (e.g., incidents of racial discrimination) and chronic features of the context (e.g., having few Black faculty or Black classmates) that are perceived, experienced, and attributed to being an ethnic minority student at a White university. These stresses are believed to be status-related, and increase the overall stress load and stress-related risk in Afro-American and other minority students. Minority student stressors are also viewed as exerting their effects on outcomes either independently (H) or mediated by sociocultural orientation (pathway F→G).

Sociocultural orientation (7) is included as an index of the adaptational styles that Afro-American students develop to cope with the stresses of a multiracial environment (e.g., racial conflict, racial identity conflicts, pressures to become fully assimilated into the dominant majority culture, etc.). This construct is based on the four patterns of adaptation described by Gibbs (1974) and can be thought of as relatively stable modes of coping that can either help or hinder functioning. These adaptations also should be viewed as having both benefits and costs, such that those that may facilitate high academic performance may do so at the expense of personal identity or psychological well-being. On the other hand, those that enhance ethnic identity and social activism may do so at the expense of academic performance.

The two primary paths are not viewed as mutually exclusive. They can occur simultaneously (e.g., when academic failure may be due to both inadequate mastery of the material and to racial discrimination). There can also be interaction between the two pathways. For example, the minority student stressor of having few Black classmates could make the more general challenges of developing friendships and selecting romantic partners more difficult. In the same vein, having a sociocultural orientation of assimilation would probably limit one's access to and use of social support provided by Black faculty, affirmative action programs, Black Studies programs, and so forth, which could help to buffer some of the intragroup and intergroup stresses.

Finally, we identify the *adaptational outcomes* (8) of interest, which are the products of the stress-coping process. These include functional outcomes (e.g., academic performance and achievement), psychological outcomes (e.g., sense of well-being, depression, anxiety), as well as physical outcomes (e.g., blood pressure levels, somatic symptoms). It is worth noting that the variables in the model might differ in the extent to which they contribute to each of these outcomes.

In sum, it is important to understand what it is about the person–environment transactions between Afro-American students and predominantly White universities that contributes to their success or failure in these settings. We suggest that an understanding of both generic life stresses and coping processes, as well as those unique to Afro-Americans, will help to identify the critical features of this transaction. The outcomes of this transaction have implications for the academic success, retention rates, and psychological well-being of Afro-American students.

The UCLA Coping with College Project

Our model was developed and initially tested by a multiethnic team of investigators in the UCLA Coping with College Project (CWCP), which was a ten-month prospective study of achievement and adjustment in a multiethnic sample of college freshmen (Prillerman, 1988). The study was designed to gain a better understanding of the factors involved in the process of freshman-year adjustment for ethnic minority students. Freshman year is the time of highest risk for attrition and adjustment difficulties for all college students, but particularly for Black and other ethnic minority students (Rugg, 1982). A self-administered questionnaire packet was mailed to all underrepresented ethnic minority freshmen and to a random sample of White freshmen at each of three points in their transition from high school to college (i.e., the summer before starting college, during their first quarter, and at the end of freshman year).

Sample Characteristics. The total sample consisted of 464 students, including 102 Afro-American students (22%), 116 Chicano students (25%), 93 White students (20%), 68 Filipino students (14%), 60 Latino students (13%), 22 Asian-American students (5%), and 3 American Indian students (<1%). Eighty Afro-American students responded to the first mailing, 60 to the second, and 45 to the third. The focus of the present discussion involves the 45 Afro-American students who responded to the third mailing when socio-cultural processes were assessed. A comparative analysis suggested that these students did not differ significantly from the 57 Afro-American students who did not respond to the third mailing.

Females comprised 67% and males made up 33% of the Afro-American sample at the end of freshman year. The students were somewhat more affluent on the average than we had expected, with 15% poor, 4% working class, 33% middle class, 31% upper middle class, and 16% upper class. Also, most of the Afro-American students in the sample came from racially integrated neighborhoods and high schools (37.8%), a sizable percentage came from predominantly White settings (22.2%), and a third came from predominantly Black neighborhoods and schools (33.3%). This sample of Black students had average SAT scores of 941.14, which is higher than the estimated national average for Blacks (722), and slightly higher than for Whites (939) who took the test in 1985 (Nettles, 1988). They also had relatively strong high school GPAs with an average of 3.36.

Approximately 13% to 36% of the Afro-American freshmen on campus responded to our study across all times, which is comparable to the rates typically obtained in mail-out surveys (e.g., 10% to 50%) (Selltiz, Wrightsman, and Cook, 1976). However, the small number of Afro-American respondents suggests considerable caution in interpreting and generalizing from our findings.

Minority Student Stress and Sociocultural Orientation. All constructs in our model were assessed in the CWCP questionnaire. However, for the purposes of this chapter, only results from two measures will be presented. These instruments, developed by the first author, assessed status-related stresses and coping strategies of Afro-American students at a White university.

A 35-item Minority Student Stress Scale (MSSS; Prillerman, 1988) was developed to measure stresses that minority students experience and attribute to their minority group status at the university. Respondents are asked to rate the stressfulness of each item on a 6-point scale ranging from "not at all stressful" (1) to "extremely stressful" (5), and including the option of "does not apply to me" (0).

Factor-analytic procedures yielded a 5-factor solution that accounted for 53% of the variance: *Environmental stresses* include items related to the demographics of the university, perceived racial attitudes, and relations between races; *interpersonal stresses* include experiences related to managing relationships with Whites, inter-ethnic relationships, and relations within one's own group; *race-related stresses* includes items that indicate a sensitivity to racism and discrimination; *intragroup stresses* include pressures from within one's own racial group, as well as challenges to group commitment and racial identity; and *achievement-related stresses* include items that describe uncertainty about one's academic potential and family expectations relevant to achievement. Alpha reliabilities of the final factors ranged from 0.76 to 0.93.

A 39-item Sociocultural Orientation Scale (SCOS; Prillerman, 1988) was also developed based on descriptions of the four patterns of adaptation of Black students to a predominantly White university offered by Gibbs (1974). This measure was developed in an attempt to assess how minority and nonminority students appraise and orient to a predominantly White university setting where incidents of racial conflict have become more frequent. This measure assessed attitudes toward one's race, toward the out-group (minorities or Whites), and toward racial issues generally. Students rated their degree of agreement with each of the 39 items on a 5-point scale from "strongly disagree" (1) to "strongly agree" (5).

The factor analysis yielded a four-factor solution accounting for 32% of the variance: The *alienation* scale described feelings of not being accepted by either one's own race or by the out-group, discomfort with the university environment, and negative feelings toward the out-group; the *affirmation* scale contained items that suggest a preference for interaction with one's own race, racial pride, commitment to one's own race, and anger toward the out-group; the *assimilation* scale described a clear preference for interaction with the out-group and discomfort with members and activities of one's own race; and, finally, the *race-avoidance/individualism* scale contained items that indicate an emphasis on individual achievement over concern for racial issues, apathy, or distancing from racial problems, and avoidance of racial issues and conflict. The internal consistency of the scales ranged from 0.68 to 0.78.

Summary of Findings

Three preliminary reports have been prepared on data from the Coping with College Project that are relevant to the issues raised in this chapter. These results should be viewed as preliminary, given the small size and nonrepresentativeness (i.e., freshmen only) of our Afro-American sample.

In one report, Barker (1988) examined the impact of race, gender, background factors (SES, multiracial exposure, SAT scores), life stresses, and minority student stresses on the four sociocultural orientation styles in Afro-American, Chicano, and Filipino students. Her results indicated that Afro-American students reported significantly higher levels of minority student stresses, were more alienated, more race-affirming, less assimilated, and less race-avoidant than Chicano and Filipino students. Personal background was significantly associated with developing race affirmation, alienation, and assimilation styles, with lower SES and less exposure to Whites prior to college associated with greater affirmation and alienation tendencies, and higher SES and more exposure to Whites prior to college associated with greater assimilation tendencies. Higher reported minority student stresses predicted both higher alienation and affirmation tendencies.

In a related report, Smedley (1988) examined the contribution of life stresses, minority student stresses, and sociocultural orientation to psychological symptoms among Afro-American, Chicano, Filipino, and other Latino students. His results confirmed our "stress load hypothesis" contending that status-related stresses contribute an additional "load" to one's level of stress and impact functioning even after considering the effects of generic stresses. These minority-status-related stresses proved to be stronger predictors of psychological symptoms than nonstatus-related life stresses. This report also looked at the direct and mediating effects of sociocultural orientation on symptoms. A race affirmation style was found to have both direct and mediating effects, with students high in affirmation being at more risk for psychological symptoms. A race-avoidance/individualism style was an important predictor of symptoms, but only in interaction with high levels of minority student stresses.

Finally, Prillerman (1988) explored the contribution of stress and coping processes to freshman year GPA, psychological symptoms, and general well-being among Afro-American, Chicano, and White students. Her results indicated that, in addition to stressful experiences, coping behaviors, cognitive appraisals, and social support satisfaction were significant predictors of outcomes for Afro-American students. Stresses and coping strategies were stronger predictors of freshman-year GPA for Black students than were SAT scores. Minority student stresses were among the best predictors of the general well-being of Black students at the end of freshman year, with lower stresses associated with greater well-being. Alienation and race-avoidance/individualism were also direct predictors of well-being, with lower alienation scores and higher race-avoidance scores associated with greater well-being.

These preliminary findings provide support for our model. Clearly, there are limitations in the interpretation and generalizability of these results. Self-selection factors may have resulted in a sample of basically functional but slightly distressed students. Black students who had outstanding academic records, those who were experiencing significant personal problems or academic failure, and those who were simply not interested or willing to participate in the project may be underrepresented in our sample.

Additionally, many of our analyses were conducted on a multiethnic sample, which raises questions as to the applicability of our findings to the subgroup of Afro-American students. However, the fact that we found significant differences between Blacks and other minority groups on minority student stresses and sociocultural adaptations supports our contention that there may be important differences among students of different ethnic groups in the way they experience and adjust to majority institutions. Our findings also indicate that Afro-American freshmen, regardless of their socioeconomic background, may experience greater psychosocial vulnerability in predominantly White university settings as evidenced by greater psychological distress. This vulnerability is heightened in those students who are also alienated, who feel a greater need for personal and racial affirmation, and by those who are unable to maintain some psychological distance from racially salient issues so that they can pursue individual achievement objectives.

Conclusions and Recommendations
for Future Research and Interventions

In this chapter we have offered a multidimensional model of stress and coping as a conceptual and methodological tool to investigate the academic achievement and psychological well-being of Afro-American students at predominantly White universities. The model identifies two pathways of influences that impact on functional outcomes. One pathway considers the impact that generic life stresses have on outcomes. These stresses are conceptualized as affecting all students, and impact outcomes both directly and mediated through coping processes (i.e., coping behaviors, cognitive appraisal, social support). A second pathway considers minority status as an additional source of stress and impetus for coping that can exert a more specific effect on the academic performance and psychological well-being of Afro-American and other ethnic students.

Our initial research has demonstrated the utility of the proposed model and has provided initial data on two instruments developed to assess important factors in this model. However, our initial findings have also raised more questions than they have answered about how Afro-American students function on White college campuses.

Our preliminary findings suggest the need for studies to investigate more specifically how Afro-American student perceptions and expectations of the university environment and of their White peers and professors impact how they perceive, interpret, and cope with their experiences. More specific attention is also needed to understand how intragroup stresses impact Black students' success or failure, and how these effects can be shaped to ensure that they are facilitative rather than injurious.

The issue of the stresses that emerge from within the group is not given sufficient attention in the literature. These stresses have both political and personal significance. On the personal level, the limited availability of a pool of potential partners exacerbates feelings of loneliness, alienation, and within-group competition. It also increases the likelihood that some Black students will broaden their social network by including non-Blacks as friends and lovers.

Afro-American students must also cope with the political dynamics that emerge given the historical imperative for Blacks to confront racist policies and practices in majority institutions. The Black student movement has been an important vehicle for social activism and social change. History has demonstrated that without this social activism there would be even fewer Black students, faculty, and administrators at White universities. However, the dynamics of social activist groups include pressures for high group identification, conformity and unity, as well as struggles over political ideology and tactics. Black students who are unclear about their political stance on these questions, or who are primarily oriented toward their academic or social pursuits, face significant conformity pressures from their more activist peers. It is reasonable to suspect, therefore, that status-related stresses from academic sources, social relationships, institutional racism, and from within the group may combine over time to confer additional risk for academic failure and early attrition. This risk should be even greater for those Black students who are already vulnerable due to deficits in their academic background.

Our research also suggests that a clearer understanding of how Afro-American students cope with these status-related sources of stress, and the impact their coping strategies have on their achievement and well-being, is potentially a very productive direction for future research. It appears from our data that, at least for freshmen, a coping style characterized by affirming one's racial group membership rather than distancing from racial issues heightens psychological distress at a predominantly White university. Black students at White universities must cope not only with the usual academic and social demands but must also cope with the pressures and conflicts over the development of racial identity, demonstrations of group loyalty, participation in group activities, and commitment to collective activism. Strong identification with one's racial group creates a sense of belonging, support, and collective strength, but it also puts the student at odds with conformity pressures of the larger university. Our data suggest that freshmen who resolve this dilemma by downplaying their racial identity or by distancing from race-related issues tend to function better during the early stages of their college careers. However, the data raise questions as to the long-term costs of this coping style on a student's self-esteem and racial identity, and questions about the adaptiveness of this style when incidents of racism and discrimination occur.

It is clear from all available data that Afro-American students will continue to attend predominantly White universities, and that their experiences on these campuses pose both significant opportunities and threats to their well-being. Therefore, it is imperative that we understand these experiences so that both preventive and corrective interventions can be designed and implemented. These should include attention to both institutional (i.e., recruiting more Afro-American faculty) and individual (i.e., teaching effective coping behaviors) strategies. Some of these interventions will have to continue to be focused on removing the psychological hazards that are integral to these settings for Blacks (i.e., incidents of racism). Other interventions will need to be targeted at some of the intragroup dynamics that emerge among Black students when they struggle to cope with these system/context obstacles and pressures. Some Black students are clearly able to navigate these difficult waters and succeed despite the significant pressures. Others become overwhelmed by the dual demands and become academic and/or psychological casualties. Research pursuing the concepts suggested by this stress-coping model offer valuable insights about the different pathways that Black students take.

REFERENCES

Allen, W. R. (1981). Correlates of Black student adjustment, achievement, and aspirations at a predominantly White southern university. In G. E. Thomas (Ed.), *Black students in higher education* (pp. 126–141). Westport, CT: Greenwood.

Allen, W. R. (1984). Race consciousness and collective commitments among Black students on White campuses. *Western Journal of Black Studies, 8,* 156–166.

Allen, W. R. (1985). Black student, White campus: Structural, interpersonal, and psychological correlates of success. *Journal of Negro Education, 54,* 134–147.

Allen, W. R. (1988). The education of Black students on White college campuses: What quality is the experience?. In M. T. Nettles (Ed.), *Toward Black undergraduate student equality in American higher education* (pp. 57–86). Westport, CT: Greenwood.

Barbarin, O. A. (1983). Coping with ecological transitions by Black families: A psychosocial model. *Journal of Community Psychology, 11,* 308–322.

Barker, L. A. (1988). *The relationship between background factors, life stresses, and sociopolitical orientation in ethnic minority freshmen at a predominantly white university.* Unpublished manuscript, University of California, Los Angeles.

Cohen, S., & Willis, T. A. (1985). Stress, social support and the buffering hypothesis. *Psychological Bulletin, 98*(2), 310–357.

Connell, J. P., & Furman, W. (1984). The study of transitions, conceptual and methodological issues. In R. N. Emde & R. Harmon (Eds.), *Continuities and discontinuities in development* (pp. 153–173). New York: Plenum.

Cronkite, R. C., & Moos, R. H. (1984). The role of predisposing and moderating factors in the stress–illness relationship. *Journal of Health and Social Behavior, 25,* 372–393.

Dohrenwend, B. S., & Dohrenwend, B. P. (1970). Class and race as status-related sources of stress. In S. Levine & N. A. Scotch (Eds.), *Social stress* (pp. 111–140). Chicago: Aldine.

Evans, G. (1986, April 30). Black students who attend White colleges face contradictions in their campus life. *Chronicle of Higher Education,* 29–30.

Fleming, J. E. (1981). Blacks in higher education to 1954: A historical overview. In G.

E. Thomas (Ed.), *Black students in higher education: Conditions and experiences in the 1970s* (pp. 11–17). Westport, CT: Greenwood.

Fleming, J. (1984). *Blacks in college: A comparative study of students' success in Black and White institutions.* San Francisco: Jossey-Bass.

Gary, L. E. (1980). A mental health research agenda for the Black community. In R. L. Jones (Ed.), *Black Psychology* (pp. 447–454). New York: Harper & Row.

Gibbs, J. T. (1973). Black students/White university: Different expectations. *Personnel and Guidance Journal, 51,* 463–469.

Gibbs, J. T. (1974). Patterns of adaptation among Black students at a predominantly White university: Selected case studies. *American Journal of Orthopsychiatry, 44,* 728–740.

Gunnings, B. B. (1982). Stress and the minority student on a predominantly White campus. *Journal of Non-White Concerns in Personnel and Guidance, 11,* 11–17.

Gurin, P., & Epps, E. (1975). *Black consciousness, identity and achievement.* New York: John Wiley.

Johnson, J. H., & Sarason, I. G. (1978). Life stress, depression and anxiety: Internal-external control as a moderator variable. *Journal of Psychosomatic Research, 22,* 205–208.

Kanner, A. D., Coyne, J. C., Schaefer, C., & Lazarus, R. S. (1981). Comparison of two modes of stress measurement: Daily hassles and uplifts versus major life events. *Journal of Behavioral Medicine, 4,* 1–39.

Keller, J., Piotrowski, C., & Sherry D. (1982). Perceptions of the college environment and campus life: The Black experience. *Journal of Non-White Concerns in Personnel and Guidance, 10,* 126–132.

Kessler, R. C. (1979). Stress, social status and psychological distress. *Journal of Health and Social Behavior, 20,* 259–272.

Lazarus, R. S., & Folkman, S. (1984). *Stress, appraisal and coping.* New York: Springer.

Lazarus, R. S., & Launier, R. (1978). Stress-related transactions between person and environment. In L. A. Pervin and M. Lewis (Eds.), *Perspectives in interactional psychology* (pp. 287–327). New York: Plenum.

Lee, C. C. (1982). Black support group: Outreach to the alienated Black college student. *Journal of College Student Personnel, 23,* 271–272.

Lunneborg, C. E., and Lunneborg, P. W. (1986). Beyond prediction: The challenge of minority achievement in higher education. *Journal of Multicultural Counseling and Development, 14,* 77–84.

Mechanic, D. (1974). Social structure and personal adaptation: Some neglected dimensions. In G. V. Coelho, D. A. Hamburg, & J. E. Adams (Eds.), *Coping and adaptation* (pp. 32–44). New York: Basic Books.

Mingle, J. R. (1981). The opening of White colleges and universities to Black students. In G. E. Thomas (Ed.), *Black students in higher education: Conditions and experiences in the 1970s* (pp. 18–29). Westport, CT: Greenwood.

Mortisugu, J., & Sue, S. (1983). Minority status as a stressor. In R. D. Felner, L. A. Jason, J. Moritsugu, & S. S. Farber (Eds.), *Preventive psychology: Theory, research and practice.* New York: Praeger.

Myers, H. F. (1982). Stress, ethnicity and social class: A model for research with Black populations. In E. Jones & S. Korchin (Eds.), *Minority mental health* (pp. 118–148). New York: Holt, Rhinehart & Winston.

Neighbors, H. W., Jackson, J. S., Bowman, P., and Gurin, G. (1983). Stress, coping and Black mental health: Preliminary findings from a national study. *Prevention in Human Services, 2,* 5–28.

Nettles, M. T. (Ed.) (1988). *Toward Black undergraduate student equality in American higher education.* New York: Greenwood.

Nobles, W. W., & Goddard, L. (1977). Consciousness, adaptability, and coping strategies: Socioeconomic and ecological issues in Black families. *Western Journal of Black Studies, 1,* 105–113.

Oliver, M. L., Rodriguez, C. J., & Mickelson, R. A. (1985). Brown and Black in White: The social adjustment and academic performance of Chicano and Black students in a predominantly White university. *The Urban Review, 17,* 3–24.

Patterson, A. M., Sedlacek, W. E., and Perry, F. W. (1984). Perceptions of Blacks and Hispanics in two campus environments. *Journal of College Student Personnel, 25,* 513–518.

Pearlin, L. I. (1982). The social contexts of stress. In L. Goldberger & S. Breznitz (Eds.), *Handbook of stress, theoretical and clinical aspects* (pp. 367–379). New York: Free Press.

Pearlin, L. I., Menaghan, E. G., Lieberman, M. A., & Mullan, J. T. (1981). The stress process. *Journal of Health and Social Behavior, 22,* 337–356.

Pfeifer, M. C., & Schneider, A. (1974). University climate perceptions by Black and White students. *Journal of Applied Psychology, 59,* 660–662.

Prillerman, S. L. (1988). *Coping with a stressful transition: A prospective study of Black student adjustment to a predominantly White university.* Unpublished doctoral dissertation, University of California, Los Angeles.

Rabkin, J. G., & Struening, E. L. (1976). Life events, stress and illness. *Science, 194,* 1013–1020.

Rugg, E. A. (1982). A longitudinal comparison of minority and nonminority college dropouts: Implications for retention improvement programs. *The Personnel and Guidance Journal, 61*(4), 232–235.

Selltiz, C., Wrightsman, L. S., & Cook, S. W. (1976). *Research methods in social relations.* New York: Holt, Rinehart & Winston.

Smedley, B. D. (1988). *Stress and coping among minority students: An examination of stressors and mediation.* Unpublished manuscript, University of California, Los Angeles.

Smith, D. H. (1981). Social and academic environments of Black students on White campuses. *Journal of Negro Education, 50*(3), 299–306.

Spaights, E., Dixon, H. E., & Nickolai, S. (1985). Racism in higher education. *College Student Journal, 19*(1), 17–22.

Suen, H. K. (1983). Alienation and attrition of Black college students on a predominantly White campus. *Journal of College Student Personnel, 24,* 117–121.

Thomas, G. E. (1981) (Ed.). *Black students in higher education: Conditions and experiences in the 1970s.* Westport, CT: Greenwood.

Tracey, T. J., & Sedlacek, W. E. (1985). The relationship of noncognitive variables to academic success: A longitudinal comparison by race. *Journal of College Student Personnel, 26*(5), 405–410.

11

What Would We Do if We Really Loved the Students?

EDWARD "CHIP" ANDERSON

Introduction

Over the past 20 years, colleges and universities have expressed increasing concern about the number of students who fail to graduate. Some of this concern has been motivated by institutional disgrace and loss of tuition income. Some of this concern has been expressed on behalf of certain student groups, such as students from historically underrepresented ethnic and cultural groups, students from low-income backgrounds, student athletes, and students in certain majors. Some of this concern has emanated from college personnel who look at student attrition as a tragic loss of opportunities for students' intellectual and personal development.

During this same 20-year period, many colleges and universities have instituted programs and services to promote academic achievement and persistence. In these efforts, thousands of committed professionals have agonized about what they and their institutions might do to retain more students and help more students gain maximum benefits from their college experience.

It is to these committed college professionals who really want to see students benefit as much as possible from the college experience that I direct my comments. I wish to share a perspective on college students' retention and achievement that comes from nearly 25 years of working in higher education. This perspective combines my experience working in retention efforts as a college counselor, instructor, and administrator, with the insights I have gained through extensive reading on the nature of college student persistence, achievement, and intellectual and personal development.

I am energized to this task by two factors. First, I believe that a college education represents the only opportunity for most students to experience significant intellectual development. And for students from low-income and historically underrepresented backgrounds, a college education is virtually their only hope and their last chance for economic and social mobility. The second factor that energizes this writing is my compassion for those college professionals who agonize over what they can do to promote student retention. To these committed individuals, I want to give my encouragement. I know how you tear your hair out trying to think of ways to promote students' academic achievement and persistence. I know how it feels to be in environments where people give lip service to caring about students and then resist your initiatives or insult you with their indifference, their ill-informed ideas, and their excuses for why your ideas can't be implemented. I know how you feel, because I've been there!

Because of the urgency of this issue and the compassion I feel toward those who want to make a difference in the lives of college students, I don't want to meander through research reports and theoretical models. So, let me take you to my bottom line. If you want to improve college student persistence and achievement, there is one question that I think you need to address in designing your programs and services. That question is, What would we do if we *really loved* the students?

I suggest conceiving and implementing retention efforts based on doing what we do when we love someone. I suggest this approach because loving seems at the core of everything that works in student retention—everything I know about, at least. We must never forget that putting forth the sustained effort to achieve, persist, and develop is a very personal matter stemming from students' personal desires and their personal motivations. From my experience, the impact of being loved stimulates persistent effort, which leads to achievement and personal development, because being loved is such a basic desire and motivation. Personalizing this point, when I have felt loved, I have tended to grow, develop, and reach for my highest potential. At these times, I have been empowered to believe in myself, because someone loved and believed in me. Because of someone's love and confidence in me, my self-esteem and self-efficacy increased. And, as others thought me worth loving, I began to view myself as worth loving. As a result, I started investing the time and energy necessary to develop myself, which in the final analysis is what produces achievement and growth.

Similarly, I have been able to promote students' achievement, persistence, and development most effectively when I have taken an active interest in them, sought to know and understand them as persons, cared for them by developing personally relevant services, respected their individuality and uniqueness, and felt responsibility for their success and development. Whether through elaborate and systematic programs, or through fledgling, half-baked efforts, when students sense that they are being loved, it makes a difference! So, then, if our aim is to promote students' academic achievement, persistence, and development, it would seem entirely reasonable to ask ourselves, What would we do if we really loved the students? And, to ask ourselves, How can I demonstrate the love I feel toward students in practical and personally meaningful ways?

Persisting and Achieving in College

In an earlier publication (Anderson, 1985), I depicted in a figure the task that students face when attempting to persist and achieve in terms of contending with various forces, pressures, and obstacles associated with the college experience. While the specific forces, pressures, and obstacles students experience differ by institution, and according to individual circumstances, they fall into general patterns. This figure depicts what I call the Force Field Analysis of College Persistence. It describes persistence in college as dependent on the number and the magnitude of the differential forces promoting and preventing progress toward the degree. Figure 11.1 also depicts various obstacles that students encounter in route to their degrees.

The critical point that this figure seeks to illuminate is that each negative internal force, each negative external force, and each obstacle requires time and energy to counteract and overcome. Thus, the task of persisting and achieving in college can be viewed in terms of the amount of time and energy students need to counteract or adjust to negative internal and external forces, and the amount of time and energy they must invest to overcome the obstacles that stand between entering and graduating from college.

While the forces (depicted as arrows) are approximately the same size on the figure, students differ in the extent to which they have

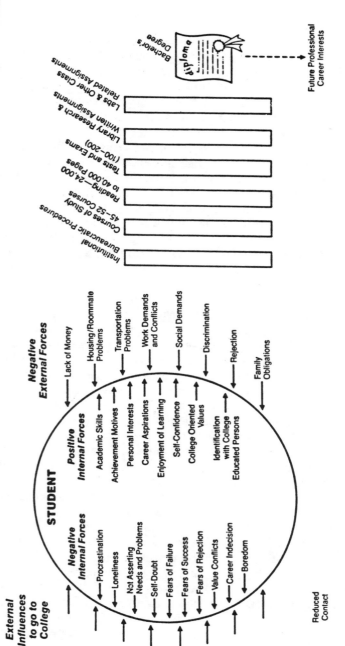

Figure 11.1 Force Field Analysis of College Persistence

well-developed positive internal forces, and the extent to which they experience negative internal and negative external forces of various magnitudes. Accordingly, the quantity and magnitude of the positive forces versus the quantity and magnitude of the negative internal and external forces strongly influence how much time and energy students will need in order to achieve and persist to graduation. The issue of available time and energy extends beyond negative versus positive forces. The task of persisting and achieving in college also involves surmounting the obstacles that students experience in route to their degrees. Once again, the issue becomes one of time and energy because overcoming each obstacle demands time and energy. Moreover, the amount of time and energy demanded for each obstacle depends on the magnitude of various internal, positive forces. Take, for example, the task of completing reading assignments. Students who have well-developed reading and comprehension skills will need less time and energy than those with weaker skills.

The Force Field Analysis scheme postulates that achievement and persistence are less likely among students who (a) experience more negative internal and negative external forces, (b) experience negative internal and negative external forces of greater magnitude, and (c) have less well-developed positive internal forces to cope with the negative internal and external forces, and to overcome the obstacles that their college experience presents.

Students who have multiple negative internal and multiple negative external forces of considerable magnitude, and who have less well developed skills to cope with these pressures, are less likely to achieve and persist because they need more time and energy to complete the tasks facing them. Or, they may fail to achieve and persist simply because they become overwhelmed and discouraged by the difficulty of their task. Or, they may fail to achieve and persist because they don't know how to direct their time and energy in productive ways or are unwilling to make the necessary choices.

In this scenario of the many internal and external forces that students must face, the concept of loving students becomes crucial. By actively knowing, caring for, respecting, and being responsible for students, college personnel can do many significant things to promote students' persistence and achievement. For example, note that upon entry to college, students typically separate themselves from the many positive external forces that influenced them to attend college (e.g., parents, high school counselors and teachers, etc.). Here, concerned professors, counselors, and advisors can increase the forces leading to persistence simply by showing a personal interest in students as well as by providing relevant services and/or by helping students from peer groups in which they support each other's achievement and persistence. Also, note the many negative internal forces mitigating against persistence, which could be addressed through relevant support services. Think about the negative external forces that could be alleviated and the obstacles that could be made easier to surmount through orientation programs, skill-building courses, problem-solving workshops, and other support services that could be created in direct response to students' problems and concerns. Finally, think about the positive internal forces that could be strengthened through academic support services, personal development classes, and advice from staff, faculty, and upperclass students.

The most basic issue in college student achievement and persistence is the amount of time and energy students have available and the amount of motivation and commitment they have to invest their time and energy in ways that produce achievement and persistence. But I am contending that responsible college personnel can make a difference in helping students address their achievement and persistence dilemmas. However, here again there is a common denominator: Someone must *actively* try to find out which students are experiencing various dilemmas; someone must *know* students well enough to understand the sources of their dilemmas; someone must *care* enough to make relevant services available to address student needs and problems; someone must *respect* students enough not to demean them because they have needs and problems; and someone must be *responsible* enough to provide needed services in a timely and effective manner. In essence, someone really needs to love the students!

The Gap Theory of Academic Achievement

I have recently been thinking about exactly what is necessary for students to achieve and persist in college. Whereas the Force Field Analysis scheme points to various forces, pressures, obstacles, and problems that tend to confound students' achievement and persistence, it fails to identify explicitly what students need to know, to be able to do, and to possess in order to achieve and persist in college. The Force Field Analysis scheme shows the importance of students having sufficient time and energy and judiciously investing their time and energy, but it doesn't depict those areas in which students need the most time and energy in order to achieve and persist. To correct these shortfalls, I am developing what I call the Gap Theory of Academic Achievement.

The Gap Theory of Academic Achievement postulates that there is a group of requisite skills, abilities, background knowledge, qualities, characteristics, and resources that college students must have in order to achieve and persist. This theory also recognizes that entering students, especially those who are admitted under special provisions, usually don't have all of the requisite skills, abilities, background knowledge, qualities, characteristics, and resources necessary for achievement and persistence, thus, the idea of "gaps."

The Gap Theory of Academic Achievement attempts to explain differential levels of academic performance by taking into consideration those student, instructor, and institutional factors that determine whether or not students who aspire to achieve high grades and who aspire to persist in college will, in fact, do so. The Gap Theory is student-centered in that academic achievement and persistence are only possible when students (a) aspire to achieve and persist, (b) assume the primary responsibility for their achievement and persistence, and (c) choose to invest the time and energy that achievement and persistence demand. It is the student's time and energy that must be invested in order to bring about achievement and persistence. Students are the ones who must have the time and energy to achieve and persist. And students are the only ones who can decide if they will invest their available time and energy in ways and to the extent that achievement and persistence demand.

An important premise of this theory is that even though professors, via the grades they award, ultimately judge whether or not students are achieving, students are responsible for putting forth the time and energy necessary to learn and achieve according to professors' expectations. It is the students who are required to close the "gap" between themselves and the expectations of their professors. Therefore, the Gap Theory of Academic Achievement considers the time and energy dilemmas students face in meeting professors' expectations to be the most crucial dimension of their college experience. The challenge that entering students face, therefore, is to learn the needed skills and background knowledge; to develop the needed qualities and abilities; to acquire the needed personal characteristics; and to amass the needed resources that will enable them to achieve and persist.

The "gaps" between what students need in order to achieve and what they possess at entry are gaps of different types, gaps of greater and lesser importance, and gaps of different expanses. Accordingly, it is the size (expanse, magnitude, or distance) of the gaps *and* the number of gaps between students and their professors' performance expectations that determine the amount of time and energy that students must invest in order to achieve academically.

The Gap Theory postulates that when there are few gaps and gaps of less expanse between students' skills, knowledge, and abilities, and what they must be able to do in order to meet their professors' expectations, academic achievement will occur. Conversely, when there are more gaps and gaps of greater expanse between what students are required to do and what they are able to do, academic achievement is less likely.

Clearly, the task of achieving academically demands time and energy. But the point is that the amount of time and energy demanded differs from student to student depending on the number and size of the gaps they have to overcome in order to meet professor expectations. For some students, achieving an "A" in a particular course demands minimal time and energy, whereas for other students in the same class achieving a "C" demands substantial time and energy. It is the number and magnitude of gaps between each student and his or her professors' expectations that will determine how much time and energy the student must invest in order to achieve at any particular level.

It is here, at the time and energy dimension of students' college experience, that academic achievement or nonachievement is determined. While each student has the same number of hours in a week, the demands on his or her time are vastly different. And, with differential demands on the student's time, there are differential demands on his or her energy.

To illustrate the Gap Theory as it applies to course achievement, consider the following example. Two freshmen, Jim and Sam, enrolled in a beginning calculus course during their first term in college. They were both highly motivated and both aspired to earn A's in their calculus course. They both came from the same high school and earned equivalent grades throughout. Now assume that everything about them, their background and their college experience, is the same except for one difference. Whereas Jim took algebra, geometry, and trigonometry in high school, Sam took only algebra and geometry.

Obviously, when Jim and Sam enroll in calculus, there is a difference or a "gap" between the two young men regarding their preparation. But the gap between Jim and Sam is not the main issue. The important issue is the gap between their respective levels of preparation and their professor's expectations. If the professor assumes that enrollees already have a firm grasp of trigonometric functions, Sam will have a real problem! That problem is a function of the gap between his skills, knowledge, and abilities, and his professor's expectations.

The ramifications of Sam's problem boil down to the time and energy he must have available and be willing to devote to mastering the trigonometric concepts and procedures on which calculus is based, plus the time and energy demanded to learn calculus. In a sense, then, Sam will be virtually taking two math courses at once—the calculus course in which he is enrolled and a course of trigonometric concepts and procedures that Sam must learn on his own. Even if the professor provides a review of assumed background knowledge in trigonometry, Sam must still expend more time and energy in order to learn what he needs to know, because there is a gap between what he knows and what his professor assumes he already knows.

In the foregoing illustration, both Jim and Sam may be able to earn A's in their calculus course provided they have sufficient motivation to invest the needed time and energy. But Sam must have more. Sam must (a) have more motivation, (b) be willing to invest more time and energy, and (c) have sufficient time and energy to compensate for the gap in his preparation. But what if Sam doesn't have the time and energy to correct for his preparation gap? What if he is not willing to invest the extra time and energy? What if Sam's calculus professor demeans him for being underprepared? What if Sam becomes discouraged about the amount of time and energy he must expend, compared to Jim or to other students? What if he has other gaps in terms of time management skills, financial resources, or self-confidence? And what if his time and energy are limited due to transportation problems, family obligations, or work demands?

Student Characteristics for Persistence and Achievement

Thinking in terms of what students need to achieve and persist in college invariably leads to questions about which student characteristics are the most critical. My answer is motivation to achieve, commitment to achieve, and self-efficacy are the most essential student characteristics needed for academic achievement and persistence.

The reason motivation, commitment, and self-efficacy are so essential goes back to the Force Field Analysis scheme of depicting the challenges and adjustments that students face in college. As previously stated, students need time and energy to overcome each obstacle and to counteract each negative force they encounter in route to their degrees. Since motivation to achieve is the source of energy, since commitment to achieve is the basis for deciding to invest time and energy in achievement activities, and since self-efficacy is the foundation for the confidence to fulfill commitments, these qualities become the most essential characteristics that students need for academic achievement and persistence. Conversely, if students lack adequate motivation to generate the energy necessary to achieve, or if they lack sufficient commitment to direct energy toward and to spend time on achievement activities, or if they lack self-efficacy to sustain the effort necessary to achieve, they simply cannot and will not persist and achieve.

The rationale for why motivation, commitment, and self-efficacy are the most essential student characteristics becomes even more evident in light of the Gap Theory of Achievement. Since the Gap Theory postulates that time and energy must be invested to close or bridge the gap(s) between students' skills, knowledge, and abilities and those required to achieve and persist, the question becomes, Do students have the energy to invest in bridging their gaps and will they choose to invest the amount of time and energy needed to achieve? In response to this question, motivation to achieve, commitment to achieve, and self-efficacy become the critical issues.

Motivation to achieve generates the energy needed to bridge gaps necessary for achievement and persistence; commitment to achieve directs the energy and invests the time needed to bridge those gaps;

and self-efficacy supplies the confidence to actually begin working toward achievement. Motivation, commitment, and self-efficacy supply, give direction to, and enable students to invest the energy needed to overcome the gaps and adjust to the forces and obstacles that college students encounter. These qualities determine whether sufficient energy will be available, whether sufficient time and energy is invested, and whether sufficient action is taken in order to make achievement and persistence a reality. Therefore, motivation to achieve, commitment to achieve, and self-efficacy are the most essential characteristics for college student achievement and persistence.

What if Students Lack the Motivation, Commitment, and Self-Efficacy to Achieve?

This is the most challenging question of all. It hits at the heart of college student persistence, achievement, and development. Because it is the most critical question, we must be extremely honest in our response.

My first response is that if a student truly lacks the motivation to achieve, commitment to achieve, and self-efficacy to achieve, there isn't anything that can be done unless this condition is corrected. All of the financial aid, housing priorities, study skill workshops, and curriculum opportunities in the world will not suffice if a student lacks the amount of motivation, commitment, and self-efficacy necessary to achieve. Said differently, motivation, commitment, and self-efficacy gaps must be addressed first, because all else depends on them. The time and energy needed to bridge other gaps depend on sufficient motivation, commitment, and self-efficacy. Likewise, the many adjustments that students must make as they encounter negative forces and obstacles within their college experience demand time and energy and thus substantial motivation to achieve, a strong commitment to achieve, and the self-efficacy to achieve.

So what should one do if students lack these essential qualities? My answer is to either establish services to build students' motivation, to enhance their commitment, and to foster their self-efficacy; or never admit such students in the first place! After all, I wouldn't consider it very loving to let students come into a college where failure is inevitable, would you?

Of course, my answer to the foregoing questions presupposes (a) that it is possible to measure students' level of motivation, level of commitment, and self-efficacy to achieve; (b) that it is possible to determine how much motivation, commitment, and self-efficacy is necessary to achieve and persist at various institutions and in specific courses of study; and (c) that it is possible to build students' motivation to achieve, to increase their commitment to achieve, and to foster their self-efficacy. Personally, I believe it is. However, relatively little has been done in this area. Instead, we have endlessly correlated aptitude test scores, grade-point averages, socioeconomic status indicators, and other demographic characteristics in an effort to make better admission decisions. And yet, I think that the usefulness of such predictors is that they are actually more representative of students' motivation, commitment, and self-efficacy to achieve than of the factors they purport to measure.

Regarding the possibility of increasing students' motivation, commitment, and self-efficacy to achieve, I believe that this is exactly what happens in our most effective support services and in our most effective programs and curricular innovations. For example, in an effective tutorial service, how much of the effectiveness is attributable to the tutors' clarification of course materials, and how much to the effect of the tutors' encouragement, interest, feedback, concern, caring, and modeling on the students' motivation, commitment, and self-efficacy?

I think that effective support services and programs are effective because they positively affect students' motivation, commitment, and self-efficacy. Therefore, I advocate more direct attempts to assess students' motivation, commitment, and self-efficacy; and to measure the amount of motivation, commitment, and self-efficacy students will need to achieve and persist at various institutions and in specific areas of study. Then, based on these assessments and measurements, I advocate that more courses and support services be specifically designed to increase students' motivation, commitment, and self-efficacy to achieve.

How Can We Increase Students' Motivation to Achieve?

Again, the critical nature of this question demands the utmost candor. Accordingly, my answer is that we can't! No one other than the student can increase his or her own motivation! A better question would be, How can we help students increase their motivation to achieve? This distinction is an important one because the methods and strategies used in support services that attempt to address motivational problems will emanate from how motivation is conceived.

Students, and everyone else for that matter, are motivated by *their perceptions* of *their needs and desires* (Maslow, 1954). Consequently, it is the students' perceptions that are all-important. Another critical issue is how students perceive that they can best meet their needs and fulfill their desires. Motivation to achieve in college is a direct extension of students perceiving that their needs can be met and that their desires can be fulfilled by achieving in college! Accordingly, professors, counselors, and student services personnel can help students increase their motivation to achieve in college by (a) helping students identify and clarify their needs and desires; (b) helping students identify and clarify their satisfactions and dissatisfactions; (c) helping students identify and clarify their questions and curiosities; (d) helping students clarify areas of desired competence; and (e) helping students identify and clarify values.

These ways of helping students increase their motivation to achieve stem from the understanding that people are self-motivated and that their motivation is based on their perceptions concerning their needs and desires. The best strategy to help students increase their motivation is to help them clarify their perceptions concerning their needs and their desires. This clarification forms the basis for motivation to achieve in college. But motivation to achieve in college also requires that students perceive achieving in college as a viable means of (a) meeting their needs and fulfilling their desires, (b) increasing their satisfaction with themselves by becoming the kinds of persons they most want to be, (c) finding answers to their questions and curiosities, (d) developing the skills and gaining the experience to become more competent, and (e) doing things that they value.

How Can We Increase Student Commitment to Achievement?

Commitment to achieve in college is an extremely critical factor in determining whether or not students will persist to graduation. Whereas motivation to achieve generates the energy needed for achievement, commitment to achieve directs energy needed for achievement to those tasks that result in achievement. Achievement in college demands a substantial investment of time and energy. And commitment to achieve is the decision-making process by which that investment is made. Without commitment, college achievement simply isn't possible.

How can we increase students' commitment to achieve? The problem we face in addressing this question is the same as that in addressing the question, How can we increase students' motivation to achieve? Simply stated, we can't! To understand why only students themselves can increase their commitment to achieve we must understand the nature of commitments and what is involved in making commitments. Commitments are promises that people make concerning what they will do and what they will accomplish. When people make commitments, whether to themselves or to others, they promise to accomplish something.

The promise to do something and to accomplish something isn't made in a vacuum, and it doesn't come from a vacuum. Promises, like all other forms of human behavior, are motivated acts, and thus stem from within a person and from other internal phenomena such as perceiving needs and perceiving desires. For this reason, no one can make a commitment for another person, and no one can increase another person's commitment to do anything—including achieving. Each person decides what he or she will commit to doing and to accomplishing.

Highlighting the fact that commitments are acts of the will is important because these *acts of the will* are not singular. They are plural. In fact, they are multiple and continuous until what a person has committed himself to has been completed. In other words, a commitment involves two acts of the will (choices or decisions): (a) to complete something, and (b) to do something. But whereas the decision to complete something remains unchanged, the process of completing something requires continuous decision making until the goal has been reached. By this I mean pursuing a desired result requires multiple choices to adjust to unforeseen obstacles, multiple decisions to generate and pursue alternate paths, and multiple acts of the will to keep trying when one is tempted to quit. So a commitment to do something involves many commitments and recommitments to keep "doing" different things in order to accomplish what one originally committed him- or herself to achieve.

Given this continuous aspect of commitment, it is little wonder that theorists such as Tinto (1975) point to commitment as a primary defining characteristic of college persisters. In fact, Tinto makes the point that the commitment to graduate from college isn't a one-time decision. Students confront the choice of persisting or dropping out over and over again.

While I agree with Tinto's point that students revisit their commitment to persist over and over again, I would add that it isn't simply the choice of persisting versus dropping out that students must make over and over again. They must make an infinite number of choices or commitments to "do" the multiple tasks that persisting to graduation requires.

In addressing the issue of helping students increase their commitments to achieve in college, I am actually confronting two types of commitments. One involves commitments to accomplish a certain goal (e.g., graduating, gaining admission to graduate school, etc.) or to achieve at certain levels of aspiration (i.e., earn certain grades, learn certain skills and knowledge, develop certain qualities, etc.). The second type of commitment involves the multiple commitments or ongoing choices that students must make in judiciously using their limited time and limited energy to accomplish their goals and to achieve at their levels of aspiration. In relation to both types of commitments, the question remains, How can students increase their commitment to achieve?

Having established the fact that students are the only ones who can increase their commitment to achieve, now I want to focus on what those of us who care about students' achievement can do to help them increase their commitment to achieve. From my experience, college professors, counselors, and student services personnel can help students increase their commitments by implementing the following strategies: (a) helping students translate their motivations and commitments for attending college into commitments to persist and achieve in college; (b) helping students clarify the relationships between their motivations and their desired outcomes of college; and (c) helping students see relationship between their motivations, their college experience, and the outcomes they desire from college.

These methods of helping students increase their commitment to achieve and persist in college center on helping students to see their college experience in ways that are personally meaningful. Whatever is meaningful to a person is motivational. And when something is personally meaningful, it is also something to which a person is willing to make commitments.

How Can We Increase Students' Self-Efficacy to Achieve?

In the preceding section, I asserted that two types of commitments are important to college students' achievement. One is a commitment to achievement goals and the other is a commitment to the process of investing the time and energy necessary to achieve. The reason I emphasized these commitments is that unless students commit themselves to the goal of achieving, and unless students commit themselves to the process leading to achievement, they simply won't achieve even if they are motivated to do so!

Now I want to discuss the process leading to making these achievement commitments. In addition to being motivated to achieve, students must be self-efficacious about their ability to achieve. Unless students are self-efficacious, they will not make the commitments necessary to achieve, and consequently, they will not invest the time and energy that college achievement and persistence demand.

Self-efficacy is the term Albert Bandura (1982) uses to describe the beliefs an individual holds regarding what he or she can accomplish through his or her own efforts. These beliefs involve (a) what a person believes he or she can accomplish and (b) how viable, strong, or effective he or she believes his or her efforts will be in accomplishing certain goals. There is, therefore, an interrelationship between self-efficacy and commitment. A person will commit himself or herself to achieving and to pursuing only those goals about which he or she is self-efficacious. Accordingly, a person must first be self-efficacious about achieving a goal before he or she will make the time and energy commitments necessary to achieving a desired goal.

Assuming that we agree that college achievement requires a substantial and sustained investment of time and energy and that students must be self-efficacious enough to make the time and energy commitments needed to achieve, the question before those who want to promote students' achievement becomes, How can we increase students' self-efficacy to achieve? To this question, I must respond as I did to the questions concerning how we can increase students' motivation and commitment to achieve. We can't! We can't increase students' self-efficacy to achieve any more than we can increase their motivation or commitment to achieve. The only person who can increase self-efficacy is the person himself or herself.

College professors, counselors, and student service personnel can do a lot, however, to help students increase their self-efficacy for achievement in college. Some of the things they can do are (a) present students with specific tasks and asking them to assess their self-efficacy to perform these tasks; (b) design diagnostic and assessment procedures that clearly portray students' strengths and abilities to themselves; (c) encourage students to work from their strengths when transitioning into college and when building skills; (d) help students define success based on realistic goals; (e) affirm students for attributing their successes to their efforts, skills, talents, and abilities; (f) focus on what students "can do" and "are willing to do" when dealing with problems, frustrations, and discouragements; (g) have successful peers disclose their struggles to achieve; and (h) design curricula in incremental steps that challenge students but that begin from students' diagnosed skills and knowledge.

Returning to the question of what would we do if we really loved the students, I can't imagine anything that is more loving than trying to help students increase their self-efficacy. In fact, I think it is the most loving thing we can attempt to do. If we can help students increase their self-efficacy, they will be more likely to achieve and persist in college, and they will become stronger persons, more able to maximize their personal and intellectual potential both while they are in college and throughout their lives.

Using the Gap Theory to Understand Students' Problems and Struggles

To promote students' achievement and persistence, we must be prepared to address any gap that impedes achievement or takes time and energy away from achievement-related activities. While I have emphasized the importance of motivation, commitment, and self-efficacy because achievement and persistence depend on them, we must be prepared to help students address any and all gaps that interfere with their achievement. Even if students are highly motivated, deeply committed, and very self-efficacious, they may not achieve or persist, for they may have too many gaps or gaps that are too large for them to overcome with the time and energy they have available.

As I listen to students describe their problems and struggles, I find it helpful to ask myself three questions: (a) To what extent are students spending their time and energy on achievement and persistence related tasks versus unrelated problems and struggles? (b) What can I do to help them be more efficient and effective? and (c) What can I do to prevent them from wasting time and energy on unnecessary problems and struggles?

While students tend to be very conscious of the problems and struggles that consume their time and energy, it is insufficient to understand students' problems and struggles only from their perspectives. In fact, students' problems and struggles are usually manifestations of gaps between what they have, know, and are able to do, and what they need to have, know, and be able to do in order to achieve and persist. Thus, we need to analyze students' problems and struggles both from the students' perspective and from a perspective that helps us understand what is causing the problems and struggles.

To illustrate the difference between how students describe their problems and struggles and what is actually causing them, let me share an experience I had. A group of students were upset about the problems they were having in a sociology course. They all said that they had really been working and trying hard to get good grades, but they were all getting "C's" or lower. They attributed their problem to their professor who, according to the students, gave disorganized lectures, assigned unrelated readings, and asked essay exam questions on topics that weren't covered either in lectures or in the assigned readings. While the students depicted their problems and struggles as being caused by their professor, I found that the students didn't understand the professor's expectations and didn't have the skills or experience to meet those expectations. The students thought that their professor expected them to amass the information presented in the lectures and assigned readings, but the professor was expecting them to learn how to analyze issues from various points of view. Therefore, the information communicated in the lectures and assigned readings was less important than the way this information was analyzed. Accordingly, when the professor asked exam questions that required students to analyze issues on topics that were never presented in the course, he was testing the students' analytic skills rather than the information they had amassed from the lectures and readings.

This experience illustrates that students' perceptions of what is causing their problems and struggles may not be accurate. But, it also illustrates the concept of gaps. There was a gap of understanding between what the professor expected his students to learn and what the students thought they were being expected to learn. But that wasn't the only gap causing the students' problems and struggles. As I eventually discovered, the students would not have been able to achieve on the exams even if they had understood the professor's expectations, because they didn't know how to analyze issues and they didn't know how to write essays for exam questions that asked them to analyze. Therefore, the students' achievement problems and struggles could be attributed to at least three gaps: (a) not understanding their professor's expectations, (b) not knowing how to analyze, and (c) not knowing how to write essays that demonstrate analytic skills.

Using this illustration, consider what could be done to help students become more efficient and effective. Since the first gap involved misunderstandings, the professor could spell out his expectations more clearly and describe to students how they should study and prepare for exams. He could give students copies of past exam questions and explain what constitutes a "good" essay in response to questions that require analysis. He could even show the students a good and bad essay answer and explain his grading criteria. He could describe his teaching techniques and explain why he is assigning particular readings. And he could give a diagnostic test on the first day of class to identify which students might need supplementary instruction to build their analytic thinking or writing skills. Of course, teaching assistants (TAs) and tutors could do many of the things suggested above. In fact, TAs and tutors could run a kind of adjunct course to teach students how to analyze and to give them opportunities to practice their analytic skills. TAs and tutors could also give practice exams to build students' analytic writing skills and confidence in an exam situation.

This list of things that could be done to help students become more efficient and effective is predicated on one condition: Someone would have to know which students were having problems and would have to analyze what gaps were producing those difficulties.

This condition then comes back to the need for ongoing relationships with students in which someone cares enough to listen to and understand their problems and struggles, someone cares enough to analyze what is causing their problems and struggles, and someone cares enough to design programs, services, and interventions that address the causes of students' problems and struggles.

Finally, there is the issue of prevention. Again using the foregoing illustration, ask yourself, what could be done? Starting from the most basic changes, printed materials on the course could describe what students are expected to know and to do. A diagnostic test could be developed for advising and placement purposes. Or a formal prerequisite for enrolling in the course might be needed. Certainly, academic advisors could provide preventative services. Advisors could explain the professor's expectations and testing standards. They could conduct informal assessments of students' skills to determine students' level of preparation and readiness for the course. Advisors could suggest courses to build analytic thinking skills and analytic writing skills that could be taken before or concurrently with the sociology course. Also, the professor might decide that these student problems were so widespread and of sufficient magnitude that a new course was needed to teach analytic thinking skills, to develop analytic writing skills, and to provide background knowledge and information on the nature of social sciences and how various social science disciplines analyze issues.

Again, these preventive measures that could help students achieve more efficiently and effectively all depend on knowing and understanding students' problems and struggles. Someone would have to take the initiative and understand the students well enough to know who needs various services and interventions. And someone would have to care enough and feel responsible enough to design preventative measures.

Using the Gap Theory to Understand Problems Encountered by Underrepresented Students

Underrepresented college students face a particular set of problems that the Gap Theory helps to illuminate. The first of these problems stems from the fact that, by definition, underrepresented students are "underrepresented," which means that they are fewer in number and percent. Being underrepresented can interfere with motivation, commitment, and self-efficacy; underrepresented students may feel alone because of their lesser numbers or alienated because they feel unwanted and unaccepted on campus. Thus, we shouldn't be surprised if these students don't persist. After all, would you want to continue attending a college, or being in any other environment for that matter, if you felt uncomfortable, unwanted, not a part of it, or rejected because of something about you that you could not change or control?

Underrepresented students may also experience discrimination on campus. By definition, discrimination involves differential treatment. According to the Gap Theory, underrepresented students would be more likely to have differential expectations placed on them. For example, underrepresented students may have professors who don't think that they are as capable of meeting their standards as "represented" students. Therefore, the task of meeting professors' expectations would be greater for underrepresented students than for represented students. Or, using the Gap Theory, underrepresented students would have to overcome larger gaps than represented students because discriminating professors hold different performance expectations for them. Underrepresented students would have to put forth more time and energy than represented students to achieve the same grades.

Finally, underrepresented students are more likely to experience prejudice as well as discrimination and alienation. With prejudice comes all of the unfavorable, negative, and demeaning judgments that, if internalized, could negatively affect their motivation, commitment, and self-efficacy, thus creating other gaps.

Because underrepresented students are more likely to experience alienation, discrimination, and prejudice, they may become less motivated to persist and achieve, less committed to persist and achieve, and less self-efficacious about persisting and achieving. The painful experience of feeling alienated on campus makes being on a college campus so displeasurable that it negatively affects underrepresented students' motivation and commitment to achieve and persist. Similarly, experiencing discrimination may make the task of achieving seem so unreachable that underrepresented students lose their self-efficacy and thus their commitment to achieve and persist. Experiencing prejudice may also cause underrepresented students to conclude that they will forever be prevented from achieving by prejudiced individuals who will continuously erect barriers to their achievement and persistence.

While the foregoing discussion centered on how the Gap Theory can be used to better understand the experience underrepresented students face because they are "underrepresented," these same students may have any number of the other gaps. If this is true, underrepresented students will have a compounding problem, because these other gaps may reinforce stereotypes and thus make it that much more difficult for the students to reach the performance expectations of their college professors. Moreover, if discriminating and prejudicial experiences have already weakened their motivation, commitment, and self-efficacy, the existence of other gaps will likely compound their motivation, commitment, and self-efficacy problems.

Finally, there is the likelihood that historically underrepresented students are also from low-income backgrounds. Therefore, to understand the experience of historically underrepresented college students and those from low-income backgrounds, we must take into consideration all of the forces that tend to affect underrepresented students' motivation, commitment, and self-efficacy due to alienation, discrimination, and prejudice; plus we must take into consideration all of the demands on low-income students' time and energy due to working, transportation, housing, and underpreparation problems. Seen in this light, the task of achieving and persisting in college for historically underrepresented students who are also from low-income backgrounds is truly monumental.

So, the question again becomes, Where should we begin in addressing the problems of underrepresented students? I must pose my theme question in order to ignite our creativity, What would we do if we really loved underrepresented students? My answer to this question is that the most important thing that underrepresented students need to experience is relationships with people whom they respect and with whom they can, in some way, identify. What is crucial about these relationships is that people affirm and invest confidence in these students. I use the word *crucial* to emphasize how important it is for underrepresented students to receive affirmations and votes of confidence. Affirmation is just the opposite of what is communicated by discrimination and prejudice, and affirming relationships are the only way to address loneliness and alienation.

A peer support system can be especially helpful in alleviating loneliness and alienation. Here is where peer counselors or peer tutors can be very helpful. The key issue here is not so much to have peer support system with other underrepresented students but to have a peer group in which students feel accepted. But, if the peer counselor or tutor is also from an underrepresented group, beneficial experiences can be shared on coping with alienation, prejudice, and discrimination.

Beyond having positive relationships, all of the approaches discussed in the previous sections may apply to underrepresented students. But, as with each of the other strategies, the bottom line remains the same: Someone needs to love the students.

Conclusions

My primary purpose has been to encourage fellow professionals who are striving to promote students' achievement, persistence, and development in college. Therefore, I conclude with some personal reflections that I hope will encourage you personally as well as professionally in your efforts.

It seems to me that to succeed in our efforts we need to have some of the same attributes that students must have. In particular, we must be motivated, committed, and self-efficacious, because the task of promoting college students' achievement, persistence, and development is almost as demanding as actually achieving, persisting, and developing in college.

Concerning motivation, I encourage you to remain true to what motivated you to enter this profession in the first place. More than likely you entered the field of education because you cared about students and wanted to help them maximize their college experience. In essence, you entered this profession because you loved students, wanted to make a difference in their lives, and believed that through achieving in college they could actualize their potential; and perhaps you wanted to help students overcome some of the difficulties that impeded your own achievement and development. Sources of motivation such as these are not only adequate for the task we confront, but they are the best sources of motivation because they combine our own needs with our desires to make a positive contribution to the lives of students.

I seldom find that fellow professionals have difficulty being motivated to promote students' achievement, persistence, and development. But we do have difficulty maintaining the level of commitment that we need to work effectively. The frustrations of the job, competing institutional priorities, and devaluing experiences with faculty, staff, and administrators distract us from the motivations that originally caused us to enter this profession. Because of these distractions, we may have difficulty making and maintaining the commitments necessary to promoting students' achievement, persistence, and development.

To counter the distractions that tend to reduce my commitment to promoting students' achievement, persistence, and development, I have found it helpful to formulate my own personal mission. I have spent many hours thinking about what I really want to accomplish. I have written, rewritten, and revised my mission many times so that each word captures my deepest desires, what I value most, and the kind of person I most want to be. Having formulated a personally meaningful mission, I now have a means of refocusing my efforts when I become distracted by frustrations and devaluing experiences. And because my mission is so personally meaningful and directly extends from my motivations, I become reenergized and recommitted to fulfill my mission each time I reverbalize it to myself or others. This is my mission:

> I want to be a person who encourages others to come to new, more positive conclusions about themselves as learners, changers, and compassionate relaters. And in the process, I want to help people discover the source of power and aliveness that only comes by being true to the deepest core of one's being.

If you haven't taken the time to set forth your personal mission, I encourage you to do so. It is the best means I know for keeping oneself focused and committed in the midst of the many distractions that threaten to confound our efforts.

Finally, there is the matter of our self-efficacy. Personally, building my own self-efficacy has been a life-long struggle. I have had to confront self doubts, feelings of inadequacy, and feelings of inferiority on a daily basis throughout my life. However, I have discovered three strategies that help me feel more self-efficacious. First, I become more self-efficacious when I stop comparing myself to other people. My natural tendency is to compare myself to others; but when I do, I become depressed, inefficacious, and inactive. Second, I become more self-efficacious when I focus my attention on my personal mission. Focusing on my mission makes me more self-efficacious in much the same way that focusing on something that is vitally important to say helps me overcome stage fright. In other words, when the *message* is more important than the *messenger,* anxiety subsides. Similarly, when one has a personally important mission, and that mission is more important than personal recognition, one becomes more self-efficacious and determined to do the things that will accomplish that mission. Finally, I become more self-efficacious when I focus on what I have control over versus what I have no control over. My natural tendency is to focus on what I can't control, but this focus makes me feel helpless and immobilizes me. When I focus on what I can do, however, and particularly when I focus on what I can do to live out my mission, I become more self-efficacious and swing into action with vigor.

Now I feel finished. I have communicated my thoughts and experience in the best way I know. I have been true to my personal mission, and I sincerely hope that I have in some ways encouraged you. I have put forth the question that I believe holds the only real hope for guiding us to the creative solutions that we must find in order to help students develop and achieve to their fullest potential. The challenge, therefore, confronting us is whether we have enough love and enough courage to truly address the question: What would we do if we really loved the students?

REFERENCES

Anderson, E. C. (1985). Forces influencing student persistence and achievement. In L. Noel, R. S. Levitz, & D. Saluri (Eds.), *Increasing student retention* (pp. 44–61). San Francisco: Jossey-Bass.

Bandura, A. (1982). Self-efficacy mechanism in human agency. *American Psychologist, 37,* 122–147.

Maslow, A. H. (1954). *Motivation and personality.* New York: Harper & Row.

Tinto, V. (1975). Dropout from higher education: A theoretical synthesis of recent research. *Review of Educational Research, 45,* 89–125.

PART IV

Psychological Interventions and Educational Leadership Strategies

12

Critical Leadership Mandates in Mainly Black Schools: Implications for School Performance and Achievement

HUGH J. SCOTT

Notwithstanding proclamations to the contrary, public education in America does not provide equal educational opportunity for all. Most Black Americans have neither experienced equal educational opportunity nor been the beneficiaries of a quality education (National Alliance of Black School Educators [NABSE], 1984). Schools in America operate in a manner that reflects a belief among many Americans that certain groups and social classes deserve better treatment than others (Oakes, 1985). In this nation, class and race are highly correlated, with Blacks and Hispanics tending to occupy the lower levels of the stratification systems in school and society (Sexton, 1967). The public schools not only reflect but perpetuate the inequities that exist among groups in the social structure (United States Department of Health, Education, and Welfare [HEW], 1972). Black students in both society and the schools are doubly disadvantaged by both race and low income (Brookover, 1985). Race and social class remain the chief determinants of success or failure in the public schools.

Most of the nearly 7 million Black students enrolled in the nation's elementary and secondary schools attend schools that are mainly minority in enrollment and located in the large cities. It has been projected that by the year 2000, one out of every three students in the public schools will be non-White. The multiple problems of large urban cities have brought about increased problems for urban school systems (Johnson, Collins, Dupuis, & Johansen, 1979). The challenges to public education in this democracy are enormous, and they are the most demanding and complex in the schools of the urban centers. The public schools in the urban centers serve large concentrations of students who are the most adverse victims of racial and socioeconomic discrimination and deprivation. For the most damaged victims of environmental supports that fall far short of meeting minimal standards of decency, humaneness, and justice, the public schools in the urban centers represent the most pronounced deficiencies of public education and the teaching profession. Urban education has come to be synonymous with the education of Blacks and other disadvantaged minorities and carries with it the connotation of failure.

To a large extent, public education for Black students remains separate and unequal (College Entrance Examination Board, 1985). The National Alliance of Black School Educators (NABSE, 1984) declared that public education for the masses of Black Americans still fails to meet even goals of adequacy not to mention excellence. In *Equality and Excellence,* it was reported that a number of indicators suggest that Black students, on the average, receive educational programs and offerings that differ in kind and content from those for White students (College Entrance Examination Board, 1985). The differences significantly influence educational achievement and later educational and career options. Pink (1984) asserts that the creation of more effective schools for students from low-income families will require fundamental changes in the ways schools evaluate, sort, label, and process students. He notes that schools routinely and systematically sort students into two different career lines: a success pathway and a failure pathway. Spring (1978) identified tracking and ability grouping of students as a means to duplicate their status in the social structure as one of the major criticisms of public schools.

Cole (1987) declared that quality education is denied to Black students by indifferent and insensitive teachers and administrators who have low expectations for Black students. Educators too often believe that the children of the poor and minority groups will either fail or have a difficult time in school (Spring, 1978). Edmonds (1979) concluded that effective schools for Black students were in short supply and that effective school systems for Black students were nonexistent.

Arguably, it may be noble but unrealistic to expect the schools for the most ravaged victims of discrimination and deprivation to produce performance results that are comparable to those produced for students from more favorable socioeconomic circumstances. Indeed, public education will be the most productive when environmental supports for both living and learning are mutually supportive. But Black students from disadvantaged socioeconomic environments can succeed in school when better teaching methods are used (Becker, 1977; Edmonds, 1979). Large numbers of Black students suffer academic deficiencies that stem, in no small measure, from poor schooling, and from inept, incompetent, and insensitive teachers and administrators. "Good" teaching and "effective" educational leadership can save large numbers of Black students from 12 or 13 years of inconsequential public education. The professional credibility of the teaching profession is severely compromised by the unacceptable reality that the public schools across this nation annually graduate high percentages of Black students whose cumulative deficiencies in reading, writing, and computational skills classify them as functional illiterates.

Leadership in Mainly Black Schools

The effectiveness of any system or organization is dependent on the quality of its leadership. Katz and Kahn (1978) identified three major components of leadership: (a) an attribute of an office or position; (b) characteristics of a person; and (c) a category of actual behavior. While authority may ultimately reside in the group, it needs a leader to help it take form and direction in goals and commitment to action (Gutherie & Reed, 1986). Merely holding an administrative position does not make one a leader (Gardner, 1986). Leadership causes individuals and groups to perform in a manner that maximizes their contributions to the achievement of the objectives of an organization (Presidents Association, 1971). Leadership is that quality that enables an individual within a setting to motivate and inspire others to adopt, achieve, and maintain organizational and individual goals (Gutherie & Reed, 1986). It is the leader who is given authority to take action, to require and receive performance of actions by others, and to direct and give decisions to others.

Members of a profession are concerned with an identified area of need or function, that is, maintenance of physical or emotional health, preservation of rights and freedom, enhancing the opportunity to learn (Howsam, Corrigan, Denmark, & Nash, 1976). In contrast to other occupations, members of a profession are expected to subordinate their own interests and to act in the best interests of their clients (Hoy & Miskel, 1987). Members of a profession should be expected to demonstrate conclusive evidence of professionalism in the discharge of their duties and responsibilities. Professionalism is the satisfactory adherence to a generally accepted set of explicit and implicit principles that govern the formulation of goals and accepted standards in the implementation of goals (Scott, 1975).

The school is physically located in the community, and its most intimate attachments to the society are or should be there (Sexton, 1967). The local school is the educational universe for most parents, and the principal is the central figure in that universe. It is the principal who must require teachers to do specific things in accordance with specific plans in response to certain timetables. It is the principal who must determine whether the performance of individual teachers is functional or dysfunctional. Effective schools do not evolve from osmosis. Effective schools are characterized by effective leadership (Edmonds, 1979). The public in the formulation of its judgments about the schools is influenced by the character and quality of those who administer the schools. While it is possible to have an effective school without an effective principal at the helm, the odds are heavily against such a consequence. Good leadership, like any other healthy organizational dynamics, enhances the possibilities of institutional policies being successfully implemented.

While definitions of what constitutes an effective school vary, particularly effective schools for children from low-income families, the correlate that effective schools have effective principals is consistent throughout the research on effective schools. The principal, at his or her best, is the architect in the development of an effective school. Paradoxically, the principal at his or her worst, is the demolisher of the productive efforts of the instructional staff. The ineffective principal is fully capable of depressing the otherwise creative, energetic, and productive behavior of teachers. On the other hand, the effective principal is capable of raising the performance standards of teachers to levels of instructional effectiveness that they might not have perceived as attainable (Edmonds, 1979).

Many principals will continue to do, if permitted, what they do often and best: prioritize the purely administrative details with limited and often ineffective excursions into overseeing individual student progress, evaluating program efficiency and effectiveness, and promoting staff development. Effective principals probably have many traits in common, but they come in many styles and diverse personalities. They vary in their race, sex, religion, and politics. But effective principals can be identified as exhibiting many of the following characteristics of educational leadership:

1. Exhibits strong curricular leadership through an achievement-oriented style while using the democratic process to incorporate teachers, students, and parent input.
2. Sets specific instructional goals and expectations with staff in reaching the goals and expectations.
3. Assumes responsibility for instructional efficiency within the school.
4. Demonstrates a legitimate concern for students that is translated into an operational climate conducive to learning and teaching.
5. Establishes an educational plan that gives preeminent emphasis to the improvement of teaching and learning.
6. Stresses a continuous program of professional development for members of the staff.
7. Knows the characteristics of all students, particularly those from low-income families and those who are from different cultures.
8. Possesses broad knowledge of the pedagogical skills, behaviors, attitudes, and values needed for successful teaching.
9. Develops with the staff a means of measuring the effectiveness of the school's program.
10. Works cooperatively with the community and demonstrates to the community that its participation is wanted and needed.

The enormity of the challenges that confront educational administrators in mainly Black schools command that they be our finest. Educational administration in mainly Black schools is no place for the "faint of heart" or for those educators who simply have their "hearts in the right place."

Psychological and Psychoeducational Variables

The behavior and performance of students in the schools are a consequence of not only what happens in the school but also what happens outside the school. Environmental factors can have an unfavorable as well as favorable impact on the intellectual development of children. The growth and development of individuals are influenced by the interaction between the person and the physical and social environments. Environmental conditions may thwart an individual's purposes and inhibit the satisfaction of his or her natural drives, and may often lead to an inadequate approach to his or her outer and inner worlds. Sometimes students miss an important learning experience because the environment failed to provide it, and some students may end up in environments that will never provide the necessary experiences (Dworetzky, 1987). The influence of the school cannot be separated from that of the student's social background and vice versa (HEW, 1972).

Most children learn easily and naturally when environmental conditions facilitate rather than impede growth and development. The maturation of an individual's potentialities is strongly affected by the effects of variables in his or her social, economic, and political environments, which serve as depressants. This is not to say that the existence of depressive factors in a child's environment present an insurmountable circumstance to educators. But it does necessitate that educators identify and confront such factors if they are to be eliminated or rectified.

A normal child is defined as one who is born with the appropriate distribution of those critical innate potentialities essential for effective participation in our society. Inherent or generic differences in intelligence between races have not been established (Sexton, 1967). No group in the United States or in any other nation finds itself lacking in innate capacities solely or primarily on the bases of race, color, or socioeconomic status. The overwhelming majority of Black Americans have been forced by society into disadvantaged environmental settings. Thus, the Black child in such environments is not disadvantaged because of any shortcomings in his or her intellectual capacities but rather because growth and development occur in disadvantaged socioeconomic environments that impose major impediments to growth and development.

Many educators believe that the problems confronting mainly

Black schools are derivatives of the problems that Black students bring to the schools. Certainly, schools do not exist independent of, or are unaffected by, the society and communities that they serve. Some of the environmental variables that exert a negative influence on the nature and effectiveness of education in mainly Black schools can neither be shaped nor controlled solely or primarily by the efforts of educators. Yet, there are variables in the nonschool environments of Black students that, though strongly subjected to powers outside of the schools, can still be made more conducive to living and learning by the professional intervention of educators. The problems of mainly Black schools should be approached in the context of the inseparability of critical variables that are both within and outside the authority of teachers and administrators. With regard to variables within the school setting that affect the overall instructional programs and their effectiveness, educators can take steps to improve measurably the instructional practices and academic performance in mainly Black schools.

There are no agnostics among the ranks of those whose decisions shape the kind and substance of education accorded to Black students. The educational administrator's behavior in a school system is not simply a function of formal expectations, individual needs, and organizational goals; he or she brings to the school a host of unique attributes, sentiments, values, needs, and motives (Hoy & Miskel, 1986). The decisions rendered by educational administrators are influenced by their sociological values and their understandings of the problems and needs faced by students in their pursuit of life, liberty, and happiness. Educational strategies are derived from the pervasive social beliefs and principal educational assumptions of those who exercise power in the determination of permissible policies and practices. Sizemore (1985) asserts that when educational administrators in mainly Black schools truly believe in the ability of Black students to learn in spite of the exigencies of racism and poverty, they form high expectations and develop effective educational programs and practices. Unfortunately, too many decision makers in mainly Black schools do not believe that Black parents and their children are deserving of respect, goodwill, and equality.

From the numerous variables that bear on the psychosocial and psychoeducational development of Black students, ten variables are presented as examples of factors that impact negatively on the life chances and the education of Black students. Each of these ten variables is presented with capsule commentary and a companion recommendation. It is conceded that the influence of leadership, as provided by educational administrators in mainly Black schools, on the ten variables ranges in its positive consequences from significant to tangential. The point of emphasis is that these 10 variables, as well as other variables, require the active rather than passive response from educational administrators. Black parents and their children should be convinced that those who direct the education of Black students are effective advocates for the unfortunate victims of an uncaring society (Green, 1973).

History, Culture, and Schools

Black Americans share values, behavioral patterns, and other cultural elements that spring from the Black experience and that distinguish Black Americans from others in the larger population (Billingsley, 1974; Banks, 1977). Clarke (1972) noted that history tells people where they have been and what they have been, and most important, an understanding of history tells people where they still must go and what they still must be. Schools promote the idea that the "Americanism" of middle-class White Americans is preferred and superior to any other culturally different background (Menacker & Pollack, 1974).

Ignorance and disrespect for Black history and culture breed low expectations and unhealthy educator assessments of Black students (NABSE, 1984). Harding (1973) cautioned that no educator should be permitted to ignore that the acquisition of knowledge and the affirmation of self are the beginnings of the long battle against the systems that have created the domination of Blacks. In the struggle to become a more viable, functioning group in a society in which power and influence are the guardians of life, liberty, and happiness, Black Americans must be keenly aware of their common history and their common predicament as Black people. Black students need to gain a knowledge of and a pride in their own history and culture in order that they can go on to discover that at the core of every distinct culture are the common imperatives of all humankind (Davis, cited in Hentoff, 1966).

Recommendation: In the overall efforts to improve the life chances and the educational lot of Black Americans, the reclamation and restoration of Black history, and recognition of and respect for the rich culture of Black Americans, must be priorities that are equal in importance to all others.

Black/White Confrontation

America is two societies, one Black, the other White, separate but unequal. The protests from Black Americans for freedom, equality, and self-determination have been directed at every major social, political, and economic institution in our society. Black consciousness has served to provide Black Americans with a rediscovered sense of dignity and self-respect. Black consciousness is Black Americans demonstrating a host of manifestations of a positive sense of their African-American identity and is the motivational force undergirding their efforts to rise above the social, political, economic, and educational constraints imposed by society. LeMelle (1967) noted that the legitimacy and maximization of a group's values and interests are a function of that group's power to deal effectively in its own behalf. While many White Americans may view the contemporary thrusts of Black consciousness as threatening, the attempts to alter elements of the social structure to produce equality of opportunity for all members of that structure are valid since no logical or empirical set of propositions can be advanced for legitimate denial of such equality (Nelson, 1965).

Recommendation: Educational administrators in mainly Black schools should demonstrate an identification with Black-directed endeavors to resolve the problems and needs of Black Americans in a racist society and should be committed to collaborative efforts to effect the elimination of, and rectify the effects of, racism in education, as well as develop educational systems that build positive and realistic self-evaluations among Black students.

School–Community Relations

Public education was never meant to be a professional monopoly. Citizens in a community hold the status of part owners of the schools (Kindred, Bagin, & Gallagher, 1984). Schools in the United States are supposed to be community affairs. (Garcia, 1983). The interdependence of school and community necessitates that each appropriately adjusts to the other in order to maximize the possibilities for the achievement of the best possible educational environment for each student. The development of sound and constructive relationships between school and community is a necessary and natural function of a publicly supported institution in a democratic society (Kindred, Bagin, & Gallagher, 1984). The citizens of the school's community should be provided information about the schools, and they should have access to pertinent facts and ideas and be permitted to discuss such among themselves and with those who administer the schools.

The distribution of Black Americans in the governance and management of public education for Black students is unrepresentative of either the high percentage of Black students in many large urban school districts or the significant number of Black Americans who reside in communities that such districts serve. Black Americans are demanding more than just a reexamination of the educational process; they are seeking to restructure the racial composition of the base of power that dictates and regulates those educational policies, programs, and practices that affect Black students.

Recommendation: Each mainly Black school should be required to establish a viable representative structure for community participation in the process of policy and program planning and implementation with the community representatives having clear and direct access to the decision-making processes.

School Desegregation

More than three decades of school desegregation have produced neither genuine racial desegregation of public education nor the extension of equal educational opportunity to the majority of Black students (Scott, 1983). Historically, the pursuit of racial balance has been the dominant feature of school desegregation since the *Brown* decision in 1954. Racial balance remedies concentrated primarily or exclusively on the reassignment of students; they gave scant attention to the inclusion of intervention components to foster improvement in the educational lot of Black students. Much greater attention needs to be directed to making *Brown* an instrument for providing effective schooling in mainly Black schools.

Black parents do not share the eagerness of most policy makers to have their children bused from familiar, friendly, supportive environments into what often can be unfriendly and hostile environments (Bell, 1972). Black parents are more interested in good, sound education for their children than they are in the need to balance themselves racially with others. The imposition of desegregation remedies that ignore the diversity among cities deprecate "Blackness," impose inequitable burdens on Black students and their parents, give scant attention to the educational essentials of equal educational opportunity, ignore the importance of Black history and culture, and/or deny Black parents some choice are not only nonproductive but are a denial of equal educational opportunity.

Recommendation: Leadership in mainly Black schools and in civil rights organizations should be advocates for school desegregation strategies that respond to the following factors:

1. The preeminent emphasis is directed to the improvement of teaching and learning.
2. The right of choice when busing is proposed is accorded to Black parents.
3. The burdens of required disruptions and dislocations are distributed equitably among all students.
4. The study of Black history and culture is incorporated into the regular curricula of all schools.
5. The policy that either White or Black students can serve as the minority student population is established.
6. A systemwide evaluation program directed to the determination of the effectiveness of instructional programs and practices is established.
7. Resources are allocated in direct relationship to the severity of the needs of students.

Collective Bargaining

The intensified push for the accountability of educators is generated, in part, by the beliefs among lay persons that collective bargaining for educators has produced more prerequisites and privileges than improved pedagogy and professionalism. The organized teaching profession has not revealed a willingness to put its self-interests secondary to such noble objectives as equal educational opportunity and quality education. The proposition that collective bargaining is good for students has its origin in politics not in education (Lieberman, 1979). As educators have become more "unionized," their relationships among themselves and with parents have become more adversarial.

Staub (1981) asserts that collective bargaining is dangerous to the health of public education. Lieberman (1981) charges that collective bargaining has produced excessive protection for incompetents. The National School Boards Association established a task force to study alternatives to collective bargaining because collective bargaining was perceived as adversarial and as impeding school reform. Collective bargaining, as it has evolved, constitutes an improper sharing of public authority with a private-interest organization (Lieberman, 1981).

Recommendation: Educational administrators in mainly Black schools should join with appropriate lay organizations in seeking the phasing-out of collective bargaining for teachers and administrators with the basic relationship of educators to the schools to be determined by the same political and policy-making processes that exist to consider, formulate, and modify public policies outside the bargaining arena.

School Climate

Schools that pursue education as a process primarily for dispensing information and for the weeding out of slow achievers contribute to the high drop-out rate among Black students. Merely attending schools, either as a right or a duty, is without meaning unless students can be guaranteed some measure of success (Squires, 1968). Very often schools are not places where individuals and groups of students can reflectively examine problems, frustrations, aspirations, proposals, and values. Schools should be open, honest, flexible, permissive, relevant, dynamic, human, and human laboratories that help students to become increasingly autonomous, self-directing, self-actualizing individuals capable of identifying and pursuing their own aims within a living societal order (Meussig, 1969).

Educators should be appreciative of and adaptable to the acquired experiential backgrounds that Black students bring with them to the classroom. Most Black children represent a peculiar set of ethnic traditions (Henderson & Washington, 1975). Schools need to accommodate and capitalize on the life-styles of Black children by adopting a multicultural base and by changing those procedures and assumptions that are antithetical to that concept (LaBelle, 1974).

Recommendation: Teachers and administrators in mainly Black schools should be required to attend in-service training programs geared toward helping them come to terms with their own behavior and attitudes toward students from different cultures, ethnic, racial, and social backgrounds.

School Discipline

Discipline is not the major task of education but a necessary function of teaching (Doyle, 1980). Discipline is the ability and will to do what needs doing for as long as it needs doing and to learn from the results (Wayson & Pinnell, 1982). The classroom teacher's performance has a profound influence on the nature of discipline in the schools (NABSE, 1984). Discipline problems, more often than not, can be traced to dysfunctions in the interpersonal climate and organizational pattern of the school than to malfunctions in the individual students. The percentage of well-behaved Black students is probably much greater than the percentage of educators in mainly Black schools who believe that Black students should not be placed in restrictive schools that seek to make them complacent and compliant individuals who will not challenge the status quo. Skilled, sensitive, and experienced teachers adjust to the multiple demands of a complex instructional environment. Motivation deserves greater emphasis as a means of promoting learning and preventing misbehavior. In mainly Black schools, just as it is true in other schools, educators must give respect if they want to receive it.

Recommendation: Educators in mainly Black schools should have a commitment to teaching alternate behavior as the aim of discipline rather than simply punishing bad or poor behavior, and should provide Black students with ample opportunities for leadership experience and a voice in making educational decisions in order that Black students may develop a sense of ownership and a sense of responsibility for what takes place in the school.

Testing

There is no completely acceptable rationale for grading the performance of students in reference to commonly applied standards of expected performance for a heterogeneous school population (Scott, 1973). Educators have accorded tests higher regard than their history warrants (Bond, 1986). Testing continues to be used as the major means of identifying the weak from the strong and exerts an undue influence on the determination of course content, performance expectations, and the success or failure of students (Scott, 1979). NABSE (1984) declared that virtually all tests fail to meet the rigorous standards of psychometric science and that standardized tests, more often than not, have been the instruments of politics rather than science. Schools have led the way in using tests to justify discriminating against the poor and minorities (Brookover, 1985).

Traditional tests lack diagnostic and prescriptive validity (Bond, 1986). Some tests do not effectively measure what they purport to measure, and some tests are used to measure factors well beyond their design and intent. The tests that are the most detrimental and culturally biased are those that are geared to the sorting and labeling of students, that limit exposure and interaction among students with different labels, and that narrow the social and occupational options open to student upon completion of school (McClung, 1973).

Recommendation: The use of standardized achievement and competency tests should be drastically curtailed with resources diverted to the development and use of more subtle, sensitive, educationally useful forms of assessment with the need for comparative data being met in ways that do not carry such massive human and individual costs.

Instructional Approaches

Kohl (1983) asserts that there is no practice of pedagogy in classrooms. Teachers do not possess a common body of validated knowledge that is transmitted in the process of professionalism, held in common with other teachers thereafter, and constantly increased through the career span of the teacher (Howsam et al., 1976). Goodlad (1984) concluded that teachers rarely establish conditions for active student learning and are overly reliant on repetitive instructional activities that foster passive student behavior. Schools do poorly in teaching higher-order skills, and students need greater opportunities to write at length and to discuss inferences of what they read (College Entrance Examination Board, 1977). Teachers need to increase the individualization of student work, whether it be in verbal instruction or in the tasks and material students are given (Goodlad, 1984). Poor classroom management and organization reduces the amount of time directed to learning (Education Commission of the States, 1983). Instructional approaches in many schools create conditions that increase the difficulty of eliminating disadvantages rather than creating circumstances that minimize and compensate for initial disadvantages in learning (Goodlad, 1984).

There is no one instructional approach that will serve every case (Wang, 1986). The major challenge in schools is not to figure out the ideal program of instruction and then impose it on all students but rather it is to create a learning environment in which all students can pursue learning according to their own style, pace, and aspiration. Instructional approaches that place the reason for failure on Black students rather than on the approaches that failed them should be categorically rejected (NABSE, 1984).

Recommendation: Black students should be provided instructional approaches that provide pedagogically sound instruction in reading, writing, mathematics, and the process of logical thought; this instruction should be accomplished with increased attention on innovations in the affective domain to temper the tendency to place an inordinate concern on information and cognitive skills, with the objective being to produce an overall rationale for instruction that capitalizes on the best of the affective and cognitive domains.

Instructional Materials

Ours is a pluralistic society, but the textbooks and other instructional materials used in the schools do not adequately reflect this reality (Cole, 1987). Racial bias in instructional materials remains a monumental and pervasive problem (Simms, 1978). Much of what is officially approved for use as instructional materials in mainly Black schools under the mandate of compulsory schooling is unrealistic, undemocratic, and uninspiring (Britton & Lumpkin, 1983).

Textbooks and other instructional materials constitute highly consequential elements in the total educational environment. The written word has always been used to convey concepts and values as well as beliefs and attitudes from one person to another and from one generation to another. Images communicated overtly and subliminally in mainly Black schools through approved instructional materials have severely limited options for people of color and for females of all races (Britton & Lumpkin, 1983). Historians, with few exceptions, have never dealt properly with Black Americans (Butterield, 1968). The study of Black Americans in American history has been neglected and not appropriately influenced by scholarship.

Recommendation: Decision makers in mainly Black school systems should unite in a collaborative effort to commission respected scholars and educators to develop textbooks and other instructional materials that are free from racial, ethnic, and sexual biases, and that correct distortions and counteract the invisibility of Black Americans in textbooks and other related materials.

Conclusion

For more than a decade, school improvement programs that draw their content direction largely from the effective schools and effective teaching research have been the most significant efforts to improve the effectiveness of schools heavily populated with Black children from low-income families. School improvement programs launched under the banner of Effective Schools Research (ESR) adopted their process direction from three interdependent bodies of related research: effective staff development, effective organizational development in education, and effective planned change (State Education Department, 1987). Most school effectiveness studies over the past decade have focused on the delineation of effectiveness characteristics in schools that are instructionally effective for students from low-income families. Edmonds (1979) and his colleagues identified the following effectiveness characteristics in schools that were assessed as instructionally effective for poor and minority children: (a) administrative leadership; (b) climate of expectations for children; (c) orderly but not rigid school atmosphere; (d) continuity in the curriculum and commitment to acquisition of basic skills; and (e) frequently monitored student progress.

The research on effective schools places the leadership of the principal as the effectiveness characteristic that sustains its relevancy most consistently. Weber (1971) saw strong leadership in a principal who was instrumental in setting the tone of the school, helping with decision making on instructional strategies, and organizing and distributing the school's resources. Edmonds (1979) declared that one of the most intangible and indispensable characteristics of effective schools was strong administrative leadership without which the disparate elements of good schools could neither be brought together nor kept together. Sizemore (1985) identified leadership in the form of a "take-charge" person who develops routines that lead toward assumption of responsibilities, which further the means to the goal. Love (1987) noted that leadership style, while a popular subject, is not as important as leadership function. What counts is what is done to facilitate teaching and learning (Love, 1987).

Mainly Black schools desperately need educational leaders who administer schools where excellence is expected of Black students and where Black students are empowered academically, culturally, psychologically, and politically (Smith, 1986). Teachers and administrators in mainly Black schools have not made appropriate use of pedagogically sound and proven instructional methods and materials. Lawler (1978) was correct when he noted that a truly scientific pedagogy locates the obstacles to learning in the practical environments of students, both in and out of the school. In a society in which the talents of Black students are often wasted and destroyed, Lawler declared that educators should approach education with an outrage at the injustices committed and with a determination to fight for the educational rights of parents and their children.

REFERENCES

Banks, J. A. (1977). The implications of multicultural education for teacher education. In F. H. Klassen & D. M. Gollnick (Eds.), *Pluralism and the American teacher* (pp. 1–29). Washington, DC: American Association of Colleges for Teacher Education.

Becker, W. C. (1977). Teaching reading and language to the disadvantaged—What we have learned from research. *Harvard Educational Review, 47*(4), 518–544.

Bell, D. A., Jr. (1972). *Trends in school desegregation law.* Denver: National Association of State School Boards of Education and the Council of Chief State School Officers.

Billingsley, A. (1974). *Black families and the struggle for survival.* New York: Friendship Press.

Bond, L. (1986). On new horizons in testing. In *Learning research development center: A twentieth anniversary profile* (pp. 21–24). Pittsburg: University of Pittsburg.

Britton, G., & Lumpkin, M. (1983). Interracial books for children. *Bulletin, XIV*(6), 4–7.

Brookover, W. B. (1985). Can we make schools more effective for minority students? *Journal of Negro Education, 54*(3), 257–268.

Butterfield, R. (1968). Search for a Black path. *Life, 65*(21), 90–123.

Clarke, J. H. (1972). *Struggle is the highest form of education.* Paper presented at the Martin Luther King, Jr. memorial forum at Bank Street College, New York City.

Cole, B. P. (1987). The state of education for Black Americans. In E. Stevens & G. H. Woods (Eds.), *Justice, ideology, and education* (pp. 443–453). New York: Random House.

College Entrance Examined Board. (1977). *Report of the advisory panel on the Scholastic Aptitude Test scores decline.* New York: Author.

College Entrance Examination Board. (1985). *Equality and excellence: The educational status of Black Americans.* New York: Author.

Doyle, W. (1980). Classroom management. *Kappa Delta Pi*, pp. 2–31.

Dworetzky, J. P. (1987). *Introduction to child development.* St. Paul: West Publishing.

Edmonds, R. (1979). Effective schools for the urban poor. *Educational Leadership, 37*, 15–24.

Education Commission of the States (1983). *Action for excellence: A comprehensive plan to improve our nation's schools.* Denver: Author.

Garcia, R. L. (1983). Residual racism in the classroom: Promises and prognoses. *Centerboard, I*(2), 17–21.

Gardner, J. W. (1986). *The nature of leadership: Introductory considerations.* Washington, DC: Independent Sector.

Goodlad, J. I. (1984). *A place called school: Prospects for the future.* New York: McGraw-Hill.

Green, R. L. (1973, November 24). *Significant and unique problems facing Blacks in American education.* Speech delivered to the National Alliance of Black School Educators, Detroit, MI.

Gutherie, J. W., & Reed, R. J. (1986). *Educational administration and policy.* Englewood Cliffs, NJ: Prentice-Hall.

Harding, V. (1973). Black reflections on the cultural ramifications of identity. In M. D. Stent, W. R. Hazard, & H. N. Rivlin (Eds.), *Cultural pluralism in education: A mandate for change* (pp. 103–115). New York: Appleton-Century-Crofts.

Henderson, D. H., & Washington, A. G. (1975, Summer) Cultural differences and the education of Black children: An alterate model for program development. *Journal of Negro Education, 44*(3), 353–360.

Hentoff, N. (1966). *Our children are dying.* New York: Viking.

Howsam, R. B., Corrigan, D. C., Denmark, G. W., & Nash, R. J. (1976). *Educating a profession.* Washington, DC: American Association of Colleges for Teacher Education.

Hoy, W. K., & Miskel, C. G. (1987). *Educational administration: Theory, research, and practice.* New York: Random House.

Johnson, J. A., Collins, H. W., Dupuis, V. L., & Johansen, J. H. (1979). *Introduction to the foundations of American education* (4th ed.). Boston: Allyn & Bacon.

Katz, D., & Kahn, R. (1978). *The social psychology of organization* (2nd ed.). New York: John Wiley.

Kindred, L. W., Bagin, D., & Gallagher, D. R. (1984). *The school and community relations* (3rd ed.). Englewood Cliffs, NJ: Prentice-Hall.

Kohl, H. (1983). Why teachers must return to pedagogy. *Learning, 12*, 28–30.

LaBelle, T. J. (1974). What's deprived about being different? In J. Menacker & E.

Pollack (Eds.), *Emerging educational issues: Conflicts and contrasts* (pp. 173–177). Boston: Little, Brown.

Lawler, J. M. (1978). *IQ, heritability, and racism.* New York: International.

LeMelle, T. J. (1967). The ideology of Blackness African American style. *Africa Today, 14*(6), 2–4.

Lieberman, M. (1979). Eggs that I have laid: Teacher bargaining reconsidered. *Phi Delta Kappan, 60*(6), 415–419.

Lieberman, M. (1981). Teacher bargaining: An autopsy. *Phi Delta Kappan, 63*(4), 231–234.

Love, R. (1987). *Effective schools program.* Chicago: Ruth Love Enterprises.

McClung, M. (1973). School classification: Some legal approaches to labels. *Inequality in Education, 14,* 17–37.

Menacker, K., & Pollack, E. (Eds.) (1974). *Emerging educational issues: Conflicts and contrasts.* Boston: Little, Brown.

Meussig, R. (1969). Change—the only constant. *Educational Leadership, 26*(6), 545–546.

National Alliance of Black School Educators (1984). *Saving the African child.* Washington, DC: Author.

Nelson, H. A. (1965). A note on education and the Negro revolt. *Journal of Negro Education, 34*(1), 99–102.

Oakes, J. (1985). *Keeping track: How schools structure inequality.* New Haven: Yale University Press.

Pink, W. (Fall, 1984). Creating effective schools. *Educational Forum, 49*(1), 91–105.

Presidents Association (1971). *Management of the educational enterprise* (Program manual for the 1971 institute for chief state school officers). San Diego, CA: American Management Association.

Scott, H. J. (1973). Reflections on issues and conditions related to public education for Black students. *Journal of Negro Education, 44*(3), 414–426.

Scott, H. J. (1975). Black consciousness and professionalism. *Journal of Negro Education, 47*(3), 432–440.

Scott, H. J. (1979). *Minimum competency testing: The newest obstruction to the education of Black and other disadvantaged Americans.* Princeton, NJ: Educational Testing Service.

Scott, H. J. (1983). Beyond racial balance remedies: School desegregation for the 1980s. *New York University Education Quarterly, 14*(2), 13–21.

Sexton, P. C. (1967). *The American school.* New Jersey: Prentice-Hall.

Simms, R. L. (1978). Correcting textbook bias: An approach that works. *Clearinghouse, 51*(9), 426–427.

Sizemore, B. A. (1985). Pitfalls and promises of effective schools research. *Journal of Negro Education, 54*(3), 269–288.

Smith, D. H. (1986, November 19–25). Educational reform is imperative. *The City Sun,* 19.

Spring, J. (1978). *American education.* New York: Longman.

Squires, R. (1968). Do students have civil rights? *PTA Magazine, 63,* 2–4.

State Education Department (1987). *Sharing a shared vision of school improvement.* Albany: University of the State of New York.

Staub, S. E. (1981). Compiling unionization and the demise of education. *Phi Delta Kappan, 63*(4), 235.

United States Department of Health, Education, & Welfare (1972). *A study of the nation's schools.* Washington, DC: Author.

Wang, M. C. (1986). On research for adaptive school practices. In *Learning research and development center, A twentieth century profile* (pp. 84–86). Pittsburgh: University of Pittsburgh.

Wayson, W. W., & Pinnell, G. S. (1982). Creating a living curriculum for teaching self-discipline. In D. L. Duke (Ed.), *Helping teachers manage classrooms* (pp. 115–136). Washington, DC: Association for Supervision and Curriculum Development.

Weber, G. (1971). *Inner city children can be taught to read: For successful schools* (Occasional paper No. 18). Washington, DC: Council for Basic Education.

13

The School Development Program: A Psychosocial Model of School Intervention

JAMES P. COMER

It is estimated that only 20% of all children enjoy and thrive in the traditional school environment. I suspect that this is the case because traditional education gives primary attention to curriculum content and teaching methods; secondary attention, and often only "lip service," is given to child development, relationship, and systems management issues. Because little attention is given to the latter issues, a social context that is not conducive to learning among many is generated in most schools. When social and behavioral science and child development knowledge are used in schools, they are generally applied to individual or small groups of students rather than to the school as a social system. But there is evidence that the application of such knowledge to management and relationship processes is needed to promote adequate teaching and learning (Biber, 1961).

Children whose families function in the mainstream of society and who receive the average expected development experience before school have the best chance of succeeding in such schools. But even among those who complete high school, many survive but do not thrive in the school setting. Finishing school is an expectation of the people with whom they identify within their social network and thus they are motivated to do so. And at some point, many understand the relationship between school completion and reasonable opportunity in the world of work and related living standards. These preparatory and motivating factors often are not operating for children more marginal to the mainstream of the society or children "locked" into antisocial networks. A disproportionate number of such children are from minority groups with a traumatic social history.

School reform efforts pay almost no attention to the social history of groups and the consequences for learning (Mackenzie, 1983). For reasons of guilt, a need to avoid societal responsibilities, or whatever, the school improvement focus has been on students and their families in the here and now. Research and evaluation in education are based on current conditions, with little appreciation for the effects of past conditions on school staffs, parents, and community. Even the best educated people in our country have little knowledge about the way past social conditions have adversely affected the community and family life and developmental experiences of minority group children.

Many—social and behavioral scientists and laypersons alike—think and act from an immigrant model of adjustment in the United States, comparing minority adjustment to it without being fully aware that they are doing so. Such an analysis holds minorities alone responsible for their situation and for improving their conditions without considering the structural, political, economic, and social policies and practices that have existed over time that the entire society must address.

Existing education research probably serves to confuse the issues more than to clarify them. The paradigm that earns the academic social and behavioral scientist the greatest rewards is the experimental research design with quantifiable outcomes. But much of what it takes to create a social climate or ethos that promotes adequate development, teaching, and learning in schools cannot be measured in a quantifiable way—attitudes, values, caring, cooperation, and their degree of application and impact are difficult to measure. This is not to say that findings from epidemiology, survey, other quantitative research, and even some experimental research are not sometimes useful. But because each school setting is complex and different, the application of most research findings across settings is difficult and rarely useful. Also, schools are dynamic, interactive social systems with interdependent components that will not allow accurate assessment of any component in isolation. For example, low interest in a mathematics class using method A may be changed dramatically by an improved climate of learning or ethos in the school overall, or a more effective teacher, rather than a change to math by teaching method B.

Traditional research leads to fragmented and limited interventions of little power, incapable of significantly changing the ecology or multiple interactions of a school. The focus on bits and pieces prevents adequate attention to systemic interventions that could be more powerful. An ecological perspective would permit both systemic and component, historical, and developmental perspectives. In this chapter, a school intervention project will be described, along with the problems it presented; the child development, social, and behavioral science theoretical framework and historical perspective used to understand the causes of school dysfunction, and the need to intervene; and the dissemination method used to carry the intervention across school and school system settings.

The Intervention Setting and Outcomes

The Yale Child Study Center initiated a joint program of school improvement and preventive psychiatry with the New Haven, Connecticut school system in 1968, after an initial planning year. The project was sponsored by the Ford Foundation and federal government funds, Title I, for low-income children. The Child Study Center team was directed by the author, a child and social psychiatrist with training in public health. A social worker, psychologist, and special education teacher comprised the other members of the team. Our initial strategy was to live in two elementary schools—a subsystem of the total school system—for a year and learn about schools rather than make assumptions based on limited research findings and understandings. Then, with theory, knowledge of history, and direct observations, we worked with staff and parents to develop an intervention research approach. We would then disseminate our approach within and beyond the New Haven school system.

Our subsystem was made up of the kindergarten through fourth grade Martin Luther King Elementary School serving approximately 300 low-income, 99% Black students, and the kindergarten through sixth grade Baldwin School, serving close to 400 low-income, 99% Black students. About 70% of the students were from Aid for Dependent Children and single-parent families (Comer, 1980).

In 1969, the schools were 32nd and 33rd in achievement among 33 schools. They were 19 and 18 months behind in language arts and mathematics on the Iowa Test of Basic Skills. The attendance was among the lowest in the city. And there were very serious behavior problems among the students who attended both schools. We left Baldwin School, after five years and a much improved social climate, rather than oppose the principal and a small group of parents and teachers who wanted to return to previous ways of managing the school. In 1977, we began to work in Brennan School, a kindergarten through fifth grade school similar in population to King and Baldwin, serving a housing project.

In 1984, with no change in the socioeconomic makeup of either school, the students at King were a year above grade level in language arts and mathematics and the students at Brennan were seven months above grade level in these areas. They had the third and fourth highest achievement rankings in language arts and mathematics among the 26 elementary schools in New Haven. King School ranked first and second in attendance during five of the previous six years and the Brennan School attendance was much improved. There had been no serious behavior problems in either school since our third year of work in them. Staff turnover is low— one teacher change in more than a decade at King. A number of the parents involved in the project returned to school and have acquired "living-wage jobs"; seven that we know of went to college and are now professional people.

In 1968, the academic program was to be directed by an instructional leader from a prestigious school of education. He and a group of ten teachers he brought with him were advocates of the open classroom approach to teaching and learning. In theory, this approach addresses child development and relationship issues. It worked successfully in a number of places. But as applied in our setting, attention was given primarily to curriculum content and teaching methods. Thus, instead of using the time before school opened to plan and develop mechanisms to create a social context that would promote desirable teaching, learning, and student growth and development, we spent time using materials that were to stimulate exciting and spontaneous learning. Little time was given to trying to understand the reasons the children were underachieving, and how we would work together as a staff and with parents to help them achieve at the social and academic level of their ability.

When school opened, there was chaos in Baldwin, and King was only slightly better. Most of the teachers were young and inexperienced. At least three classrooms were totally out of control. Students were frightened, crying, wandering off, abusive of each other and staff, and acting up in a variety of other ways. Most new, young teachers are apprehensive and insecure during the first few days. But usually established policies and practices, and peer and administrative leadership permit them to work effectively, gain confidence, and gain greater competence. In our case, aside from three experienced teachers in Baldwin, the teaching experience of the balance of the staff was about one year. Much of this latter group had pushed for their version of the open classroom approach as opposed to teaching and learning within a framework of structure and planning. They were understandably defensive and insisted that there was no problem other than inadequate supplies and administration. As a result, they could not adequately respond to the crisis.

The parents had been promised a meaningful role in the management of the school program. But several key decisions had been made in opposition to their wishes. Teachers who were not asked to remain in the school criticized the project, some telling the parents that their children would be used as guinea pigs by Yale University. Some principals in nearby schools advised parents of children with problems to enroll them at Baldwin School because they had a number of child-care specialists. It was the year of Martin Luther King's assassination and Black community feelings were strong and often directed against authority figures and institutions. Some individuals and groups attempted to exploit the unrest for personal gain. The parents eventually prevented such exploitation, but ambivalent and distrustful from the beginning, they had their worst fears confirmed by the way the program was initiated.

Our Yale Child Study Center team was forced out of our "learning posture" and was forced to try to save the project. We had to respond to parental wishes and return to the more hierarchical, top-down, authoritarian organization and management style. And for the most part, the open classroom approach was abandoned. A tenuous control was established. But there was much anger, little cooperation, little learning, and many behavior problems among staff, parents, and students. We did manage to establish a building level governance and management team made up of representatives of parents, teachers, administrators, and our Child Study Center team.

Our Mental Health Team was able to help the teaching staff with a number of behavior problems, but continuous staff strife almost led to termination of the project. The potential that parents observed in the work of the representative governance and management team and the Mental Health Team probably enabled the project to survive.

Perhaps because of the conditions of the first year, we learned more about school problems than we would have in a more stable but poorly functioning school over the same period of time. We observed well-intentioned, highly motivated young teachers losing their confidence and performing below their potential, experiencing much anguish. We observed an ethos or climate that changed from high hopes to hopelessness and despair, and the effects on adults and students alike. We observed difficult parent, staff, and student interactions that simply did not occur in schools 30 years before, no matter what the quality of learning. We noted that open, inadequately managed schools were less effective than the hierarchical, authoritarian approach. We observed the direct connection between inadequate organization and management, difficult staff–parent–student relationships, and difficult student behavior.

All that we observed confirmed our suspicion that the social context of learning was being inadequately addressed in schools, which in turn created problems that made teaching difficult, regardless of the methods. The content quickly became meaningless to many students. And because many of the students were not prepared for academic learning prior to school, a difficult social context was even more troublesome for them. Most important, we realized that educators paid little to no attention to child development issues, and such issues directly affected the context of schooling. It was obvious that our intervention had to address the social context of schools.

But there were other important questions. Why were there difficult and undesirable behaviors between parents, teachers, and students of a kind and degree that did not exist 30 years before? And why were schools serving Black students adversely affected in disproportionate numbers? We felt that without an understanding of these questions it would be difficult for the staff to maintain desirable attitudes, hope, and high expectations for the students. We postulated that desirable interactions between staff, parents, and students were necessary to improve learning. It was here that we combined knowledge of child development, relationships, and history in an ecological perspective. The study of interactions—past and present, individuals and society—gave us the understanding we needed to develop an effective intervention.

Child Development, Economic Change, and Social Change

Children are born into the world totally dependent. At birth, they have only biological potentials that must be developed, and aggressive energy that must be channeled and sublimated into learning, work, and play activities or it will be destructive to themselves and to others. They are also born with the capacity to form relationships. By about 18 years of age they are expected to be able to carry out all adult tasks—to obtain advanced education or work, to live in and support a family, to find satisfaction and meaning in life, and to become responsible citizens of their social network and society. A great deal of development must take place between birth and adulthood.

Because of children's dependency, it is necessary for parents or caretakers to provide for them. In the process, an emotional attachment and bond takes place between caretaker and child. Almost from the beginning, the child learns by imitating, identifying with, and internalizing the attitudes, values, and ways of the caretaker. This interaction allows the caretaker to aid the child's growth along many developmental pathways, at least five of which are critical to academic learning: social interactional, psychoemotional, moral, speech and language, and intellectual–cognitive. Academic learning is actually a by-product of overall good preparation and development along these critical developmental pathways.

Almost all interactions enable parents to aid the development of their children: teaching greetings to friends, taking trips to the grocery store, teaching safety precautions, managing conflict with other children, reading bedtime stories, and the like. Children who have such experiences mediated by mature adults are able to present themselves to school people at five years of age as appropriately mature and able students, capable of spontaneity and curiosity at appropriate times, capable of control and investment in a task at appropriate times.

Appropriate behavior elicits a positive response from school people and, in turn, permits an attachment and bond to take place between the child, school people, and school activities similar to that made with parents. This development makes activities in school relevant and meaningful to children. These conditions make it possible for school staff, reinforced by parents, to promote adequate academic learning. Because the school is a mainstream institution, parents from mainstream social networks are usually providing their preschool children with the kind of experiences and the level of development they will need to perform adequately in school. Economic and social changes during the first half of this century raised the level of development needed to participate in the mainstream of the society.

Prior to the 1950s, the level of overall development and education needed to earn a living and carry out adult tasks was not very high. In the agricultural, and then early industrial economy, through 1900, it was possible to earn a living with no education or training, and only a moderate level was required during the heavy industrial economy age between 1900 and 1945 or 1950 (Nash, 1964). And for these reasons, only about 20% of all children finished high school prior to World War II (Synder, 1987).

Also, the small-town, rural-area nature of the United States through 1900, when even cities were collections of small towns, facilitated desirable family functioning and child development. This situation existed to a great extent through World War II. Young people less often challenged the authority of parents, school people, and other adults. The low level of transportation and communication promoted a strong sense of relatedness and community. The school was a natural part of the community. Thus, there was less acting up and acting out in school, and again, children who were not succeeding could leave.

After World War II, education became the ticket of admission to a living-wage job. Success in school, requiring a higher level of development than was ever before necessary, became a necessity. Simultaneously, the United States became a nation of metropolitan areas with high mobility. Mass communication, particularly television, became commonplace. These conditions brought children models of behavior from around the world, bypassed adult authority figures, and went directly to the young. These changes also permitted adult authority figures to live long distances from schools and other places in which they worked, increasing suspicion, distrust, and sometimes alienation between different groups of adults. All of these changes made acting up and acting out more possible in school at the very time when children needed more adult support—home and school—to reach a level of development needed to achieve in school and in a more complex society. Black, Hispanic, and Native American families were hurt most by these changes because of their more traumatic social histories.

A comparison of the Black experience with that of European and Asian immigrants will be helpful here. While the latter experienced great hardship, both groups experienced a great amount of cultural continuity. They brought with them a language, religion, and other aspects of their culture. They often moved in large numbers from the same place in the old country and lived together in the new country until they were assimilated. This led to a great deal of group cohesion. In addition, they got the vote in one generation. Because of group cohesion, they were able to get political, economic, and social power in one generation. This power created a kind of push–pull phenomenon: Opportunities in the society serve as a pull on groups, families, and individuals, and thus promote a push from within for individual and group development and academic learning.

The coming of the immigrants—1815 to 1915—paralleled the three generations of industrial change. Heads of households were able to earn a living in the agricultural and early industrial economy without an education, and with only a moderate education in the heavy industrial period up until the 1940s. This adequate family functioning made it possible for more children to acquire a high level of education and to have a reasonable opportunity to function well in the late industrial stage between 1945 and 1980, and in the postindustrial period beginning in the 1980s. Thus, these groups were able to undergo three generations of movement and development. As a result, most families among these groups have functioned within the mainstream of American society and were able to provide their children with an adequate developmental experience.

The Black, Hispanic, and Native American experiences were quite different. This discussion will be limited to the Black Experience. The Black experience was characterized by extreme cultural discontinuity with a loss of the protective and adaptive political, economic, and social institutions of West Africa (Gibbs, 1965). Slavery was a system of forced dependency in a society that highly valued independence. A slave could achieve adequacy only by pleasing the master, an inherently inferior position. Regardless of how hard they worked, there was no better future for slaves. Our present knowledge of human functioning tells us that these conditions lead to negative psychosocial consequences.

Psychosocial trauma was experienced by many, and then transmitted from generation to generation among a significant segment of the population (Comer, 1972). Religion, or the Black church, and better conditions during slavery protected many Blacks from the most severe trauma, but all were negatively affected to some degree, particularly from a racial and individual identity standpoint. The level of group cohesion was diminished. And, in addition, a large segment of the Black population did not get the vote until the 1960s. Without the vote, it was extremely difficult for the group to develop political, economic, and social power in the mainstream of the society in the very areas in which they existed in large numbers.

Without opportunity within the mainstream of the society, many of the troublesome behaviors that developed during slavery could not be extinguished. And many from well-functioning families, despite their development and education, were closed out of opportunities because of the high level of racism that was possible by Blacks being denied political and economic power. As a result, there was less of a push–pull phenomenon, although it did exist among the most successful families. But opportunity was limited to professional service areas needed to maintain racial segregation. Opportunity did not exist in business and industry in the mainstream of the society.

Because of these conditions, Blacks were denied educational opportunities in large numbers, and to an extreme degree. As late as the 1930s, four to eight times as much money was being spent on the education of a White child as that of a Black in the eight states that held 80% of the Black population (Blose & Ambrose, 1936). The disparity was as great as 25 times in areas that were disproportionately Black. The same disparity existed in higher education. In fact, as late as the mid 1960s, two prestigious White women's colleges had a combined endowment that was about one half that of Harvard, and the one half endowment of Harvard was more than that of the more than 100 Black colleges put together (Council for Financial Aid to Education, 1967).

When education became the ticket of admission to living-wage jobs in the 1950s, Blacks, undereducated in the past and working at the margins of the economy, were forced to remain there. Coupled with the loss of the supportive rural and Black church culture as a result of migration and urbanization, many families that once functioned well now functioned less well. Simultaneously, changed societal conditions requiring higher levels of social and academic development made it even more difficult for such families to function well.

A growing number of families from all backgrounds began to have more difficulty functioning well. Because of their difficult social history, a disproportionate number of such families were Black. Some of these families were simply marginal to the mainstream of the society and had somewhat different attitudes, values, and ways. Others became increasingly antisocial as a result of the stress they experienced and the distrust and alienation they felt in relationship to the mainstream. A large number of such families were not and are not now in a position to give their children the kinds of experiences that will prepare them to succeed in school and to have the best chance to succeed in life.

In many cases, they want to support their children's development but simply do not know how to do so. Such families frequently live under such stress that they are not able to provide the developmental support, even when they know how. Such children often present themselves to school people underdeveloped along the critical pathways necessary for academic success. They often lack social-interactive skills, good personal control, the ability to invest in a task, and so on.

Because the discipline of education is not driven by child development principles, most teachers and administrators are not adequately prepared to respond to such children. They generally view expressions of underdevelopment—fighting rather than negotiating, inability to share—as bad behavior and the inability to succeed at academic tasks as a lack of ability. In turn, they punish or have low expectations for such children, which often leads to a struggle for power and control between children and teachers. This struggle decreases the possibility of the kind of attachment and bonding so necessary for children to be able to imitate, identify with, and internalize the attitudes, values, and ways of school people and activities. Antagonism between home and school develops and low-level academic achievement and acting-up behavior are the results.

Even so, many such children will do reasonably well until about third grade. At that point, the academic expectations of the school become more abstract and difficult to manage for children with cognitive underdevelopment in the first place. Also, children develop the capacity to understand how they and their families are different from school people and many are forced to actually make a choice between the attitudes, values, and ways of home and those of school. And around this age, children are seeking greater independence and are less accepting of adult influence. If academic achievement has not already become an internalized value, parents and school staff are less likely to be able to help make this the case in the future.

All of these factors are at play in the education of low-income Black children. Our model is designed to take these many factors into account, build on the strengths of all involved in the education enterprise, and overcome obstacles to adequate academic achievement.

The School Development Program (SDP) Model

We did not begin our work in 1968 with the understanding described above. It emerged as we analyzed and adjusted to the conditions and behaviors in our project school, the school system, and the communities around us. We used our personal experiences and insights gained from growing up in low-income Black communities and in racially integrated schools; we also used our knowledge of adult behavior, child development and behavior, systems functioning and their impact on behavior—all within an interactional or ecological context—in order to understand the needs of all involved in the schools and to intervene in ways that best met the needs of most. In short, the mechanisms and operations of our School Development Program model are based on psychosocial and developmental needs of people and institutions created by past and present interactions or experiences.

The model that evolved is a systems-level, primary-prevention approach that addresses all aspects of a school's operation, not a particular group of individuals or any pretargeted specific aspect of a school. The school itself is viewed as a social system. Again, addressing any subsystem of the school in isolation does not provide sufficient power to bring about overall school improvement. In our process model, through a coordinated effort, all of the adults involved (and students where possible) identify problems and opportunities, prioritize needs, establish goals, mobilize resources, and develop creative program implementation approaches. The process is monitored and adjustments are made as necessary. This method creates a synergism that generates sufficient power to bring about and sustain desirable school change.

There are three program components or mechanisms and three major program operations. The key program component is the building-level representative governance and management body, referred to as the School Planning and Management Team (SPMT) in New Haven. The second component is the Mental Health Team. The third component is the Parents' Program.

The school Mental Health Team provides child development and relationship knowledge and skill to the work of the governance and management body, and to its own prescriptive activities with individual or small groups of students. The mental health team works in both preventive and treatment modes. Parents support the program of the school through participation as selected representatives on the governance and management body, through membership in a parents' group, and through support of academic and social activities that are developed through, and with, the management body.

Three critical operations are carried out or supervised by the School Planning and Management Team—a comprehensive school plan, a staff development program, and an assessment and modification effort. A Comprehensive School Plan that outlines goals, objectives, and strategies is developed by each school SPMT. The plan addresses two areas: social climate and academic climate. In New Haven, there is also a public relations component to the plan. The activities in these areas are based on felt need, research, and analysis of school functioning, and student achievement. The Staff Development Program is based on training needs that arise from the school plan goals. Central office supervisory personnel provide support for staff development activities initiated at the building level. A systematic near year-end assessment complements an informal, ongoing assessment, and serves as the basis for program modification and adjustment in the next school year.

School Planning and Management Team

The School Planning and Management Team is led by the principal and is made up of teachers selected by their colleagues, parents selected by the parents' group, and a mental health team member, as well as representatives from other adult service providers in a school. In middle schools and high schools, students should be represented directly, or indirectly. The SPMT coordinates all the resources and activities of the school. They are, to use familiar analogies, the engine or nervous system of the school. The operation of this governance and management group becomes unwieldy when there are more than 12 to 15 people involved.

The work of the SPMT—and eventually all the groups and activities of the school—is guided by several key philosophies, beliefs, and resultant practices. First, there is a no-fault policy. The focus is on problem solving, not on blame. Second, the members of the team are advisory to the principal and cannot paralyze him or her. But the principal understands that he or she cannot use the members of the group as a "rubber stamp." A genuine effort must be made to work collaboratively and cooperatively. Toward this end, decisions are made by consensus rather than by vote in order to avoid "winners" and "losers," and related behaviors. Indeed, a major task of this group is to develop a consensus of attitudes, values, and ways that will lead to school success for staff, parents, and children. They help to generate a desirable ethos or climate that eventually permeates the attitudes, values, and ways of the entire school. A central attitude or belief is the notion that all kids can learn and behave socially and academically at an acceptable level.

Mental Health Team

The mental health team can be led by the principal but may be led by a mental health team member who reports directly to the principal. The social worker, psychologist, special education teacher, or any other support service person in the school serves on the mental health team. The team provides help to any individual child or group that is experiencing a problem, as in the traditional method of providing pupil support services. But a more important function of the team in our model is prevention. Often using incidents and problems that come to their attention through work with individual children, the team attempts to spot procedures, attitudes, and ways of thinking within the school that contribute to the problems of children. They work with the governance and management team to bring about needed changes.

For example, after a frightened transfer student kicked a teacher, the mental health team helped the staff appreciate the anxiety the student experienced and developed an orientation program for new students that the governance and management team adopted. This program greatly reduced transfer anxiety and the acting-out behavior and disruption related to it. An incident that pointed up the need for greater adult–student continuity led to a program of keeping students with the same teacher for two years. In similar ways, programs such as Discovery Room, Crisis Room, and a number of others were established to decrease students' anxiety, permit them to make positive attachments to the school staff and program, and help them to manage the school environment and to grow along the critical developmental pathways necessary to succeed in school.

Parents

The parent group worked in support of the school program primarily by supporting the social calendar of the school. At one point in our original project schools, a parent worked in each classroom as an assistant to the teacher, helping with academic and social matters. Assistants formed the core of a group of 30 to 40 parents. With the school staff, they sponsored activities designed to create a good school climate. The parent activities were developed as an integral part of the Comprehensive School Plan. The strategy was to create conditions that would allow staff and parents to serve as meaningful role models and guides for students. As with the innovations developed by the mental health team, the parent program made it possible for students to make a positive attachment and bond with their parents, or community people like their parents, school people, and the program of the school. The parents' group selected the parents to serve on the governance and management group. As a result of their meaningful involvement and positive interaction with school people, they felt a sense of mutuality and common cause with the staff (Schraft & Comer, 1979).

Great care was given to involving parents in the program of the school. In one case, a teacher served as the liaison and as a facilitator for the parents' group, and in another case the social worker had this role. The staff member helped parents gain the skills to manage their group as well as to interact with the staff. Without doing so, parents might well get into an adversarial relationship with the staff, particularly before trust is established and before significant school improvement is observed.

Many low-income parents have numerous failure experiences. Parent projects were carefully designed and well supported so that they would experience success. Success breeds success and increases the desire of parents to participate. Also many have had bad experiences with school themselves. Many expect that their children will not succeed. Often they are only called to school when there are problems. Parent activities designed to improve the climate of the schools involve parents during good times rather than bad times, and allow them to interact with staff in social situations as opposed to meeting only around more threatening academic performance issues.

Social Skills Curriculum for Inner-City Children

As various groups and programs experienced success, a climate of good feeling emerged in the schools. Behavior problems decreased and the higher social and academic potential of the students became apparent. Eventually, there was adequate time and energy for teaching, and this, in turn, improved learning. The school staff responded to improved student performance in ways that promoted still higher performance. Eventually, the staff began to believe that the students could equal the performance of students from better educated and/or middle-income families if they were systematically provided with experiences in school that the latter gain simply by growing up with their parents. Out of this thinking grew a program entitled, "A Social Skills Curriculum for Inner-City Children" (Comer, Schraft, & Sparrow, 1980).

The parents were asked what kind of careers and life experiences they wanted for their children as adults. They wanted essentially the same outcomes as better-educated parents. With staff, they considered the areas in which their children would need expertise in order to perform adequately as adults. Staff and parents together decided that the children would need skills in politics and government, business and economics, health and nutrition, and spiritual and leisure activities. In what would have been free or elective times, units were developed. In this way, no time was taken away from the teaching of basic skills. In each unit, there was an integration of the teaching of basic skills, social skills, and artistic expression. Artistic expression promoted the channeling of aggressive energy. The use of basic academic skills in these four adult activity areas demonstrated their utility and importance.

The first unit was built around a mayoralty contest that was occurring in the city. The students wrote letters to the candidates inviting them to come in and give a campaign speech and wrote thank-you letters after the visit. Parents used money from activities they sponsored in support of the school program and, with staff, rented buses and took the children on field trips around the city. They discussed the relationship of conditions in the city to the role of government. They returned to school and talked and wrote about their experiences. They were taught how to be hosts for the candidates and their parents. They were taught how to raise questions to the candidates in a way that was respectful while soliciting specific answers. They put on a dance-drama program for other students, staff, and the candidates.

Language arts, social science, social skills, and artistic expression were involved in a meaningful way in all of these activities. Our assessment showed that the activities made the learning of basic academic skills relevant and important. Indeed, it was after the development of the social skills curriculum that we saw the most dramatic improvement in academic achievement.

Dissemination

Dissemination of our school improvement approach was a part of our original plan. Doing so became even more important after some observers suggested that the effectiveness of our approach was due to the direct involvement of the Child Study Center. And while we have not been directly involved in the original project schools since 1980, we are still involved in other New Haven schools. Thus, perhaps our presence is still felt. We decided to develop models in other school systems within and outside of the state. We also employed different training and program implementation approaches, in part, as an accommodation to the needs of other school systems, but also as an opportunity to study their different effectiveness. In all cases the systems use the same basic model and psychosocial principles.

We are now involved in 11 almost all-Black elementary schools in Benton Harbor, Michigan, and 24 such schools in the urban segment of Prince George's County, Maryland, just outside of Washington, D.C. We have new programs in Norfolk, Virginia, a southern urban district; and in Lee County, Arkansas, a rural southern district. We briefly had a program in one school in an affluent urban–suburban school district in Connecticut.

We used a "Trainer of Trainers" technique in all but one of these school districts. We asked the superintendent of the participating district to select a facilitator who would report directly to him. The selection was based on criteria agreed on by our staff and the superintendent: good interpersonal skills and respect for and from peers, knowledge and sensitivity to child development and relationship issues, good management skills, and a track record for success in these areas. The facilitator then spent time in New Haven learning the model and returned to his or her district to implement it under the supervision of the superintendent, with minimal support from our staff. We felt that it was not necessary for the facilitator to have extensive training in child development, but he or she should know how to apply the basic principles to problems and opportunities in school.

Program Impact

We have examined the program's impact on children's academic performance and psychosocial adjustment in school. Significant positive effects have been noted on standardized achievement scores, suspensions, and self-esteem among students who have been exposed to the program (Haynes, Comer, & Hamilton-Lee, 1988).

The most significant improvements in achievement in the shortest period of time have occurred in Prince George's County (Englund, 1988). Data provided by the research and evaluation office of the Prince George's County Public Schools on the California Achievement Test (CAT) indicate that between 1985 and 1986 third and fifth graders in the initial ten program schools significantly exceeded the gains reported for the district as a whole. The district gains were three and two points respectively for mathematics, zero and two points respectively for reading, and one and two points respectively for language. Among the ten original program schools, the seven judged by an independent evaluator to be implementing the program most efficiently have shown the greatest gains. The average gains among third and fifth graders in these schools were 9 and 16 percentile points respectively in mathematics, 8 and 7 points respectively in reading, and 11 and 6 points respectively in language.

Significant gains were also reported in Benton Harbor where the lowest-achieving schools, using the SDP model, have equaled or exceeded district and national averages on the California Achievement Test during the past five years (Haynes et al., 1988). In addition, suspension rates have declined significantly in program schools by about 19% during the past several years, while districtwide suspension rates increased about 34%. Our assessment of self-esteem has shown that children in program schools have experienced more significant positive change in their self-perceptions, particularly their school-related self-concept, than children in nonprogram control schools (Comer & Haynes, 1987).

Facilitator Findings

One facilitator spent an entire year at our center and in project schools in New Haven. No other participants from her district spent time observing in New Haven. When she returned, she was working in isolation with little local appreciation and support for what she was trying to do. In response to this problem, we developed a model in which a facilitator spends four weeks learning the model in New Haven. During that time, three groups of about ten people, representative of all the adults in the facilitator's school system—school board, teachers, support staff, administrators, parents, and so on— visit New Haven for a two and one-half-day orientation workshop. The facilitator then trains and works with principals to help them carry out the program when they return to the district. Our staff makes brief presentations in the district. This model has been the most successful. The least successful model has been our effort to work in single schools in a district: one in an affluent school district and the other in a low-income school district.

Resistance to change is human. Professional training, as currently carried out in education and other disciplines, often implies that there is a "right way." This thinking reinforces resistance to change. Bureaucratic structures and operational inertia make change difficult even when the need is obvious. When a change project is limited to one school, the usual forces of resistance can easily undermine the effort. Problems peculiar to a particular setting, such as insecure leadership, inadequate acceptance of the need for change on the part of the staff, staff–parent conflict, and so on, promote resistance. In affluent schools, the high achievement of students from well-educated families often causes school staff to place the academic achievement problems of low-income students on the students themselves and on their families, thus seeing little need to address relationship issues.

We have observed that when approximately ten schools are involved, three to four principals and staff will be highly successful in employing the model. Four to six will have moderate success, and three to four will not do well at all. There are multiple factors involved here: issues of basic competence, attitudes, style, local administrative issues, resistance to outside intervention, and others. But the success of several schools helps others change.

What is clear from all these experiences is that the relevant psychosocial and developmental principles involved in our program can be learned by educators with modest behavioral, social science, and developmental backgrounds, and applied successfully in their own school systems. This application is necessary if the model is to have widespread dissemination potential.

The different personnel, political, social, and economic conditions in a community and school, and personality factors, all suggest why it is difficult to use research findings from one school setting in another. We found our observational skills, influenced by a theoretical framework drawn from human ecology and child development, to be much more useful in understanding needs and helping to develop school improvement processes. This finding suggests that anthropology and the ethnographic approach, or the case study approach used to educate business people, may be a more useful way of understanding and changing schools than the experimental research approaches that are still most highly regarded and most often used.

Conclusions

Low-income families are often marginal to the mainstream of the society and often operate under great economic and social stress. As a result, children often do not receive the kinds of preschool experiences that will allow them to succeed in school. The problem is greatest among minorities with traumatic social histories. Because of the organization and management of schools and the training of staffs, the school is not able to respond in a way that makes it possible for such children to succeed. School underachievement on the part of students, staff, and parents is the result.

Our School Development Program changes the organization and management of the school from an authoritarian hierarchical approach to a participatory approach. It permits the staff to learn and apply child development and relationship principles to every aspect of the school program. It permits the staff and parents to work together to support the program of the school. In the process, children are able to form positive emotional attachments and bonds with school staff, parents, and the school program in a way that promotes their overall development, and in turn facilitates academic learning. The model is designed to gradually overcome resistances inherent in schools. We have also demonstrated that the principles of the model can be used in sites outside of New Haven without intensive and sustained involvement of our staff.

REFERENCES

Biber, B. (1961). Integration of mental health principles in the school setting. In G. Caplan (Ed.), *Prevention of mental disorders.* New York: Basic Books.

Blose, D., & Ambrose, C. (1936). *Statistics of the education of Negroes, 1929–30; 1931–32* (U.S. Office of Education Bulletin No. 13). Washington, DC: U.S. Department of Interior.

Comer, J. P. (1972). *Beyond Black and White.* New York: Quadrangle/New York Times.

Comer, J. P. (1980). *School power: Implications of an Intervention Project.* New York: Free Press.

Comer, J. P., & Haynes, N. M. (1987). Dimensions of children's self-concept as predictors of social competence. *Journal of Social Psychology, 127*(3), 321–329.

Comer, J. P., Schraft, C. M., & Sparrow, S. S. (1980). *Social skills curriculum for inner city children: Final report.* Unpublished manuscript.

Council for Financial Aid to Education (1967). *Voluntary support of America's colleges and universities: 1964–65.* New York: Author.

Englund, W. (1988, January 10). Scores, morale soar in Prince George's. *The Baltimore Sun,* p. 1.

Gibbs, J. L. (Ed.). (1965). *Peoples of Africa.* New York: Holt, Rinehart & Winston.

Haynes, N. M., Comer, J. P., & Hamilton-Lee, M. (1988). The school development program: A model for school improvement. *Journal of Negro Education, 57*(7), 11–21.

Mackenzie, D. E. (1983, April). Research for school improvement: An appraisal of some recent trends. *Educational Researcher,* pp. 5–17.

Nash, G. D. (Ed.). (1964). *Issues in American economic history.* Boston: D.C. Heath.

Schraft, C. M., & Comer, J. (1979). Parent participation and urban schools. *School Social Work Quarterly, 14,* 309–325.

Synder, T. D. (1987). *Digest of education statistics 1987.* Washington, DC: U.S. Government Printing Office.

14

Afro-Americans and Academic Achievement: Pathways to Excellence

GORDON LaVERN BERRY

Seeking a Positive Perspective Toward Afro-Americans and Achievement

The historical and present-day social, economic, political, psychological, and educational experiences of Black Americans have all combined to shape their social status in American society. Clearly, the previous chapters in this book argue well for the notion that family, community, school, employment, health, and governmental policies are linked together to determine the educational achievement opportunities for Americans in general, and Black Americans in particular. The implications are clear from the central themes of the chapters that no longer can social scientists simply turn their research to cognitive, linguistic, and parenting deficits of underclass Afro-Americans as if these isolated variables can explain their academic achievement status in the broader society. Rather, there is a multiplicity of economic, political, and psychosocial factors that are related to both the successful and maladaptive behaviors of Black Americans. Indeed, many of their academic behaviors stem from social experiences that must be interpreted not only from a culturally holistic perspective but also by the quality of the environmental conditions that many of them have been forced to experience by the policies and practices of the broader society.

A broader perspective of the academic achievement behaviors of Afro-American children, youth, and adults might well influence social scientists and policy makers to move away from a major reliance on Western-oriented learning constructs, toward more of a culturally diverse world view on the meaning of educational and academic achievement motives in those Black Americans with special needs. The concepts presented in this chapter shift the focus away from the "blame the victim and cultural deficit" perspectives related to Afro-Americans in the educational pipeline. At the same time, the concepts do not ignore or romanticize the role that a group of people have for improving their own achievement level. Rather, the article assumes that even with the complexities of those retarding social forces, especially faced by underclass Black people, a conceptually sound, humane, success-oriented, and culturally relevant educational program can tap the untapped potentials of African-American school-age children and young adults. It is, therefore, to this call for a commitment to excellence within a framework of cultural relativity to which this chapter is addressed.

A Capsule Overview of Structural Factors and Academic Achievement

There can be little doubt from the introduction to this chapter and the general thrust of the book that there is a belief system stating that structural or societal forces have brought on many of the educational achievement problems of African-American children and youth. That is to say, cultural attributes found in the family, community, and peer groups do not by themselves explain the lower levels of academic and social achievement experienced by some Black people. There have been, of course, an assortment of views offered to both explain and justify the lower academic and social status of Blacks. Hare (1987), while acknowledging the relative under-attainment of Black Americans, argues for an ideological perspective that suggests the relative academic and economic failure of Black Americans in this country is functional, if not intended, given racism and the differential distribution of wealth, power, and privilege in the social structure.

Significantly, this notion of the differential distribution of those experiences and opportunities that will lead to higher achievement becomes especially salient when you study many of the educational programs offered to Black students. For example, a comprehensive report on the educational status of Black Americans conducted by the College Entrance Examination Board (1985) highlighted some of the recent policy trends that are being practiced in various parts of the country. Taking just one phase of the report related to the equality in the school curriculum, it pointed out that a number of indicators suggest that Black students, on average, receive educational programs and offerings that differ in kind and content from those of White students.

Contrary to much of the conventional wisdom, Black families, even of the so-called underclass, believe in education and schooling as a pathway to a better life. Frequently, however, the socioeconomic circumstances and experiences of the parents do not adequately provide the early educational orientation that prepares the child to be successful in a classroom that does not value the strengths of his or her life-style.

Programmatic Pathways Toward Improving Academic Achievement

At the very core of the philosophy of this book has always been the notion that the old labels of the past that have inferred cognitive, motivational, self-esteem, and learning deficits of Black children, youth, and college-age young adults should be looked at with a jaundiced eye. Rather, our concept has been to recognize that there are real problems of student underattainment in the Black community and they must be identified and changed. We feel that African-Americans are at a pivotal point in their development where students have made some very significant gains in achievement and educational success over the last 20 years. At the same time, there is a clear risk of having those gains eroded by the damaging drop-out rates on all levels of education, teenage pregnancy, drug use, and crime that are all factors impacting negatively on the educational achievement of a large segment of Black people.

It is clear that even with the high-risk nature of the problems, there is a possibility of positive change and growth. Programs on how to change a community school and other proposals in the book demonstrate that committed strategies can and do make a difference. In this sense, human nature and behaviors are not, as historically felt, rooted so firmly in early socialization modes that they cannot be modified. If we are to submit to the notion that defeating or retarding behaviors are somehow irretrievable, we will have given into an attitude suggesting that an entire upcoming generation of Afro-American children and youth are lost. Such a thought is culturally, intellectually, and personally repugnant.

The task of bringing about those structural changes in the broader society, as well as the changes that must be undertaken by Black people themselves, is not easy. Too many young people no longer believe, as did their elders, that high educational attainments are the route to a better life for themselves and Black people as a group. Affecting change in societal structure, as well as in individuals and the groups, will call for a genuine commitment on the part of the major decision makers from the White House to the council chambers in the smallest cities. Such change also means that large groups and small family units will have to take control and become involved in making personal decisions about their life-style and those societal forces that influence it.

Many of the chapters in this book have looked at prenatal and health issues, psychological constructs related to motivation and self-esteem, community factors, the drop-out problem, issues faced by the family and the school, higher-education success issues, and model programs that are committed to making changes in schooling. Given the scope of the previous chapters, this final one will only highlight some of the changes and challenges faced by governmental units, the private sector, the family unit, and the school.

Governmental Units

Despite all of the statistics, reports, and forecasts of how great it has been for Americans during the last eight years, one third of all Black families live below the poverty level of $10,989 a year for a family of four. The jobless rate for Black teenagers, particularly males, is close to 40%, which is twice that of White teenagers (Whitaker, 1988). These and similar pictures on housing, child care, and other social and economic conditions mean that the governmental units on all levels must move to correct this condition among poor people.

It should not be surprising to anyone that there is a relationship between educational achievement and the social conditions faced by a group. Several contributors in previous sections of this book have called attention to the fact that young Blacks' view of social reality and how their vision of the future is shaped relates to their perception of employment opportunities. Ogbu (1978) supports this notion about the importance of employment opportunities by pointing out that lower school performance on the part of Blacks is an adaptation to their lower social and occupational positions in adult life. In order to be competitive with the underground economy in many Black communities, governmental agencies will have to become involved in cooperative career-oriented programs that will lead to meaningful and competitive jobs geared for the future economy of the country.

Financial support for those researchers and school professionals who are truly looking for ways to break the cycle of poverty and stimulate *all* children, regardless of ability, should be encouraged through governmental grants. One implication for research grants is that they should provide an opportunity for people, communities, and institutions who have a track record of minority involvement to become leaders in the research enterprise. For too long, community folk and Black institutions have not be able to provide their input into the research effort because major institutions have simply had the resources and political connections to pick and choose from those grants offered by governmental units.

Industry and Private Units

Industry groups and private foundations must join in the research and action program efforts. A major requirement of these groups would be to provide resources that could stimulate the effective programs related to the teaching, research, and learning, especially in the public and other schools, where large numbers of urban and rural children attend. This proposal also relates to a need for these groups to build functional and working linkages that will establish productive work and training positions for young people and will update the scientific and technical knowledge base of teachers, students, and the school curriculum.

The private sector has a major role to play in support and cooperative programs that will also foster liberal arts education and those cultural activities that will broaden the perspective of the individual. Too many potentially talented Black children have a superficial view of their own cultural heritage and that of the world in general. Black Americans, just as it is true with other groups, need to understand the liberal arts and develop a world view.

The Family Unit

It is axiomatic to state that at the core of the issue of academic achievement is the Black family and its function in a community that has significantly changed. And yet, both the family and the changing Black community have a type of cultural momentum drawn from religious and extended family traditions that seem to still produce—albeit too few—many achievers despite the major social and economic problems.

Barbara Shade (1979) concluded that the most significant variance between Black achievers and nonachievers was related to the behaviors of the parents and guardians. Shade (1979, pp. 62–63) drawing on the work of Coleman (1969), Solomon, Scheinfeld, Hirsh, & Jackson (1971), Greenberg and Davidson (1972), and others, cited the most common parental behaviors that are related to Black achievers as:

The maintenance of a quality of communication that tends to stimulate the child's problem-solving ability, independence, and productivity;

The expression of warmth, interest, affection, and encouragement;

The establishment of close family ties;

The maintenance of some structure and order for the child;

The establishment of goals of performance;

The use of control mechanisms that include moderate amounts of praise and blame, moderate amounts of punishment, and no authoritarian tactics;

The giving of assistance when requested or when the need is perceived.

Significantly, there are many strengths in the Black family. At the same time, there is a clear need to institute school and community programs that will emphasize solid parenting skills because they are so important to the future achievement of the child, his or her self-esteem, and the survival of Black people.

I would submit that much of the research in this area should focus on how successful families, with what appear to be similar backgrounds, manage to rear academic achievers. That is to say, we need to begin to study successful family life-style models along with the unsuccessful ones.

The School Unit

The school is a social system with a complex set of rules. Schools serving young Black children create a climate from which they take their cues. Every child understands those cues that communicate the messages: that he or she is respected as an individual; that there is an expectation that, to the best of your ability, you can be successful; that the professional staff is here to help you; that your African and Afro-American heritage is as important as people with other cultural roots; that there are high but fair standards to be observed; and that you can strive for excellence.

Far too often, however, schools and higher-education institutions do not communicate to people of color in general, and Black students in particular, these positive and success-oriented messages as part of the folkways and mores of the educational enterprise.

Conclusions

Recent articles, reports, studies, and a host of media offerings have been concerned with many of the issues presented in this book. Few of the proposals from many of the recent studies have received enough national support to impact on the educational status of Afro-Americans and low-income groups in general. Significantly, too few of the proposals truly confront the issues of both excellence and equity as parallel components for meaningful change.

An especially disturbing aspect of many of the recent conclusions concerning the improvement of educational opportunity for Afro-Americans are two questions that seem to emerge directly or indirectly. The first question is, "What type of educational program do the Black children and youth *need?*" My answer to that question is that they need an educational system that strives for excellence without compromise, but with a full understanding and appreciation for the strengths of the child and his or her life-style. The second stated or implied question from the literature asks, "What type of education and schools do Black people *want?*" To this question, I can only suggest that they want schools and teachers who strive for excellence within a framework of cultural understanding.

The chief advantage of my answers to such complicated questions is that they both begin with a philosophical commitment that is based on a positive approach to the *needs* and *wants* of Afro-Americans. Both of these answers assume that Black youngsters can master a strong curriculum that is well planned and well taught. These answers also assume that the parents want, appreciate, and desire a strong school program that will help their Johnny and Jane to be competitive in society. In general, my approach to the questions does not begin with how different these children and their parents are, because it has been this "different doctrine" that has brought to the urban schools a rash of watered-down and do-nothing programs. These programs have often been operated by people who purport caring about children of color, but fail to teach them how to read and compute. That is to say, we have classrooms that function on a type of "care for them and leave them approach" to the teaching–learning process.

There are also powerful voices within the Black communities who call for "blackening" the curricular content and the total school for their children. If they mean we must set the history, English, and scientific textbooks straight concerning the culture and contributions of minority groups, I totally agree. If they mean we must integrate and enrich the school curriculum with the nature of, and concern for, the "Black Experience," I can very much agree. On the other hand, we should be prepared to reject from the brothers, sisters, liberals, radicals, or conservatives any attempt to call for school programs that are anything less than solid in their content, humanistic in their concerns, and relevant to the needs of the community. In addition, the curriculum should be broad enough to help Black youngsters to understand humankind in the community and the world. Briefly, Afro-American children need competent teachers and a curriculum that includes content taught in an intellectually honest manner.

Excellence for Black students, stated a report from the College Entrance Examination Board (1985), will not become a reality unless and until they receive enriched curricular opportunities in elementary and secondary schools, sufficient financial assistance to pursue higher-education opportunities, and the appropriateness of courses and achievement measures intended to enforce high standards. I would conclude by stating that we must build programs based on equity and excellence in spite of the fact that many of these young people uniquely challenge our educational systems from grade schools to colleges to meet their needs. In the final analysis, our tasks as adults, professional educators, social scientists, political leaders, and researchers are to be creative and committed enough to Afro-Americans and all students to modify their weaknesses, to tap their strengths, and to unshackle their positive potentials to achieve.

REFERENCES

Coleman, A. (1969). The disadvantaged child who is successful in high school. *Educational Forum*, 95–97.

College Entrance Examination Board (1985). *Equality and excellence: The educational status of Black Americans*. New York:

Greenberg, J., & Davidson, H. H. (1972). Home background and school achievement of Black urban ghetto children. *American Journal of Orthopsychiatry, 42*, 803–810.

Hare, B. (1987). Structural inequality and the endangered status of Black youth. *Journal of Negro Education, 56*(1), 100–110.

Ogbu, J. V. (1978). *Minority education and caste: The American system in cross-cultural perspective*. New York: Academic Press.

Shade, B. J. (1979). Social-psychological characteristics of achieving Black children. In G. Henderson (Ed.), *Understanding and counseling ethnic minorities* (pp. 60–69). Springfield, IL: Charles C Thomas.

Solomon, D., Scheinfeld, D., Hirsh, J. G., & Jackson, J. (1971). Early grade performance in inner city Negro high school high achievers, low achievers, and dropouts. *Developmental Psychology, 4*, 482.

Whitaker, C. (1988). A generation in peril. *Ebony, 63*(10), 34–36.

Epilogue

Unity in Diversity: Thirty-Three Years of Stress

CHESTER M. PIERCE

The given theme for this meeting, "Unity in Diversity," is apt for a speaker memorializing Dr. Solomon Carter Fuller. His life as the pioneer Black psychiatrist in the U.S.A.—and probably the world—shows that indeed diversity can contribute to and strengthen unity. His example models much of what has happened and must continue to happen for colored minorities in the U.S.A. in all instances of interaction with the general population. Further, on an individual level, as each colored minority member negotiates existence, the ever-present stress is to decide about and act upon the quality and quantity of diversity or unity to be presented to the total community. Our incessant struggle is this: How and when do we accommodate to racism versus how and when do we resist racism. Our constant problem is when and how do we seek assimilation into the total society versus when and how do we insist on separation from the total society. Our ongoing existential doubt is whether we are warmly welcomed or merely tolerated when accepted by the general community. The psychological resolution of these conflicts on either group or individual basis claims an extraordinary amount of our time and effort. The nature of the resolution is framed always by racism-inhibitors that define the limits of hope, desire, probability, and possibility.

Fortunately, the total society is augmented because people like

AUTHOR'S NOTE: Presented as the Solomon Carter Fuller Lecture, American Psychiatric Association Meeting, Washington, DC, May 12, 1986.

Dr. Fuller, despite the heavy cost in terms of stress, defy these racism-inhibitors and push back the boundaries of what is probable and possible for minority people to hope for, desire, and achieve. As a result, the infusion of different input and viewpoint serves to promote unity and strength for everyone. You will not be surprised to learn that a group of Black psychiatrists first proposed to seek formal recognition of Solomon Carter Fuller as a champion of our cause on the evening of Martin Luther King's assassination. On that night, 17 years ago, it happened that a small collection of Black psychiatrists from all over the U.S.A. were meeting in a hotel in New York City, to polish plans for a confrontation with the American Psychiatric Association leadership in regards to institutional racism.

Formation of these plans, which included the establishment of the Black Psychiatrists of America, were interrupted by the somber pressures of the evening. Since each planner made repeated calls to his home town, we were able to monitor the grisly event from first-hand reports from all over the nation. In the course of this surveillance, it was mentioned how important it was for Blacks to select, revere, and cherish their own heroes. At least two of the most senior members of the group knew Solomon Carter Fuller and told the group that he was our first Black psychiatrist.

What may now surprise some people is that there was instantaneous agreement, without further discussion, that Solomon Carter Fuller should become widely appreciated and acknowledged. This spontaneous and unanimous agreement reflects our indigenism in a way that will be commented on later. Suffice to say that it indicated an unspoken, shared certainty that Dr. Fuller by virtue of his pioneering efforts as a Black man had to have suffered untold hurt, frustration, humiliation, and degradation. Nevertheless, his success was pivotal for the social advancement of medicine and of the whole society.

No thinking Black person can gaze at the celebrated photo of Freud in his first visit to America, taken at Clark University in Worcester, Massachusetts, without knowing that Solomon Carter Fuller had overcome obstacles and resentments that did not affect the others in the photograph. In addition, one could be certain that unlike the others in the picture, Dr. Fuller, in spite of any achievement, would never be free to pursue his career without the burden of being suspect in the eyes of his peers in terms of ability, effectiveness, or efficiency. Finally, the Black viewer of the picture would know intuitively that throughout his career Dr. Fuller would have had to do more work for less reward and that at each instance of advancement he would have had to demonstrate superior qualifications and credentials than a White colleague aspiring for the same advancement.

In short, the unity that Dr. Fuller sought to bring to American psychiatry was accomplished under inestimable stress and duress. To this day all colored minority psychiatrists are beneficiaries of this legacy. Regrettably, to this day, all colored minority psychiatrists must continue to adapt to the same burdens that afflicted Solomon Carter Fuller.

What will be submitted by this lecture is that being Black in America means being stressed more because you are Black. Being a Black psychiatrist means you are stressed more because you are a Black psychiatrist. In the resolution of the psychological conflicts, all Blacks have a requirement to consolidate, integrate, and make sense of the diversity that being Black, and thereby marginal, brings with it in all interactions with the general society. Therefore there is a need to unify the diversity even as one struggles with the issue of when and how to unite.

A different sort of unification of diversity is imposed on Blacks, especially Black professionals, who by reason of skin color and historical circumstances are fractionated and widely distributed across a plethora of activities in the pursuit of their goals. As a result, Blacks must bring together or unify countless diversions that accompany being both marginal to the society and fractionated across the society.

Like Solomon Carter Fuller, Black psychiatrists today in their personal and professional lives operate in many circumstances of marginality and fractionation. Coordinating and controlling these operations, all of which are under the aegis of extra stress, may constitute the largest and most difficult developmental task for any Black citizen. Each citizen must order these operations according to his or her own perception of truth.

For the remainder of this lecture, I will survey the ordering of my own life's diversity in the effort to find unity and minimize stress. It is my contention that all Black psychiatrists since Solomon Carter Fuller have had to go through this process as the chief influence in career development and professional satisfaction.

Thus in a real sense how each of us resolves this process exerts extreme impact on all patients whom we serve, all persons whom we teach, and all administrative endeavors we undertake. My own bottom line is this: Since it is usually impossible for me to be conscious more than 30 minutes without thinking of my race, all of my professional life can be described as an effort to live as a Black in the U.S.A.

Permit me to share with you how I ordered my diverse background and diverse activities as a Black psychiatrist living in the U.S.A. seeking to find unity and reduce stress. I embark on the conceptualization in the hope that it may help young Black psychiatrists to have an overview of how one person managed for a third of a century, the stress inherent in our situation. It follows that my life, like all others, is idiosyncratic. Therefore, what I present is highly selective and peculiar to myself. However, I will attempt to distill what lessons or general guidelines were precipitated in the hope that some may find them useful.

Diversity in Background: The Consequences of Being Marginal and Being Fractionate

I did not know Dr. Fuller. As a child, however, I was a playmate of someone destined to become his daughter-in-law. Had Dr. Fuller observed our group of playmates it is unlikely he would have thought that any who followed him into psychiatry would engage in the sort of diverse activities that have characterized my career. In fact, even my teachers in psychiatry would not have anticipated such diversity.

The generalization I distill is that even though a combination of temperament, inclinations, and circumstances resulted in such diversity, I was much more likely to have had such a career than a peer. Always being forced to be fractionated in my activities, and frequently being viewed as marginal in the conduct of these activities, became strong determinants for demanding even more diverse activity.

I have wondered how much such determinants were at work in Solomon Carter Fuller's life in which he engaged in activities from neuropathology to psychoanalysis. The problem with being obliged to massive diverse professional activity is that it is impossible to become an expert in depth. There are, however, many advantages including the immensely important one of allowing one to have an unusually interesting life. Yet the advantage I distill from the forced obligation to be diverse is that it has been a major protector against the ravages of racism. Working in situations where there is no critical mass of Blacks often has reduced negative responses. More important, not being able to be or needing to be connected with only one or two groups of colleagues has facilitated withdrawal from majority immersion. The salient fact is that I have never mourned feeling I was not a full-fledged part of the bulk of collegial processes in which I engaged. This has provided crucial minimalization of wariness and defensiveness, which often is an implacable part of a Black's response in interracial situations.

Just as there are pros and cons to being marginal in this pluralistic society, there are advantages and disadvantages of being fractionated. The same factors of skin color and historical circumstances made it more likely, perhaps, for me, in comparison to a White peer, to devote considerable effort to community concerns and civic and social actions that affected both majority and minority groups. Besides this fractionation in general and minority community activities, there may have been more insistence and opportunity to work in organized professional groups that deal with either general or minority professionals. Here too the forced diversity, associated with being an outsider, made it even more difficult to concentrate sufficiently in any one area of life to stay at the cutting edge of that aspect of human existence. On the other hand the fractionation of experience over a widely dispersed range brought the benefit of a broad perspective about how the society functions. This broader view may have made integration and ordering of experience more arduous, but it may have increased the richness of the experience.

As a result of being nearly always marginal and fractionated, my experience and view probably has more overlays than underlays with any Black at any point in U.S. history. Thus we Blacks bring as background to any situation a great diversity. And we must make more effort to synthesize and orchestrate these diverse experiences so that they are functional and united.

Over the course of many years, forced to be both marginal and fractionated in professional life, has made me travel great distances in time and space, both literally and figuratively. I traveled these distances to find where my diversity would be joined in unity with the least amount of stress. In terms of space, my work took me to all seven of the earth's continents. In terms of time, my work traversed considerations from the ancient Greeks to the future of astronauts.

In all these journeys, I encountered a wonderful and marvelous diversity of colleagues from many countries, representing equally diverse and wonderful disciplines. Two thoughts emerge from this statement. One is that, as is often the case in cogitations about inter-racial matters, I have considered many times what envy my good fortune would incite in collective White America. Surely if they knew what fun I had in my search for unity in diversity, which the collective generated, methods would be found to stop it. Like all Blacks in all walks of life, I tried to discover and focus on what things I could enjoy regardless of racism. And like many Blacks in all eras of history, I found some success in this effort.

The second thought is less happy. That thought speaks to the fact that wherever I went, whatever I did, and with whomever I worked, my never-ending preoccupation had to be on how to survive as a Black. It is to these survival observations that I now turn. The distil-late from all my diverse activities, which were occasioned by the di-versity of background, addresses Black survival in the U.S.A. The unity in diversity from being Black and therefore marginal and frac-tionated comes from synthesizing multiple experiences. Such syn-thesis aids Black survival, that is, how one attenuates and dilutes the stress from racism.

The conclusions reached and the lessons learned may seem trivial or obvious or mundane or even wrong. Further, given all that occurs in a third of a century to any person, the items that instructed me may seem unremarkable or exotic or romantic or even far-fetched. Nevertheless, from the array of diverse activities these have been the most arresting speculations about survival of Blacks in the U.S.A.

Diversity in Activity: Surviving Racism

During my career the array of activities that have instructed me most about racism have come from diverse areas usually far remote, at first approach, from any possible racial relevance. From working with animals such as elephants, skua birds, whales, seals, and penguins, I have learned about victimization and have contem-plated human-specific behavior that differentiates Homo sapiens from other fauna. From working with prisoners and people inhabiting extreme environments, such as submariners or polar expeditioners, I have sharpened my thinking about inhabitants in an inner city. From working in sleep laboratories and doing investigations about medical aspects of history and music, I refined my knowledge about the pervasiveness of ideas about skin color. Yet throughout my life there have been specific constellations of activity that resulted in a particular insight about racism that might or might not have been novel to my previous observations. These insights always seemed to illuminate and define the canons of American society and expedite banishment from the tyranny of racial injustice.

1953-1964

When I entered psychiatry in 1953, I had sincere and profound doubt about whether or not I could earn my living. At that time, it did not seem likely to me that enough White patients would pay to come see a Black psychiatrist, nor did it seem likely that enough Blacks would have wherewithal to afford a psychiatrist.

These doubts were still a part of me when I entered the Navy during the Korean War. The Navy taught me what it was like to be White. For as an officer, I was saluted by enlisted people and I was segregated from them. I had no ill feeling for what they did in their private lives nor did I have any special desire for them to suffer. I was astonished by how much servitude enlisted recruits invited onto themselves. Without bidding they would bring me coffee, help me off with my coat, inquire solicitously about the welfare of my family. All of this was done in their misguided belief that I had far more power than I possessed relative to getting them out of the Navy. The first major lesson about racial stress that I learned as a psychiatrist was because as an officer I was socially "White." The lesson was that the oppressed invite a great deal and sometimes most of their own oppression gratuitously and unnecessarily. The oppressed accepted and expected as unremarkable an etiquette system that was based on their volitional deference. It occurred to me that Blacks all too frequently were pro-racist in behavior and thereby contributed to their own victimization.

Lesson two occurred also while I was in the Navy. A research project required that we measure a number of qualities in football players. Some of these players had been in the National Football League.

Others had never played high school football. Speed, strength, and lateral reaction time could be measured. What we could not measure was experience or motivation. These proved to be the most elusive variables in predicting success in football. The second lesson was that it might also be true in race relations that objective measures had limited predictive value in terms of performance and behavior because people had different subjective experience and motivation. This could help account for the commonplace observation that two people brought up in quite identical situations would fare differently under the same racial assault. What is needed still is for psychiatry to help find methods to maximize experience and incite motivation in ways that everyone, Black or White, can use to reduce racial conflict.

By the late 1950s, after return to civilian life, I was involved in a project aimed at discovering when a nurse would tell a doctor that the doctor was in error. The experiment consisted of determining how a nurse would respond to a telephone order to give what she knew would be an overdose of a medicine. To the astonishment of all the chiefs of service who cleared this project to be done, routinely nurses accepted the order, often times pouring out the placebo, which they thought was potent, while speaking on the phone. Only after they were told that they had been observed, did we witness any evidence of stress.

Here the lesson extended the guidelines derived from the experience in the Navy. Perhaps, as strange as it sounds, Blacks are under little duress over racial inequity until they are made aware of their acceptance of this inequity. Since it would seem that gross and obvious racial inequity needed no exposure, it occurred to me that the microscopic, everyday response to inequity may remain concealed from the victim.

Later, around 1963, lesson five suggested itself to me as a further evolution of the first four lessons or guidelines. At this time female astronaut candidates were being tested in a situation of drastic sensory reduction while being submerged in water. One of my assignments was to interview these candidates about previous stress that they may have encountered.

Some of these female test pilots had gone through what to me were incredible events. Yet, I learned about them only in an offhand, casual manner, sometimes only in informal conversations following the interviews. A woman who denied any sort of unusual stress in her flying career might mention how she had only one hour of instruction on a new type of bomber before ferrying it across the ocean to be in combat. Or that she once mistakenly landed an aircraft being piloted to one combatant onto enemy territory. The question this raised as a guideline was whether Blacks not only deny stress, like the nurses, but that in addition we tend to underestimate and minimize the impact of stress, like the female astronaut candidates.

About this time, I was traveling to various countries as a senior consultant for the Peace Corps. Often volunteers seemed to be living in conditions bordering on privation. Yet, they maintained lofty ideals and many verbalized that this experience had altered their career directions and ambitions. They became more ardent to serve others and more hopeful for human progress. The seventh major speculation as a Black psychiatrist revolved around the importance of the combination of lofty ideals and hardship in finding a justification for existence.

Blacks, like the Peace Corps volunteers, often have lofty ideals and hardship. What we can't mobilize as easily as the volunteers is the hope that we can translate lofty ideals and willingness to sacrifice into rewarding social contributions. Our continuing dilemma is how people essentially trapped in hopelessness can infuse hope into their children.

The final lesson from these years, upon which I'll comment, began at this time but took a decade for me to fathom. One of the first national committees on which I served was deciding who should join us. Many names were offered. All were rejected with the terse but mystifying statement, "He's not one of us."

Who was "one of us" was baffling to me since at the table there were psychiatrists from rural and urban areas, psychoanalysts and state hospital administrators, men and women, researchers and practitioners, academicians and colored minority people. Years later, I realized what constituted "one of us."

At that time, another group met. Invitees were told that continental breakfast would be available a half hour before the meeting was to start. Also they were told: (1) Bring your golf clubs, and (2) do not schedule your return flight before 5 p.m. the last day of the meeting.

Only one person arrived with golf clubs. He had scheduled his return flight for 7 p.m. on the last day. His greatest blunder however was to arrive only five minutes earlier than the meeting was scheduled to start. By that point, "all of us" were on item three of the agenda. Almost predictably someone had said at 8:15 a.m., "we're all almost here, let's start." Further, predictably someone suggested we work extra hours rather than play golf, so that we could finish by noon rather than 5 p.m. on the last day. "All of us" had arranged early afternoon departures despite an admonition to the contrary.

It hit me with monstrous impact that what is especially complicated about being Black in the U.S.A. is that, even while resolving whether acceptance signifies being welcomed or being tolerated, there are compounding subtle variables that must be factored into the resolution. The "one of us" incident taught me many things. Not the least tuition was that an inherent and considerable stress, in almost all situations in which there is some degree of acceptance, in either homoracial or heteroracial circumstances, is that we can never be sure how much acceptance depends on skin color and how much depends on interpreting what constitutes being "one of us."

1964–1975

During the first phase of my professional life, the time spent in training, in the Navy, and on two university faculties had emphasized the overwhelming importance particularly for a Black of possessing unquestionable clinical skills. Thus, by the beginning of the second phase, I was much immersed in clinical endeavors. By now these endeavors were associated with administrative tasks as I became a chief of a large service.

Everyday decisions were about such matters as whether the inpatient census should go up to 80, whether a certain outpatient secretary should get a raise, how we should go about unlocking a ward, which citizens we should ask to be on our ombudsmen committee, what were the issues we needed to anticipate in a day center. In all these decisions, everyday, I was obliged to handle the extra stress that came from needing to reckon racial concerns of my own and of many others of all races, about what I decided, how I did it, why I did it.

No White in a similar position would have had these concerns in the same qualitative and quantitative way that any Black would have. Nor would the Whites' decisions be as likely to be scrutinized and sharply criticized—or reversed—because of racial aspects in

the decision. All minority people will concur that the stress in maintaining unity in diversity is because in the U.S.A. skin color com-
pounds and complicates every facet of behavior.

Accordingly, at this stage in my professional maturation, I became consciously aware of the three diverse strands that had to be
integrated since they all influenced and informed each other in a
special way in a Black psychiatrist's life. Automatically such integration entailed the acceptance of added stress in my life, as well as the
yielding of other alternative life possibilities.

The diverse strands were: (1) professional responsibilities in
terms of clinical, research, teaching, and administrative duties; (2)
organizational responsibilities in terms of being in a position to provide input into policies by general and minority professional
groups; and (3) civic and social responsibilities in terms of being in a
position to provide input into policies by general and minority community groups. For me, the three strands were at once blurred and
indistinguishable and distinct and separated. Yet the tie binding all
three strands was responsibility to my family.

In my mind, the strands were a trilogy. Each was worthy of full-
time attention and could stand alone. Yet each of the three diverse
strands was obligated intrinsically to each other. For me, this trilogy
operated in this stress-producing way purely because I happened to
be Black. That is given the accidents of birth, time, and place, I was
compelled to develop all three strands lest none of them could develop nor would I be able to meet responsibilities to my family.

As I pursued these three diverse strands, each of which had, by
virtue of my Blackness, extreme diversity within them, I made a
conscious conceptualization about my career. This concept functioned to explain to myself what I was doing but had the added virtue of showing me ways to reduce the stress in being a Black
professional in the quest for unity. The concept was that compared
to my peers I had to work as a scout and not a wagon master.

The scout ranges across much more distance, sees a far greater variety of things, and estimates risks, advantages, and possible paths
of action. The scout integrated diversity. By the time I made this
conceptualization and I had calculated the major strands of activity,
I was aware more consciously of my habitual mode of thinking. This
was to search for racial analogies in whatever I was doing.

Such considerations prepared me for the main lesson I learned
during these years. This occurred in 1966 during my second visit to

Antarctica. Our research team was scheduled to go to Vostok, a Soviet base in the high altitude. We were to be at a landing strip at a certain hour. When we awoke, the senior member of our team reasonably enough turned on a light so that we could see to get dressed and organized. However, a half dozen other men in the room were not arising at that time. My immediate thought was, "Well, Goddam, they'll think I turned on the light."

A couple of weeks later, by chance for the first time during the trip, I was alone with the other Black on our team. We had decided to spend the day exploring an ice cave. My colleague said to me, "Remember that day we were going to Vostock? Well, when the light was turned on, right away I thought, 'Well, Goddam, they'll think I turned on the light.' "

This incident addressed the quintessence of our indigenism. Thus, it was not remarkable to me that the night Martin Luther King died, Solomon Carter Fuller was acclaimed worthy of heroic status without discussion. Just as in Antarctica, the experience of being Black made some things so obvious that discussion was not needed, for in fact, people might even be thinking the same words at the same time.

In Antarctica, both Black men were thinking defensively, apologetically, and deferentially, certain that we would be falsely accused and pictured in unflattering terms. The great lesson was not only in general reference to indigenism but specifically that we are stressed because we are made always to feel we are on the defensive. Much of the behavior illustrated in the lessons from early professional life was generated by this defensive and deferential thinking. Our blind spots, our attention to subtleties, our focus on nonverbal cues comes from this type of thinking. In fact, since most racism is kinetic, not verbal, our defensive and deferential thinking may be the chief way we invite gratuitous degradation and thwart hope.

How we are placed on the defensive and the consequences of it, in terms of stress, continued to occupy much of my attention during these years as I entered into diverse activities in all three strands in which I was dedicated. For instance, when a Tarahumara witch doctor asked me to see a participant in a 250-mile foot race, I was able to put together how magnificent biological assets can be overcome by the unknown, the unpredictable, and the uncontrollable.

This meant that if one rehearsed for and anticipated offenses, one might endure. At another site diverse to common psychiatric practice, I attempted to learn more about how someone is made offensive and what the differences are between offense and defense.

The lesson derived from being an assistant freshman football coach at Harvard. It showed me the importance in race relations of microaggressions, most of which are kinetic. These subtle, minor, stunning, automatic assaults are a major offense mechanism by which Whites stress Blacks unremittingly and keep them on the defensive, as well as in a psychologically reduced condition. An example of microaggression is the customary etiquette whereby a Black is expected to hold open a door for a White should they both arrive at the door in the same instance.

It appeared that what kept us diverse, and simultaneously caused us to seek diversity, somehow involved our own collaboration in accepting demeaning microaggressions, whose aim often was to influence nonverbal behavior. Microaggressions simultaneously sustained defensive–deferential thinking and eroded self-confidence in Blacks. Further, by monopolizing our perception and action through regularly irregular disruptions, they contributed to relative paralysis of action, planning, and self-esteem. They seem to be the principal foundation for the verification of Black inferiority for both Whites and Blacks.

These ideas of the stress brought on by racism were taken to still more diverse settings. About this time, following participation in planning meetings for *Sesame Street,* professional interests and projects resulted in keen attention to how children are portrayed in the media, especially television. Children seemed to be even more oppressed on television than Blacks, in terms of certain content analyses. Closer examination revealed the common ingredients of this oppression. The important guideline hypothesis that precipitated was this: Mathematically, any oppression is proportional to the obligatory restriction of one's space, time, energy, and mobility. The oppressor at every possible instance curbs and controls these conditions in such a way that the oppressor's own space, time, energy, and mobility take precedence in a way to save and convenience the oppressor at the expense of the dominated, for example, the Black being assumed to donate space, time, energy, and mobility to open a door for a White. Microaggressions are basic in keeping any Black donating to the quality and perhaps the quantity of life for any White at the expense of the Black's own quality and quantity of life.

1975–1986

When the third phase of the quest for unity in diversity began it seemed of paramount importance that Blacks in any situation become aware of how to anticipate, assess, and counter microaggressions. Since they are ubiquitous and omnipresent in nearly all interracial interactions, the Black in terms of psychic economy must be especially sensitive about which microaggressions should be neutralized.

This turns out to be an enormously complex job. It may be that the immense psychic energy required to be Black is most drained in electing which of many daily microaggressions one must undercut. The mere vigilance process also consumes much psychic energy.

However, during these years a variety of activities brought me to the appreciation that what intensified this process of vigilance and selective defense was the need for rapid estimation in each microaggressive assault about how much of it was human-specific, how much was cultural-specific, how much was ethnic-specific and how much was specific to individual cumulative experiences of the actors. To best accomplish this reckoning one needed to know a great deal about one's own indigenism as well as what seems to be human-specific and animal-specific behavior.

The reason any person is able to be involved in cross-racial interactions with success is that crucial appeals can be made to human-specific emotions and sentiments by all parties. Even so, to isolate and manage a microaggression, other life features need to be disentangled.

As in other human events, factors of chance, fortune, and serendipity must be included in any interpretation or response to a microaggression. Similarly, frequently, as in other human events, there are potent effects secondary to sheer bodily constitution realities. All of this makes the management of a microaggression the key ingredient to handling diversity by a Black, a very trying and uncertain practice. The clarification of how to negotiate microaggressions continues to occupy a great deal of attention by any Black.

Meanwhile some other lessons or guidelines about racism have percolated from making analogies during these years. One, following studies on dog sled mushers who raced 1100 miles across Alaska, concerned the need for a clear goal. The mushers, despite organic brain signs at the end of the race, had been able to reach this goal without mishap. This seemed staggering. It suggested that, in spite of obstacles, having a clearly focused goal and informed resolution of conflicts would be valuable for Black's individual and community survival. This means that each Black, in our instance as Black psychiatrists, must do things to help Blacks and ourselves to make such resolutions and goal formulations.

One consideration that seems important for Black professions to emphasize is service to the international community. Compared to White America we are in short supply of skilled and educated people. Compared to many countries of the world, especially third-world countries, Black America has a superabundance of skilled and educated people. Another opportunity to bring unity out of diversity would be for us to initiate more strong actions to bring our skill and education to other areas, even while we extend our slender resources to alleviate conditions in the U.S.A.

This view can be defended on the basis of historical and humanitarian needs. Also philosophically, due to our acquaintance with oppression, we might, as a group, find more ready congeniality to work on planetary projects. Politically, the model would help Blacks in the U.S.A. and help the country abroad. Psychologically, for those able to do it, it would be an avenue in which to utilize lofty aspirations and our willingness to sacrifice.

As a scouting report, it can be said that for a variety of reasons Black Americans are about to be recruited to wider efforts on a scale never before approached. Here is an instance where we should prepare for unity when our diversity is sought.

Time prevents an extensive survey of lessons learned in this third phase. There is one problem from which there has as yet been no distillate. This is the problem about why it is that we are undeniably gifted in competing in and understanding games of sport, but don't transfer these advantages into other places such as games in academia, business, or government. Related to this problem is perhaps an inability to decipher critical micromessages.

A young Black and myself both had had extensive education in "White" settings. Both of us had been college athletes. Both of us had had far more than usual experience working in Black causes. Neither of us saw what several independent White readers saw in a letter sent to the young man. To all of them, it was immediately clear that the Black had asked for too much money to work in a large corporation, but that otherwise the job was his. We were not "one of them." They played one game; we were playing another game. No matter how much we read, we couldn't see the covert message, much less to see it as clearly and as obviously as did the Whites. Have we Blacks been so consumed by microaggressions that we are not able to recognize other micromessages important to our comfort?

Conclusions

The quest for unity in diversity by Black psychiatrists since Solomon Carter Fuller has been to take account of racism in the U.S.A. and find professional satisfactions in spite of it. To do this means the acceptance of constant extra stress in all undertakings.

One possible route in the quest has been to adjust to being marginal and fractionated by traveling widely as a scout over virginal terrain, which might be more or less naive to racism and would keep one from too intimate or too sustained contact and involvement with any single group that might exert discrimination.

Other routes will be equally or more promising for physicians in the next couple of decades. We should have not only lots of wagon masters but also many settlers. The wagon masters will get us to destinations. The settlers will be rooted and able to prevail and flourish so that we can be more significant contributors to help more people to live longer and better.

Whichever route our doctors take, they will have to resolve conflicts. At present it seems to me that these ever-present conflicts usually must be resolved more toward the conservative direction. We must resist racism, we must be protective of our own indigenism, and we must assume, when we are accepted, that we are tolerated but not wanted.

All of us should work, even though it means extra effort and stress, in the service of our profession, our professional organizations, and community groups. All of us must do what we can to shore up the Black family, especially the Black male child, who by all indicators is the most likely person in our society to have his space, time, energy, and mobility controlled. And he is told not only that he is inadequate but that in almost all ways he is not needed.

It remains for me to thank numerous people who have allowed me a career as a scout, with concerns reaching from the submolecular to the extragalactic. It has been absorbing to spend one day talking about hormone studies to be done in Black hypertensives and the next day to talk about planning a mission to Mars. I would emphasize that everywhere I've been, I've been not a psychiatrist, but a Black psychiatrist. Thus, from Sisoguichi to Siberia, from Singapore to the South Pole, I have had to be first of all a Black seeker of unity.

My special indebtedness is to colleagues and teachers at numerous and far-flung institutions, especially at the University of Cincinnati, the U.S. Navy, the University of Oklahoma, and Harvard. Also, there are many who helped me in all sorts of professional and community groups. My greatest debt is to my wife and daughters, whose support enabled me to have the honor of being here.

Finally, despite popular and scientific literature, which dwells on the rigidity of Black matriarchy, I wish to thank Black females, for this addresses a subject of monumental present concern about the future of every American. Any Black male who has survived in the U.S.A. as well as I have, has had much indulgence and encouragement from Black females such as mother, wife, daughters, aunts, nieces, cousins, fictive kin, and associates. They have counterbalanced what the incessantly negative microaggressions convey, by proving to a Black male that even if he is not needed, he is still very much wanted. All of us must help Black females continue, as they have done for decades, to support Black boys in becoming effective men and citizens against woeful and terrible odds.

About the Contributors

WALTER R. ALLEN (Ph.D., University of Chicago) is Professor of Sociology at the University of California, Los Angeles. Among the many honors he has received are The Rockefeller Foundation Post-doctoral Fellowship, the Senior Fulbright Lecturer-University of Zimbabwe, and American Educational Research Association Distinguished Scholar Award. Dr. Allen's research and teaching focus on family patterns, socialization and personality development, race and ethnic relations, and higher education. He has had more than fifty articles appear in such journals as *Journal of Marriage and the Family, Phylon,* and *Sociological Quarterly* and has coauthored *The Colorline and the Quality of Life in America* (with R. Reynolds Farley) and *Beginnings: The Social and Affective Development of Black Children* (with Geraldine Brooks and Margaret Spencer).

EDWARD "CHIP" ANDERSON (Ph.D., University of California, Los Angeles) is currently a member of UCLA's Graduate School of Education. His professional experience includes designing and directing academic support service programs for low income, historically underrepresented, Vietnam veterans, and under-prepared college students as well as campuswide orientation, advising, and tutorial programs. Dr. Anderson's current research interests include sources of college student motivation strategies for promoting college student achievement, and methods of increasing minority student persistence. He applies research to help students gain maximum benefits from their college experience, particularly those who are "at risk" of not doing so. The perspective he brings to this process is explained in "Forces Influencing Student Persistence and Achievement," in *Increasing Student Retention,* edited by Lee Noel, Randi Levitz and Diana Saluri.

JOY KEIKO ASAMEN, Ph.D., is an Assistant Professor of Psychology at Pepperdine University, Graduate School of Education and Psychology. Her instructional foci are in the areas of sociocultural issues and research methods. Dr. Asamen's doctoral studies were completed at the University of California, Los Angeles in Educational Psychology/Counseling. She has published in professional journals in the area of cross-cultural counseling. Dr. Asamen has diverse experiences as a counselor, teacher, and researcher, and has acted both as a clinical and research consultant.

GORDON LaVERN BERRY, (Ed.D., Marquette University) is Professor in the Educational Psychology Division of the Graduate School of Education at UCLA. Dr. Berry's research interests are in multicultural counseling psychology and the study of media and social behavior. His most recently published works are *Television and the Socialization of the Minority Child,* four instructional guides for the multimedia series, *Learning Values with Fat Albert and the Cosby Kids,* and a handbook, *Successful Strategies for Teaching in Central City Schools.* He has published more than fifty articles in scholarly psychology, counseling, media, and educational journals. Dr. Berry has been an advisor to such television shows as *Captain Kangaroo, Fraggle Rock, Fat Albert and the Cosby Kids, 30 Minutes,* and *Zoobilee Zoo.* He is a member of the American Psychological Association, the American Educational Research Association, the Association for Counseling and Development, and the American Psychological Society.

JAMES P. COMER is the Maurice Falk professor of child psychiatry at the Yale University Child Study Center, and he is the director of the school development program at the center. He earned the M.D. degree at the Howard University College of Medicine, and did his training in psychiatry at the Yale University School of Medicine. Dr. Comer's research interests include preventive psychiatry through school improvement, child development, and race relations. His articles appear in numerous professional and popular journals and periodicals, including a regular column in *Parents Magazine.* His latest book is *Maggie's American Dream: The Life and Times of a Black Family.* This book is a personal family story that combines his interest in education, child development, and race relations.

SANDRA GRAHAM is an Associate Professor at the Graduate School of Education, UCLA. She received the Ph.D. in educational psychology from UCLA in 1982. Her research interests include attributional processes in motivation, particularly as applied to minority group children, and the development of emotional understanding from an attributional perspective. Professor Graham is a recipient of the APA Division 15 (Educational Psychology) Early Contribution Award. Some notable publications include "Race, Class, and the Attributional Process" (with Anna Long) that appeared in the *Journal of Educational Psychology* (1986) and "Attributional Mediators of Expectancy, Evaluation, and Affect" (with Jonathon Brown) that appeared in the *Journal of Personality and Social Psychology* (1988).

JANICE HALE-BENSON (Ph.D., Georgia State University) is Associate Professor at Cleveland State University and a director of early childhood education programs. She has served as Assistant and Associate Professor of early childhood education at Clark College in Atlanta and as a Research Fellow and visiting lecturer in the Laboratory of Comparative Human Cognition at the University of California, San Diego. Dr. Hale-Benson has authored numerous articles and wrote *Black Children: Their Roots, Culture, and Learning Styles.*

MARCIA L. HALL is a recent Ph.D. graduate of the Sociology Department at the University of Michigan. Her research focuses on race consciousness in Black students on White campuses. Publications include Dreams Deferred: Black Student Career Goals and Fields of Study in Graduate/Professional Schools (with A. Mays and W. Allen) and Race Consciousness and Achievement: Two Issues in the Study of Black Graduate and Professional Students (with W. Allen).

LOUIS E. JENKINS (Ph.D., Pennsylvania State University) He is particularly active in the area of family, life-style, and health-care issues as a teacher, lecturer, and workshop presenter. He also serves as a consultant to health-care professionals and schools, and is a clinical-behavioral science instructor for family medicine residents. He is currently an Associate Professor of Psychology at Pepperdine University Graduate School of Education and Psychology, and Clinical Professor of Psychology for the Department of Family Medicine and the Department of Psychiatry and Human Behavior at the Charles R. Drew University of Medicine and Science.

GLORIA JOHNSON POWELL, M.D. is Professor in the Division of Mental Retardation/Child Psychiatry, Department of Psychiatry at the Neuropsychiatric Institute and Hospital at UCLA. For the past eight years Dr. Powell has been Director of the Family Support Program, and evaluation and treatment program for sexually abused children and their families. Dr. Powell is involved in ongoing research as well as the legal and social policy issues involved in child sexual abuse. She is senior editor of *Psychosocial Development of Minority Group Children* and author of *Black Monday's Children: The Effects of School Desegregation,* and *The Last Closet: The Lives of Sexually Abused Children* (in press).

ROSLYN ARLIN MICKELSON (Ph.D., University of California, Los Angeles) is Assistant Professor of Sociology and Adjunct Assistant Professor of Women's Studies at the University of North Carolina at Charlotte. Her research interests include race, gender, and class equity in educational processes and outcomes. She is the author of "Why Does Jane Read and Write So Well? The Anomaly of Female Achievement" and "The Attitude-Achievement Paradox Among Black Adolescents," both of which recently appeared in *Sociology of Education.* Currently she is examining the corporate-sponsored school reform movement and its implications for educational equity.

HECTOR F. MYERS is an associate professor of psychology at UCLA. He is also director of the Biobehavioral Laboratory at the Charles R. Drew University of Medicine and Science. He is an active researcher with numerous publications to his credit on the role of stress in the mental and physical health of Black and other minority populations.

THOMAS A. PARHAM, (Ph.D., Southern Illinois University) is Director of the Career Planning and Placement Center, and adjunct faculty member of the University of California at Irvine. Dr. Parham is an active member of the Association of Black Psychologists, and also has affiliations with the American Psychological

Association and the American Association for Counseling and Development. He also served on the editorial board for the *Journal of Multi-Cultural Counseling and Development* for five years, and is currently on the editorial board of the *Journal of Counseling and Development.* For the past nine years, Dr. Parham has focused his research efforts in the area of psychological nigrescence, and has authored several articles in the area.

WILLIAM D. PARHAM (Ph.D., Southern Illinois University) is a licensed psychologist whose professional time is spent in several areas. He is a staff psychologist at the UCLA Student Psychological Services, a position he has held since 1981. Dr. Parham is also a member of the part-time faculty, in the Department of Psychology, at Loyola Marymount University. He joined their faculty in 1983 and since that time he has taught courses in cross-cultural counseling, group counseling and psychotherapy, and childhood and adolescense. He also maintains a part-time private practice in Los Angeles, where he provides psychological as well as consultation services.

Dr. Parham is very active in several professional and civic organizations, and he was recently appointed by the governor to be on the Advisory Board of Metropolitan State Hospital.

CHESTER M. PIERCE, professor of education and psychiatry at Harvard, is affiliated with the Massachusetts General Hospital and MIT. Dr. Pierce is a past president of the American Board of Psychiatry and Neurology and the American Orthopsychiatric Association. He was founding national chairman of the Black Psychiatrists of America and has served as national consultant to the surgeon general of the U.S. Air Force. He is an internationally recognized scholar in several areas of psychiatry. He is a member of the Sigma Xi and Alpha Omega Alpha honor societies, the Institute of Medicine, and the National Academy of Sciences. Dr. Pierce also has honorary degrees from Westfield and Tufts.

SHELLY L. PRILLERMAN (Ph.D., University of California, Los Angeles) is a National Institute of Mental Health Postdoctoral fellow in the psychology department at UCLA. Her research interests include the role of race-related stress and coping processes in the functioning of Afro-Americans with a focus on college students at White universities.

KATHY SANDERS-PHILLIPS (Ph.D., John Hopkins University) is a developmental psychologist who is currently an Assistant professor of pediatrics at the Charles R. Drew University of Medicine and Science in Los Angeles, California and an Assistant professor of pediatrics at the UCLA School of Medicine. She completed an internship in pediatric psychology in the Department of Pediatrics at the University of Maryland Hospital in Baltimore. Dr. Phillips' primary research interests are in infant development, particularly the development of high-risk infants. She currently serves as director of the Infant Study Laboratory at the King/Drew Medical Center. She has published in the area of early infant feeding behavior, specifically focusing on the effects of obstetric medication on the sucking response of neonates. She has recently been funded by the March of Dimes Foundation to continue studies of the effects of prenatal exposure to PCP and cocaine on infant feeding capacities and development during the first six months of life.

HUGH J. SCOTT (Ed.D., Michigan State University) has served as Dean of Programs in Education at Hunter College of CUNY since July 1, 1975. Prior to his deanship at Hunter College, he served as professor of education in the Department of Educational Leadership and Community Service at Howard University in Washington, D.C. From 1970 to 1973, he served as superintendent of schools for the public schools of Washington, D.C. Dr. Scott is the author of *The Black School Superintendent: Messiah or Scapegoat?* (Howard University Press). His articles reveal major interests in the problems of educational leadership and the implementation of the concepts of equal educational opportunity and quality education. He recently completed a study of the views of Black school superintendents on Black consciousness and professionalism.

BRIAN D. SMEDLEY is an advanced doctoral student in clinical psychology at UCLA. He earned the A.B. from Harvard University in 1986, and the M.A. in psychology from UCLA in 1988. He is currently a Ford Foundation predoctoral fellow, and both his clinical and research interests relate to the mental health and adjustment of Black and other college-age populations.

STEPHEN SAMUEL SMITH is a Ph.D. candidate in political science at Stanford University. His research interests include political violence, political behavior, theories of the state, and the politics of class and race. His dissertation research focuses on mass beliefs about state violence in the United States and the effect of these beliefs on political activity.

ROMERIA TIDWELL (Ph.D., University of California, Los Angeles) is an Associate Professor of Education and Counseling Psychology in the Graduate School of Education, UCLA, and a California licensed psychologist and educational psychologist. Dr. Tidwell's research is concerned with counseling psychology with an emphasis on educational/psychological measurement, and the therapeutic process as it relates to gender, ethnicity, and socioeconomic status.

NOTES